COOKING
with the STARS

**HEALTHY, DELICIOUS RECIPES
FROM CELEBRITIES' OWN KITCHENS**

Edited by

Michael F. Jacobson, Ph.D.

☆

Jennifer Douglas

*To Joyce Goldstein,
Thanks for the terrific recipe
Mike Jacobson*

Center for Science in the Public Interest
Washington, D.C.

ACKNOWLEDGMENTS

This cookbook could never have been done without a lot of help from many friends, relatives and strangers. Our colleagues at the Center for Science in the Public Interest deserve the loudest applause. Michael Rudof worked hard identifying celebrities, analyzing the nutritional quality of the recipes and working with expert cook Catherine Evans to improve the taste and healthfulness of some of the recipes. The nutritional expertise of Jayne Hurley (assisted by Ingrid Van Tuinen) helped tremendously. Emily Gray wrote several of the recipe introductions.

Many friends and colleagues were generous in helping to obtain recipes and giving us suggestions for contacting elusive celebrities. A hearty thanks to Anne Bancroft, Roberta Baskin, Ty Braswell, Marie Brown, Carol Tucker Foreman, Tim Lang, Diane MacEachern, David Levine, Esther Peterson, Maria Rodriguez and Deborah Szekely. Our thanks also go to the people who tested recipes, especially Elaine Greenstone, Belle Jacobson, Craig Jenkins, Frensch Niegermeier, Miranda Otradovsky and Joyce West.

— Michael F. Jacobson, Ph.D.
— Jennifer Douglas

COVER DESIGN: Javier Romero Design, Inc.
BOOK DESIGN: Tim Miles
COPY EDITOR: Brenda Koplin
INDEXER: Rose Grant

ISBN 0-89329-031-9

First printing October 1993
Printed in the United States of America

10 9 8 7 6 5 4 3 2 1

CONTENTS

Main-Course Salads

Pasta, Rice and Other Grains

Fish and Seafood

Poultry and Other Meat

Vegetable Side Dishes

Desserts

Introduction

Michael F. Jacobson, Ph.D.
Executive Director and Co-Founder
Center for Science in the Public Interest

I've never eaten dinner at Alan Alda's house or Martina Navratilova's or Al and Tipper Gore's. But if the recipes they contributed to *Cooking with the Stars* are any indication, I—and you—have been missing some wonderful experiences.

This star-studded cookbook celebrates the Center for Science in the Public Interest's more than twenty years of advocating better nutrition. In a way, the book is a culmination of what we've advocated: that people should enjoy delicious meals made from healthful, wholesome ingredients.

Over the past two decades, my own diet and the diets of millions of other Americans have changed radically. In the 1960s, I was a pretty average eater. I ate my vegetables, but I certainly wasn't going to let them crowd out my hot dogs, bologna sandwiches (white bread, of course), potato chips and soda pop. In 1970 I moved to Washington to work with Ralph Nader. My first assignment (which, in a way, has never ended) was to write a book concerning the safety of food additives—a subject about which I knew absolutely nothing. Gradually, I began learning about foods. First the additives, then the nutritional value of the foods themselves. With each discovery of a possible problem—sodium nitrite, brominated vegetable oil, saccharin, dyes—my diet changed a little bit for the better.

The most important conclusion I came to while writing *Eater's Digest* was that the nutritional content of foods has a far greater impact on health than do the additives. With that realization, I began focusing more and more on the bombshell health effects of diets dripping with grease, sweetened with tons of sugar, infused with cholesterol and seasoned with copious quantities of salt: obesity, tooth decay, constipation, high blood pressure, diabetes, coronary heart disease and certain cancers.

Back in the early 1970s, the only people who seemed to care about nutrition were hippies hanging around college campuses and older die-hard "health-food nuts" whose guru was Adelle Davis. This cookbook shows just how far the health movement has come. Nutrition has gone mainstream, upscale, downtown; it has reached everywhere from the U.S. Congress to Hollywood to the fanciest restaurants to baseball stadiums. I am grateful that so many stars have contributed their favorite healthful recipes.

My own personal goals in eating are to eat as many delicious foods as I can while minimizing the fat, cholesterol, sodium and other junk. That means plenty of whole grains, beans, veggies, fruit, non-fat dairy products, fish and an occasional skinless-chicken dish. A good diet doesn't have to be vegetarian, but we'd all do well to move a long way in that direction.

During the preparation of this book, I looked forward with excitement to my daily mail. Practically every day brought new mouth-watering recipes from famous actors, musicians, athletes, politicians, scientists, chefs, cookbook writers and restaurateurs.

We encouraged those people to contribute recipes low in fat, cholesterol, sodium and refined sugar, and loaded with dietary fiber, vitamins and minerals. We encouraged, but didn't insist on, whole-grain flour in breads and pasta.

Though preparing a book like this would seem to be fairly straightforward, I must say that of all the books I have worked on, this one was the most difficult. I originally thought we could just write letters to famous people and they would promptly send back tasty, healthful recipes. As it turns out, though, it's practically impossible (as every teeny-bopper discovers) to actually get our letters to those stars, let alone get answers back.

Furthermore, most stars don't have recipes, they have cooks. Robert Redford's assistant was kind enough to tell us that much as he'd like to provide a recipe, "The truth of the matter is Mr. Redford doesn't cook—at all." And Joseph Heller (author of *Catch 22*) told me, "I'd rather starve than have to cook another meal myself."

We didn't have strict and specific nutritional criteria, but we did have our limits. Several contributors were kind enough to modify, or allow us to modify, their recipes and bring them in line with our health concerns. Some recipes, however, were beyond redemption.

And even many stars who do remember what a kitchen is for apparently never took a nutrition class. Vanna White's salad made with Jell-O and Cool Whip didn't make the grade. "Isiah's Favorite Cheesecake," contributed by Detroit Pistons basketball great Isiah Thomas, crashed into our fat and cholesterol guidelines. Chris Evert's chicken salad was fine, but we had to dump "Chris's Spaghetti," in which the four onions don't come close to canceling out the fat provided by six pounds of ground beef. From the Houston Oilers came a recipe that was based on a gallon of ice cream and a bottle of liqueur. Another recipe started with "1 box of Velveeta cheese." Don't bother searching through this book for those gems.

We also thought that we could just print the recipes as they were sent to us. But even some famous chefs were adding far more fat or salt than was really needed, accidentally listing one cup of thyme when they meant one teaspoon, or forgetting either to list ingredients that were used or use the ingredients that were listed. Testing recipes was clearly necessary!

For the technically minded, the fat content of recipes is generally below 30 percent of calories and sodium below 200 milligrams per 100 calories. We also preferred fruit or fruit juice to sugar, fresh foods to canned foods and whole-wheat flour and brown rice to white flour and white rice. If you can find organically grown ingredients, terrific.

Each recipe is accompanied by nutrition information. In general, you should try to eat less fat (especially the saturated variety), cholesterol, sodium and refined sugar...and more foods rich in dietary fiber (it's only present in foods derived from plants). Believe it or not, you needn't worry too much about calories. Most people automatically eat about the same number of calories every day—the body has a means of ensuring that it takes in as many calories as it expends. If you eat lots of bulky, low-fat foods, like vegetables, fruit and whole grains, you'll find that the calories usually take care of themselves.

The following benchmarks will help you interpret the nutrition information in the recipes:

Daily Nutrient Levels

	2,000 calorie diet 120-pound person	2,500 calorie diet 180-pound person
Protein (15% of calories)	75 g	94 g
Carbohydrate (65% of calories)	325 g	406 g
Fat (20% of calories)	44 g	56 g
Saturated Fat (5% of calories)	15 g	19 g
Cholesterol	200 mg max.	250 mg max.
Sodium	2,000 mg max.	2,500 mg max.

If your diet meets those guidelines, you'd likely also consume adequate amounts of most vitamins and minerals.

Each recipe lists protein, but don't worry about it. Practically everyone consumes much more protein than is needed. On the other hand, carbohydrate is something we should be eating more of, because something has to replace the fat that I hope you're going to be eating less of. Just be sure that the carbohydrate comes from fruit or starchy foods, rather than refined sugar. Not many recipes in *Cooking with the Stars* contain sugar, though some contain a little. White sugar is not a poison; we just shouldn't eat too much of it.

You should also get plenty of dietary fiber—twenty to thirty grams a day. We couldn't list fiber levels, because many ingredients simply haven't been analyzed yet.

The nutritional analyses are based on the items called for in the recipes. However, when an ingredient (often salt) is marked "optional," it was not included in the analysis. When a choice of ingredients is given, the first ingredient was generally the one used in the analysis. In recipes calling for stock, the analysis is based on no-salt-added stocks. Because such products are hard to find at grocery stores, we've included no-salt-added chicken and vegetable stock recipes on page 21.

4

You should feel free to modify the recipes if you would like more or less of any ingredient. These recipes are not written in stone, and half the fun of cooking is adding your own special twist. Many recipes call for salt. If you're concerned about sodium, you could try cutting the amount of salt in half or eliminating it entirely (possibly replacing it with herbs, salsa, or pepper). You can always add salt, pepper or spicy seasoning to a soup or stew, if you think it's a little bland. The high sodium levels in canned beans and tuna can be cut by 40% and 82% respectively by rinsing the food in a colander for about a minute. Cutting one-half teaspoon of salt (about 1,000 milligrams of sodium) out of a recipe that serves four reduces sodium by 250 milligrams per serving. The following chart will help you estimate how sodium changes when you add or subtract salt from a recipe:

Change in Amount of Salt	*Change in Milligrams of Sodium Per Serving*				
	Number of Servings Recipe Yields				
	1	**2**	**4**	**6**	**8**
¼ teaspoon	500	250	125	85	60
½ teaspoon	1,000	500	250	170	125
¾ teaspoon	1,500	750	375	255	190
1 teaspoon	2,000	1,000	500	335	250

Creative health-conscious cooks can make other changes. You can increase the nutrient level of any pasta dish by using whole-wheat instead of ordinary pasta. You can try cutting down on the fat or cholesterol content a little, but most recipes are at their limit (one alternative is to "sauté" vegetables in water, not oil). You can replace one vegetable with another, or fish with chicken. In some recipes you could further reduce cholesterol by replacing an egg yolk with an egg white (two whites in place of one whole egg). One change I often make is to cut down on the amount of chicken or fish and increase the amounts of vegetables or starchy foods in a meal. So, cut the salt, leave out a spice or add one you like or make other changes—cooking should be fun!

One final word. Several recipes call for specific brands of packaged foods. Those are the choices of the cooks; the Center for Science in the Public Interest does not endorse any brands of food. You might well find another brand of fat-free salad dressing or low-sodium spaghetti sauce that is tastier, more convenient or cheaper—chances are it'll be just as good.

I hope you enjoy these recipes as much as we enjoyed obtaining and testing them and that they add a special zest to your mealtimes. After all, this will probably be the closest you and I ever get to bringing the likes of Anne Bancroft, Whoopi Goldberg, Jimmy and Rosalynn Carter and Paul and Linda McCartney into our dining rooms for a fabulous dinner party.

Washington, D.C.
October 1993

BREAKFAST AND MUFFINS

David Baltimore and Alice Huang's
Frensch Niegermeier Granola   *15 servings*

☆☆

David Baltimore, who was president of Rockefeller University and is now a professor there, is famous for sharing the 1975 Nobel Prize for Physiology or Medicine and for his early cautions on genetic engineering. Little known, though, is that this cookbook's senior editor (M.F.J.) was David's first graduate student, initially at the Salk Institute and then at MIT. Alice Huang (David's wife) is herself a well-known virologist at New York University and also taught that editor how to dance. Alice named this granola after a fun-loving friend and says, "I cannot live without it, and many of my friends are hooked." Granolas are good sources of fiber, and often fat, but this is a terrific no-oil-added granola. You'll love it.

  4 **cups rolled oats**
 ⅔ **cup unsweetened toasted wheat germ**
  2 **tablespoons sesame seeds**
  1 **ounce sunflower seeds**
 ¼ **cup chopped pecans**
 ¼ **cup slivered almonds (or pine nuts or peanuts)**
 ½ **cup maple syrup (or packed brown sugar)**
 ¼ **cup apple juice**
  3 **teaspoons vanilla**
  1 **cup raisins (or chopped dates)**

1. Mix first 6 ingredients.
2. Shake maple syrup, apple juice and vanilla together. Pour into dry mixture and stir well.
3. Spread in 1 or 2 baking pans so that the granola is about ½ inch thick or less.
4. Bake at 325° for about 20 minutes. Remove and stir every 5 minutes (to prevent burning) until oats are a toasty color. Let cool, stir in raisins (or dates). and store in an airtight container.

PER SERVING (2 oz.):

Calories: 202	Fat: 6 g (25% of calories)	Cholesterol: 0 mg	Protein: 6 g
	Saturated Fat: <1 g	Sodium: 7 mg	Carbohydrate: 34 g

Bill Bradley's
New Jersey Blueberry or Cranberry Muffins *12 servings*

☆☆

Senator Bill Bradley, a New Jersey Democrat, was reelected for a third term in 1990. In recent years, he has focused much of his energy on solving America's racial crisis.

Prior to politics, Senator Bradley starred for ten years with the New York Knicks, who won the National Basketball Championship twice with Bradley as a starting forward. The senator is partial to these muffins, because New Jersey ranks second in the production of both blueberries and cranberries, but the muffins taste almost as good with berries grown elsewhere. Either type of berry adds vitamins A and C to your breakfast.

    1 cup whole-wheat flour
    1 cup sifted flour (unbleached)
    ½ cup sugar
  2 ½ teaspoons baking powder
    ½ teaspoon salt
    2 well-beaten egg whites
    1 cup skim milk
    ⅓ cup vegetable oil
    1 cup fresh (or thawed), well-drained blueberries or cranberries
       paper muffin cups

1. Sift first 5 ingredients (dry ones) into a bowl.
2. In a small bowl, combine egg whites, milk and oil. Add to dry ingredients. Stir briskly until all ingredients are blended. Gently stir in blueberries or cranberries.
3. Preheat oven to 400°. Line muffin tins with 12 paper muffin cups. Fill ⅔ full and bake for about 25 minutes.

PER SERVING:

| Calories: 175 | Fat: 7 g (33% of calories) | Cholesterol: 0 mg | Protein: 4 g |
| | Saturated Fat: <1 g | Sodium: 174 mg | Carbohydrate: 26 g |

ℛ

Mike Farrell's
Mike's Fruit-Yogurt Refresher   *2 (12 fluid ounce) servings*

☆☆☆☆☆☆☆☆☆☆☆ ☆☆☆☆☆☆ ☆☆☆☆☆☆☆☆☆☆☆☆☆☆ ☆☆☆☆☆☆☆☆☆☆☆☆☆

Mike Farrell is best known for his eight years as B.J. Hunnicutt on "M*A*S*H" and also as a writer and director on the show. In real life, Mike has championed many causes, most notably the international refugee aid organization CONCERN.

Mike warned us that he is not so much a cook as a blender jockey. Mike says, "It's best to keep the blender going throughout the procedure (look out for the spray) so the powders don't all stick to the sides of the jar." This recipe adds a health-food punch to a more traditional breakfast-in-a-glass of blended fruit, fruit juice and yogurt. You'll have to go down to your local health-food store to find the optional ingredients. The optional ingredients thicken the drink (and the spirulina darkens it—sometimes to a blackish purple), but believe it or not, they don't change the taste very much.

1 cup fruit juice (cranberry nectar preferably)
1 banana
1 cup low-fat, non-fat or non-dairy (soy) yogurt with fruit
½ cup fresh or frozen berries (preferably raspberries or blueberries)
1 tablespoon spirulina powder (optional)
2 tablespoons lecithin granules (optional)
1 tablespoon protein powder (optional)
2 tablespoons acidophilus culture (optional)
1 tablespoon Sunrider Herbal mix (optional)
1 gram vitamin C powder (optional)

Combine all ingredients in a blender.

PER SERVING (12 FLUID OUNCES):
Calories: 279   Fat: 3 g (9% of calories)   Cholesterol: 5 mg   Protein: 7 g
                Saturated Fat: 1 g   Sodium: 43 mg   Carbohydrate: 58 g

%ə

Carol Tucker Foreman's
Rachel's Blast-Off Bran Muffins   *18 servings*

☆☆☆☆ ☆☆☆☆☆☆☆☆☆☆☆☆☆☆☆☆☆☆☆☆☆☆☆ ☆☆☆☆☆☆☆☆☆☆☆☆

Carol Tucker Foreman was inducted in 1991 into the Center for Science in the Public Interest's "Nutrition Hall of Fame" for overseeing the publication of the government's land-mark Dietary Guidelines for Americans, *which replaced namby-pamby advice to "eat a variety of foods" with that of emphasizing the reduction of fat, cholesterol, salt and sugar. Carol was then serving as an assistant secretary of agriculture under President Jimmy Carter. She is now a partner in the Washington, D.C., lobbying firm of Foreman & Heidepriem, a leading advocate of effective meat and poultry inspection, and one of this cook-book's senior editor's (M.F.J.) dog's best friends whenever Carol delivers a load of used ten-nis balls. When you are in the mood for muffins, cook up this great fiber- and vitamin-rich recipe. Carol's Black Beans are on page 73.*

1½ cups unprocessed bran
¼   cup canola oil
½   15-ounce box raisins (about 1¼ cups)
½   cup boiling water
2   egg whites
2   cups plain non-fat yogurt
2   tablespoons molasses
1⅛ cups whole-wheat flour
1¼ teaspoons baking soda
4   ripe bananas, puréed
    paper muffin cups

1. Mix bran with oil, raisins and boiling water.
2. In a separate bowl, mix together egg whites, yogurt and molasses and add to the first mixture.
3. Mix together flour and baking soda and add to the above.
4. Purée bananas and add to the mixture. Stir just enough to mix all ingredients. Cover and let stand for 1 hour.
5. Preheat oven to 400°.
6. Line muffin tins with 18 paper muffin cups. Fill ⅔ full and bake 20 to 25 minutes. Remove from oven and allow to cool.

PER SERVING:
Calories: 150   Fat: 4 g (22% of calories)   Cholesterol: 0 mg   Protein: 3 g
                 Saturated Fat: <1 g   Sodium: 78 mg   Carbohydrate: 26 g

Michael Jacobson's
Green and Spicy Scrambled Eggs   *2 servings*

☆ ☆

Center for Science in the Public Interest executive director Michael Jacobson, the senior editor of this cookbook, offers up his favorite egg dish for health-conscious people who don't feel satiated with bran cereal and skim milk for breakfast. Michael's Turkey and Vegetable Soup is on page 25. Michael says:

Eggs are great foods once you get rid of the cholesterol. And egg-white scrambled eggs or omelets are scrumptious, if they're made with plenty of spices and vegetables. You can throw practically anything from mushrooms to fresh tomatoes to shrimp to zucchini into egg whites for a great meal. Season with spicy salsa, tangy mustard or just herbs. This is a basic recipe. Open up your vegetable drawers and spice cabinet and use your creativity to whip up your own favorite cholesterol-free, low-sodium scrambled eggs.

 1 **small green pepper, diced**
1⅓ **cup broccoli, diced**
 2 **teaspoon soft margarine**
 4 **tablespoons skim milk**
 6 **egg whites**
 3 **tablepoons salsa (medium)**
 1 **teaspoon oregano**
 1 **teaspoon basil**

1. Sauté green pepper and broccoli in margarine until soft.
2. In bowl, add milk to egg whites and beat.
3. Stir salsa and herbs into egg whites and pour over vegetables. Stir occasionally over medium heat. Serve with hot tea and whole-wheat toast spread with honey.

PER SERVING:

Calories: 135	Fat: 4 g (27% of calories)	Cholesterol: 1 mg	Protein: 14 g
	Saturated Fat: <1 g	Sodium: 247 mg	Carbohydrate: 11 g

Nancy Kassebaum's
Oatmeal Muffins

12 servings

☆☆☆ ☆☆☆☆☆☆☆☆☆☆☆☆☆ ☆☆☆☆☆☆☆☆☆☆☆☆☆☆ ☆☆☆☆☆☆☆☆☆☆☆☆☆☆☆☆

Nancy Kassebaum, a moderate Republican, has been senator from Kansas since 1978, before which she served on the Maize, Kansas, school board. Her father, Alfred Landon, chose a poor time (1936) to run for president on the Republican ticket. The senator's Oatmeal Muffins are a great way to start the day.

1 cup uncooked oats
1 cup buttermilk
2 egg whites
¼ cup brown sugar, firmly packed
½ cup whole-wheat flour
½ cup all-purpose flour
½ teaspoon salt
½ teaspoon baking soda
1 teaspoon baking powder
2 tablespoons oil
2 tablespoons honey
paper muffin cups

1. Soak oatmeal in buttermilk for 1 hour.
2. After soaking period, add egg whites and brown sugar; beat well.
3. Sift together flours, salt, baking soda and baking powder. (You can reduce the salt to cut the sodium.) Add to liquid mixture.
4. Preheat oven to 400°. Beat together oil and honey. Stir into mixture. Line muffin tins with 12 paper muffin cups and divide batter evenly. Bake for 15 to 20 minutes. Muffins can be frozen after cooling.

PER SERVING:

Calories: 120	Fat: 3 g (22% of calories)	Cholesterol: 1 mg	Protein: 3 g
	Saturated Fat: <1 g	Sodium: 182 mg	Carbohydrate: 20 g

Bob Keeshan's
Carrot-Zucchini Muffins

12 servings

☆☆☆☆☆☆☆☆☆ ☆☆☆☆☆☆☆☆☆☆☆ ☆☆☆☆☆☆☆☆☆☆☆ ☆☆☆☆☆☆☆☆☆☆

Millions of former kids fondly remember Bob Keeshan as the kinder, gentler host of "Captain Kangaroo." The CBS show began in 1955, ran for nearly 30 years and won six Emmys. Today's children can enjoy the show on public television. Bob, a six-time grandfather, remains committed to quality children's programming with shows like "CBS Storybreak." Bob recently wrote an autobiography, Growing Up Happy, *and is serving as the national spokesperson for the Coalition for America's Children, a grass-roots advocacy group.*

The shredded carrots in Bob's cholesterol-free muffins give a nice blast of beta-carotene.

  3 tablespoons vegetable shortening
½ cup brown sugar
  2 egg whites, lightly beaten
⅔ cup skim milk
1¾ cups quick-cooking or old-fashioned oats, uncooked
  1 cup flour
  1 tablespoon baking powder
¼ teaspoon nutmeg
  1 cup shredded carrot
½ cup shredded zucchini (about 1 small squash)
    paper muffin cups

TOPPING:
¼ cup oats, uncooked
  1 tablespoon chopped almonds
  1 tablespoon melted vegetable shortening

1. Combine shortening and brown sugar in large bowl. Beat at medium speed with electric mixer or stir with fork until blended. Stir in egg whites and milk gradually. Combine and add oats, flour, baking powder and nutmeg. Add shredded carrot and zucchini. Stir until just blended.
2. Preheat oven to 400°. Line muffin tin with 12 paper muffin cups. Divide batter evenly. Cups should be almost full.
3. For topping, combine oats, nuts and shortening. Sprinkle over each muffin. Press into batter lightly. Bake for 20 to 25 minutes or until golden brown. Serve warm.

PER SERVING:
Calories: 180   Fat: 6 g (28% of calories)   Cholesterol: 0 mg   Protein: 5 g
                 Saturated Fat: 1 g   Sodium: 101 mg   Carbohydrate: 28 g

Graham Kerr's
Quiche Kirkland

6 servings

☆☆

Graham Kerr made his fame and fortune as television's "Galloping Gourmet" in the sixties. But twenty years later, Graham has abandoned mountains of butter and deep-frying techniques for a diet built to American Heart Association standards. His book, Graham Kerr's Smart Cooking, *and "The Graham Kerr Show" feature what he calls "minimax" (food with minimum fat, sodium and cholesterol and with maximum flavor) and "ACT" (healthful food with Aroma, Color and Texture). Graham has another "minimax" recipe, Golden Threads Squash, on page 177. Graham says:*

Depending, of course, upon how deep the quiche is, the nutrition risk often comes as much from the crust as from the filling. In a classic butter-made crust, there are about 21 grams of saturated fat, which runs about 63% of calories from fat. That really isn't good news for pie fanciers (like me!). However, here is an unusually tasty crust that goes a long way toward making this recipe an acceptable alternative: it's actually made from rice. I always serve quiche with an attractive salad.

PARMESAN RICE CRUST:
  2 cups cooked long grain rice
  ½ teaspoon salt
  1 egg white, beaten
  ¼ cup freshly ground black pepper to taste

QUICHE FILLING:
  7 sun-dried tomato halves
  ¼ cup matchstick-sliced Canadian bacon
  1⅓ cups thinly sliced mushrooms
  ¼ cup diced green pepper
  ¼ cup diced red pepper
  1 tablespoon fresh thyme leaves
  1 tablespoon fresh chopped basil leaves
  ¼ teaspoon freshly ground nutmeg
    freshly ground black pepper to taste
  ¼ cup freshly grated Parmesan cheese
  1 whole egg
  4 egg whites
  1½ cups skim milk

GARNISH:
  ½ tablespoon fresh chopped basil
  ½ tablespoon fresh chopped parsley
    pinch of cayenne pepper

1. In a medium bowl, mix together all the crust ingredients. Press into a 9-inch non-stick pie pan. Bake at 375° for 25 minutes, until it looks dry and just golden brown around the edges.
2. Preheat the oven to 400°. Soak the sun-dried tomatoes in warm water to plump, about 15 minutes. Drain and dice finely.
3. In a medium skillet, sauté the Canadian bacon, mushrooms, peppers and sun-dried tomatoes. Notice the great colors! Sprinkle with the thyme leaves, basil, nutmeg and black pepper. Cook the vegetables until they are just tender and their flavors blended, about 5 minutes.
4. Turn the cooked vegetables into a fine mesh strainer and drain any excess liquids. Turn them into the cooked pie crust and sprinkle with half of the Parmesan.
5. In a medium bowl, beat the egg yolk, egg whites and milk. Pour the custard on top of the vegetables. It should just cover them. Sprinkle with the remaining Parmesan cheese.
6. Bake at 400° for 25 minutes, or until the crust is set. To serve, sprinkle the quiche with fresh basil, parsley and cayenne pepper. Cut into wedges and delight your guests!

PER SERVING:

| Calories: 164 | Fat: 3 g (17% of calories) | Cholesterol: 52 mg | Protein: 10 g |
| | Saturated Fat: 1 g | Sodium: 456 mg | Carbohydrate: 23 g |

Douglas La Follette's
Oat-Nutmeg Waffles
4 servings

☆☆☆☆☆☆ ☆☆☆☆☆☆☆☆☆☆☆ ☆☆☆☆☆☆☆☆☆☆☆☆ ☆☆☆☆☆☆☆☆☆☆

Douglas La Follette has used his position as secretary of state in Wisconsin to campaign for a better environment, and he has long been a nutrition activist. He's a whole-grain kind of guy and says about his high-fiber waffles: "This tasty, healthy breakfast, lunch or dinner is great served plain or with real maple syrup, peanut butter, honey, molasses or any combination of the above. It is also excellent with yogurt and any kind of fruit topping. These waffles make a perfect end to a day of hiking, skiing, biking or canoeing. ENJOY!"

1 **cup skim milk**
1 **tablespoon vegetable oil**
1 **teaspoon vanilla**
1 **tablespoon honey or maple syrup**
1 **cup quick-cooking oatmeal (or whirl 1 cup regular in food processor for 4 seconds)**
1 **cup oat bran**

2 teaspoons nutmeg (freshly ground is best)
1 tablespoon baking powder
4 egg whites, beaten until firm but not dry
nonstick cooking spray

1. Mix milk with the oil, vanilla and honey. Stir in all the dry ingredients, adding milk to achieve the desired consistency. You may have to add more liquid during the mixing and cooking process as the oats and oat bran will absorb some.
2. Fold in the well-beaten egg whites. Let stand for 3 to 4 minutes before cooking on waffle iron. Be sure to spray the iron lightly each time with vegetable spray.

Note: This batter can also be used to make pancakes.

PER SERVING:

Calories: 253	Fat: 7 g (29% of calories)	Cholesterol: 1 mg	Protein: 13 g
	Saturated Fat: 1 g	Sodium: 326 mg	Carbohydrate: 34 g

Mark Medoff's
A Playwright's Breakfast
1 serving

☆☆☆☆☆☆☆ ☆☆☆☆☆☆☆☆☆☆☆☆☆☆ ☆☆☆☆☆☆☆☆☆☆☆☆ ☆☆☆☆☆☆☆☆☆☆☆

Playwright Mark Medoff won a Tony Award for Children of a Lesser God *and was nominated for an Academy Award for the screenplay. Among his half-dozen movies is* Clara's Heart, *with Whoopi Goldberg. He serves as Dramatist in Residence and Professor of Theatre Arts at New Mexico State University. This breakfast is simple and simply delicious and is just as good with fat-free yogurt as milk. As proven by the following, Mark can turn even a recipe into a work of art.*

½ cup low-fat granola (or ¼ cup each of different granolas)
3 teaspoons raw oat or wheat bran
splash of toasted wheat germ
1 teaspoon honey
1 cup skim milk
fresh berries or sliced fresh fruit

Get up at five in the morning. Look at the children, make sure they're breathing. Go downstairs in the dark, hoping no one has left anything on the stairs and that your left knee doesn't lock, sending you end over end to the tile below. Take from the freezer and grind fresh coffee (three quarters decaf, one quarter regular). While the coffee is brewing, turn on the word processor. Go out front, look up at the stars (and at the satellite that sits high in the eastern sky). Start thinking about granola choices. Pick up newspaper. Look at front page and shake head in despair at the bad news. Think what an effective antidote good granola is for an inhospitable world. Go in the house. Have first cup of coffee and read the sports section. Refill coffee. Go to the word processor. Put on headphones. Turn on music. Write until seven. Wake up children. Cuddle, coax out of bed. Refill coffee. Write until seven-thirty. Save knees by using one phone line downstairs to call children upstairs on the other line. Tell them to move it! Then mix the granola, wheat bran and germ, honey, milk and fresh fruit. Kibitz with children until mixture is almost soggy. Enjoy!

PER SERVING:

Calories: 395	Fat: 8 g (20% of calories)	Cholesterol: 4 mg	Protein: 15 g
	Saturated Fat: 3 g	Sodium: 281 mg	Carbohydrate: 66 g

ॐ

Esther Peterson's
Utah Muffins
24 servings

☆☆

Esther Peterson is simply one of the most splendid persons on earth. Starting out as a gym teacher in Utah, Esther became a leading national and international spokesperson on consumer, women's and labor issues. She served as consumer advisor to Presidents Lyndon Johnson and Jimmy Carter, fighting valiantly for a (still-needed) Consumer Protection Agency. Esther then became the consumer spokesperson for Giant Foods, a leading East Coast supermarket chain, where she pioneered the use of unit pricing and open dating. More recently, she was the International Organization of Consumers Unions's ambassador to the United Nations, where she advocated a code of ethics for multinational corporations.

Esther is also a first-rate cook and you don't have to be from Utah to enjoy her Utah Muffins. Her Quick and Easy Brown Bread is on page 62.

- 2 cups whole-wheat flour
- ¼ teaspoon salt
- 1½ cups bran cereal
- ½ cup bran flakes
- ½ cup chopped dates
- ⅓ cup chopped nuts
- ⅔ cup raisins
- ½ cup boiling water
- 2 teaspoons baking soda
- ⅔ cup brown sugar
- ⅓ cup margarine
- 3 egg whites
- 2 cups buttermilk or 2 cups skim milk with 1 teaspoon vinegar
  paper muffin cups

1. Mix flour, salt, bran cereal, bran flakes, dates and nuts in a large bowl.
2. Cover raisins with boiling water. Add soda and let cool.
3. Cream brown sugar with margarine. Add egg whites and beat well. Add buttermilk. Add raisin mixture and brown sugar mixture to flour mixture. Cover and refrigerate for at least 12 hours.
4. Preheat oven to 375°. Line 2 muffin tins with 24 paper muffin cups, filling about ⅔ full. Bake for 20 minutes. Bake only as many muffins as you need. The rest of the batter can be stored in the refrigerator for up to 2 weeks, to be baked "as the spirit moves."

PER SERVING:

Calories: 130	Fat: 4 g (26% of calories)	Cholesterol: 1 mg	Protein: 4 g
	Saturated Fat: 1 g	Sodium: 179 mg	Carbohydrate: 24 g

SOUPS

Jimmy and Rosalynn Carter's
Cream of Broccoli Soup—With No Cream
4 servings

☆☆☆☆☆☆☆☆☆☆ ☆☆☆☆☆☆☆☆☆☆ ☆☆☆☆☆☆☆☆☆☆ ☆☆☆☆☆☆☆☆☆☆

Jimmy and Rosalynn Carter served as president and first lady of the United States from 1977 to 1981. Afterwards, not content to sit around and play golf, the former president founded The Carter Center in Atlanta to address health, hunger and other critical issues. The Carters have been ardent supporters of Habitat for Humanity, which helps build housing for low-income people. The Carters enjoy this broccoli soup, which Rosalynn makes often. It's a good source of fiber and vitamins A and C.

    1 medium onion
    1 garlic clove, crushed
    1 teaspoon sunflower or other vegetable oil
    1 bay leaf
    1 pound green broccoli, chopped
2½ cups vegetable stock (see page 21) or low-sodium canned broth
    1 small potato, cubed (for thickening)
       salt and pepper (optional)
       juice of ½ lemon
   ¼ cup low-fat or non-fat plain yogurt

1. Sauté onion and garlic in the oil with bay leaf until soft, about 8 minutes.
2. Add broccoli, stock and potato. Simmer gently, covered, for 10 minutes. The broccoli should be tender but still bright green. Remove bay leaf and let soup cool a little.
3. Purée in a blender (but not so it is entirely smooth). Season to taste and add lemon juice. May need reheating in clean pan before serving.
4. Add a dollop of yogurt before serving.

PER SERVING:

Calories: 156	Fat: 4 g (17% of calories)	Cholesterol: 1 mg	Protein: 11 g
	Saturated Fat: <1 g	Sodium: 105 mg	Carbohydrate: 30 g

ℛ

Annemarie Colbin's
Curried Apple-Squash Bisque
8 servings

☆☆☆☆☆☆☆☆☆☆ ☆☆☆☆☆☆☆☆☆☆ ☆☆☆☆☆☆☆☆☆☆ ☆☆☆☆☆☆☆☆☆☆

Annemarie Colbin is the author of The Natural Gourmet: Delicious Recipes for Healthy, Balanced Eating. *She is a leader in the world of natural-foods cooking and since 1977 has operated The Natural Gourmet Cooking School in New York City. She describes this bisque as "a lovely soup, delicate and with an unusual flavoring touch provided by the very tart Granny Smith apples." The butternut squash adds a good dose of beta-carotene. Her spiced Glazed Pears with Tofu Cream is on page 187.*

1 tablespoon unsalted butter or cold-pressed sunflower oil
1 medium onion, chopped
1 tablespoon curry powder, or to taste
2 Granny Smith apples
1 butternut squash, peeled, seeded and cubed
5 cups vegetable stock (see page 21) or low-sodium canned broth
1 teaspoon sea salt, or to taste
1 tablespoon brown sugar (optional)
1 tablespoon fresh lemon juice

1. In a 3- to 4-quart pot, heat the butter or oil and sauté the onion and the curry powder over medium heat until the onion is translucent, about 10 minutes.
2. Meanwhile, peel and seed one of the apples; cut into cubes. When the onion becomes translucent, add the cubed apple, the squash and the stock. Bring to a boil, reduce heat and simmer, covered, for 20 to 30 minutes, or until the squash is tender. Add the salt and correct the seasoning to taste.
3. Purée the soup in a blender. Peel the remaining apple, grate it and toss in a bowl with the lemon juice. Serve hot or cold, garnished with the freshly grated apple.

PER SERVING:

Calories: 90	Fat: 2 g (18% of calories)	Cholesterol: 4 mg	Protein: 1 g
	Saturated Fat: 1 g	Sodium: 269 mg	Carbohydrate: 18 g

℮а

Alan Cranston's
Senate Bean Soup   *8 servings*

☆☆

Alan Cranston, a California Democrat, served in the United States Senate from 1968 to 1992. He concentrated on world peace, housing and environmental protection. An avid runner, Senator Cranston began the sport long before it became popular, starting in high school and continuing for the next six decades.

Senator Cranston loves hearty soups, as evidenced by these two recipes. The first is the official recipe for what is probably the most famous soup in America (you can leave out the ham hocks and cut the salt, if you wish). Legend has it that Senator Fred Thomas Dubois of Idaho, who served from 1901 to 1907, gaveled through a resolution requiring that bean soup be a daily feature on the Senate Restaurant's menu. Who needs All-Bran when you can get your fiber from bean soup!

2 pounds small Michigan navy beans, washed and run through hot
  water until white
4 quarts hot water
½ pound smoked ham hocks
1 onion, chopped
1 tablespoon butter
1 teaspoon salt
  black pepper to taste

1. Combine beans and water in large pot. Add ham hocks, cover and boil
   slowly for approximately 3 hours.
2. Lightly brown onion in butter and add to soup. Season with salt and
   pepper just before serving.

PER SERVING:
Calories: 289   Fat: 7 g (22% of calories)   Cholesterol: 22 mg   Protein: 19 g
      Saturated Fat: 3 g   Sodium: 629 mg   Carbohydrate: 38 g

Alan Cranston's
Split Pea Soup

6 servings

☆ ☆☆☆

     1 pound green split peas, raw
1 to 2 ham hocks (or ½ ounce ham)
     2 quarts water
     1 onion, chopped
     2 or more carrots, chopped
     2 cloves of garlic, minced
     2 bay leaves
     1 teaspoon thyme
      pepper to taste

1. Combine all ingredients. Bring to a boil. Reduce heat and simmer for 2
   hours, stirring occasionally.
2. Remove ham hocks and bay leaves. Purée through a sieve or use a food
   processor and return to pot. If necessary, dilute with broth or water.

PER SERVING:
Calories: 185   Fat: 1 g (3% of calories)   Cholesterol: 1 mg   Protein: 10 g
      Saturated Fat: <1 g   Sodium: 55 mg   Carbohydrate: 42 g

CSPI's
Celebrity Chicken Stock

Yield: 1 quart

☆ ☆

You don't need to panic or resort to a salty canned broth when a recipe calls for chicken or vegetable stock. For this chicken stock, you can supplement the bones with chicken meat, but to keep the fat content low don't add skin and fatty pieces.

      At least 2 cups of raw chicken bones, without skin
4 to 5 **cups water**
     1 **onion, with outside peel, washed, cut in quarters**
     1 **carrot, scrubbed, cut in half**
     ½ **stalk celery, cut in half**
     1 **bay leaf**
     1 **pinch thyme**
     5 **black peppercorns**
3 to 4 **parsley stems**

1. Put the bones in a pot and cover with cold water. Add onion, carrot and celery.
2. Bring to a boil. Lower heat to simmer and skim off any of the foam on top. Add herbs and spices.
3. Simmer for 3 hours, adding more water if necessary.
4. Strain off all the liquid and cool. Discard bones and vegetables. Refrigerate as soon as possible.
5. Before using, carefully remove all fat.
6. Freeze extra in plastic containers or Ziplock bags.

ॐ

CSPI's
Celebrity Vegetable Stock

Yield: 1 quart

☆ ☆

Making vegetable stock is a creative endeavor. All you need to do is put assorted vegetables and/or vegetable scraps and peelings with spices into water and let them simmer for a while. The following recipe is only a guide. Feel free to add other vegetables and spices, such as the ones listed.

     4 **celery stalks, cut in half**
     1 **yellow squash, cut into ½-inch pieces**
     1 **leek, sliced**
     1 **yellow onion, sliced**
     6 **mushrooms, halved**

1 onion, peeled, halved and studded with 2 cloves
4 carrots, scrubbed, cut in half
1 clove garlic, sliced
6 cups cold water

BOUQUET GARNI:

6 sprigs of parsley
2 sprigs each of fresh marjoram and sage (or ½ teaspoon dried of each)
1 large bay leaf
12 black peppercorns
12 allspice berries

1. Place the vegetables and bouquet garni in a large stockpot filled with the water.
2. Simmer for 35 to 40 minutes.
3. Strain. Discard vegetables and bouquet garni (or use in a soup or stew).

Other vegetables: green beans, broccoli stalks, pea pods, fresh corn kernels
Other spices: thyme, kombu seaweed, allspice berries, white peppercorns

༄

Phyllis Diller's
Gosh...It's Gazpacho! *10 servings*

☆☆☆

Phyllis Diller—comedienne, actress, author and pianist—has had a long and varied career. She played the lead role in Hello, Dolly! *on Broadway, starred in several television series and movies, headlined in six countries as a stand-up comic and has written best-selling books about the wacky side of suburban life. Judging from this gazpacho recipe, rich in beta-carotene and vitamin C, she also could have been a great chef.*

3 cups peeled, coarsely chopped and cored tomatoes (about 3 tomatoes)
1½ cups peeled and coarsely chopped cucumbers (about 1 cucumber)
1 green pepper, cored, seeded and coarsely chopped
1 clove garlic, minced
½ cup water
1 tablespoon olive oil
¼ cup wine vinegar
2 slices untrimmed whole-wheat bread, cubed
⅛ teaspoon cayenne pepper
¼ teaspoon salt
black pepper to taste
6-ounce can of low-sodium tomato juice (if desired)

SUGGESTED GARNISH:
- 1 **cucumber, finely diced**
- ½ **onion, finely diced**
- 1 **green pepper, finely diced**
  croutons, optional

1. Purée all vegetables (except garnish and the remaining ingredients) Chill.
2. Serve in well-chilled soup bowls. Garnish as desired. If the soup is too thick, add 1 or more cans of low-sodium tomato juice.

PER SERVING:
Calories: 50   Fat: 2 g (32% of calories)   Cholesterol: 0 mg   Protein: 2 g
                 Saturated Fat: <1 g   Sodium: 100 mg   Carbohydrate: 8 g

Arlyn Hackett's
Spicy Borscht
8 servings

☆☆☆

Arlyn Hackett is the author of Health Smart Gourmet Cooking, *host of a public-television series of the same name and has taught cooking at the Pritikin Longevity Center. He is also co-owner and managing chef of Doorstep Diets, a cooking school and delivery business in San Diego. Arlyn says, "Carrots, yams and apples provide the sweetness in this version of borscht, rather than the traditional sugar. The sweetness is beautifully complemented by the spices." Americans don't eat nearly enough borscht! Give this great recipe a try. His Vegetables with Thai Marinade recipe is on page 75.*

- 3 **beets, peeled and cut into ½-inch cubes**
- 1 **cup sliced carrots**
- 1 **cup diced yam or sweet potato**
- ½ **cup coarsely chopped red onion**
- 2 **tablespoons fresh ginger, finely minced**
- 1 **teaspoon cinnamon**
- ¼ **teaspoon allspice**
- ¼ **teaspoon cayenne pepper**
- 5 **cups water**
- 2 **cups red cabbage, shredded**
- 2 **red apples, cored and finely diced**
- ½ **cup red wine vinegar**
- ½ **cup unsalted tomato paste**
- 1 **lemon, cut into 8 wedges**
- 1 **orange, cut into 8 wedges**

1. In a soup pot, combine the beets, carrots, yam, onion, ginger, spices and water. Simmer 40 minutes.
2. Add the cabbage and apples; simmer another 15 minutes.
3. Add the vinegar and tomato paste; stir to thoroughly blend the mixture. Cook another 5 minutes and serve.
4. Garnish each bowl with a wedge of lemon and orange.

PER SERVING:

| Calories: 90 | Fat: <1 g (4% of calories) | Cholesterol: 0 mg | Protein: 2 g |
| | Saturated Fat: <1 g | Sodium: 28 mg | Carbohydrate: 23 g |

Jean Hewitt's
Anytime Vegetable Soup   *8 servings*

☆☆☆☆☆☆☆☆ ☆☆☆☆☆☆☆ ☆☆☆☆☆☆☆☆ ☆☆☆☆☆☆☆☆☆☆☆☆☆☆☆☆☆☆

Jean Hewitt, author of The New York Times New Natural Foods Cookbook, *is a four-time winner of the R.T. French Tastemaker Awards. She has been food and equipment editor of* Family Circle *magazine since 1975 and was a food reporter and critic at the* New York Times. *In 1991, the James Beard Foundation and the Oldways Preservations and Trust Society honored Hewitt for her contributions to food journalism. Her Marinated Vegetables are on page 174.*

Jean says, "Good country bread with a hearty soup is my choice for weekend lunches in the country. There's always plenty for family or friends who stop by and leftovers go into the freezer. The ingredients in this soup change with the seasons and can include leftover vegetables, too."

1 onion, chopped
2 tablespoons olive oil
2 cloves of garlic, minced
1 celery stalk, sliced
1 large carrot, thickly sliced
2 cups fresh or frozen vegetables such as corn kernels, peas, lima beans, cut green beans
1 16-ounce can stewed tomatoes (no salt added)
¼ cup small elbow macaroni
4 cups low-sodium vegetable stock (see page 21) or low-sodium canned broth
2 tablespoons chopped fresh basil
1 tablespoon chopped fresh oregano
1 teaspoon salt
¼ teaspoon freshly ground black pepper
1 small zucchini, cut into ¼-inch slices
grated Parmesan cheese, if desired

1. Sauté the onion in olive oil in a large saucepan over medium heat until soft, about 5 minutes. Add garlic and cook 1 minute longer. Add celery, carrot, 2 cups vegetables, tomatoes, macaroni, stock, basil, oregano, salt (reduce salt to cut the sodium, *eds.*) and pepper. Bring to a boil, cover and let simmer until vegetables are crisp-tender, about 6 minutes.
2. Add zucchini and cook 5 minutes longer or until macaroni is al dente. Serve with freshly grated Parmesan cheese, if desired.

PER SERVING:
Calories: 114   Fat: 4 g (30% of calories)   Cholesterol: 0 mg   Protein: 3 g
                 Saturated Fat: <1 g   Sodium: 302 mg   Carbohydrate: 17 g

ဖြင

Michael Jacobson's
Turkey and Vegetable Soup   *18 servings*
☆☆☆ ☆☆☆☆☆☆☆☆☆☆ ☆☆☆☆☆☆☆☆☆☆☆☆☆☆☆☆☆☆☆☆☆☆☆☆☆☆☆☆☆

This recipe comes from Michael Jacobson, executive director and co-founder of the Center for Science in the Public Interest and this cookbook's senior editor. Michael's Green and Spicy Scrambled Eggs is on page 9. Michael, who has a Ph.D. in microbiology, has a decidedly non-scientific approach to preparing soup:

Winter is soup time! I love making a huge pot of soup on a cold Sunday afternoon and having it for lunches and dinners (along with freshly baked whole-wheat bread) during the week. My greatest (and perhaps only) culinary breakthrough came the day I understood the theory of making soups. Previously, I followed recipes slavishly. Now I don't measure anything or plan ahead. I just add ingredients until the soup's about as thick, colorful and spicy as I want. This is a basic recipe that you can vary however you wish. Are you a vegetarian? Just replace the turkey with black beans. Out of potatoes? Then add cooked or uncooked brown rice, or no starchy ingredient at all. Like a thicker soup? Add less stock or water or purée several cups of soup in the blender.

5 cups vegetable or chicken stock (see page 21) or low-sodium canned broth
6 cups water
4 turkey drumsticks, medium (or 16 ounces cooked turkey chunks)
7 ribs celery, chopped (12 ounces)
1 pound carrots, cut into disks and chunks
1 can tomatoes (28 ounces), chopped
5 medium white potatoes (2 pounds), chunks
2 medium onions, diced
8 ounces mushrooms, chopped
3 garlic cloves, crushed or finely diced

2 teaspoons margarine
1 teaspoon black pepper
3 teaspoons oregano
12 fresh basil leaves, diced (or 2 tablespoons dried basil)
grated Parmesan cheese (optional)

1. Start cooking drumsticks in large (8-quart) pot boiling stock or water. Add celery, carrots, tomatoes and potatoes. Sauté onions, mushrooms and garlic in margarine until browned. Add pepper, oregano and basil. Cook for about 1½ hours.
2. Remove drumsticks from soup and place on cutting board; remove meat from bones and skin. Chop meat into chunks and return to pot. Freeze half of soup.
3. When serving, sprinkle on a little grated Parmesan cheese, if you wish.

PER SERVING (10 OUNCES):

Calories: 95	Fat: 1 g (12% of calories)	Cholesterol: 20 mg	Protein: 7 g
	Saturated Fat: <1 g	Sodium: 104 mg	Carbohydrate: 15 g

Norman and Audrey Kaplan's
Red Pepper Soup

4 servings

☆☆☆

Dr. Norman and Audrey Kaplan are the authors of Travel Well, A Gourmet Guide to Healthy Travel. *Norman, an expert on hypertension and the prevention of heart disease, teaches at the University of Texas Southwestern Medical Center at Dallas. Not content to stay in the classroom, he has hosted a PBS-TV series on health, "Here's to Your Health," which was nominated for an Emmy. This reduced-calorie and lower-cholesterol rendition of a traditional red pepper soup recipe is one of the Kaplans' favorites. Peppers are a great source of vitamin C.*

6 large red bell peppers, roasted, peeled and chopped
1 tablespoon corn oil margarine
2 medium onions, finely chopped
3 cups chicken stock (see page 21) or low-sodium canned broth
¼ teaspoon freshly ground black pepper
2 teaspoons apple cider vinegar
½ teaspoon salt (use less to reduce sodium)
1½ tablespoons sugar
basil leaves for garnish
⅓ cup non-fat plain yogurt
1 16-ounce carton part-skim ricotta cheese
1 tablespoon skim milk

1. Slit each pepper and place on cookie sheet. Place under preheated broiler 4 to 6 inches from heat. Roast and rotate until peppers are charred and blistered. Remove and place in paper bag. Close bag and put in freezer for 10 minutes to facilitate removal of skins. Remove seeds and skin.
2. Heat margarine and sauté onions until translucent. Add peppers and chicken stock. Bring to a boil, reduce heat and simmer uncovered slowly for 20 minutes or until peppers are tender.
3. Add black pepper, vinegar, salt and sugar. Purée soup in a food processor. Chill overnight covered.
4. To make light cheese, blend yogurt, ricotta and skim milk in food processor or blender. Refrigerate in tightly covered container. Add a tablespoon to each serving of the soup.

PER SERVING:

Calories: 132	Fat: 5 g (29% of calories)	Cholesterol: 5 mg	Protein: 5 g
	Saturated Fat: 1 g	Sodium: 338 mg	Carbohydrate: 19 g

ౚ

Casey Kasem's
Vegetable Soup
6 servings

☆☆☆ ☆☆☆☆☆☆☆☆☆☆☆☆☆☆ ☆☆☆☆☆☆☆☆☆☆☆☆ ☆☆☆☆☆☆☆☆☆☆☆☆

Millions of Americans adjust their schedules to include Casey Kasem's "American Top 40" countdown of the most popular songs on the radio. Casey's friendly "crackling" voice style has taken him to the top of his profession. A highly respected character actor in films and a veteran of commercials and cartoon shows, Casey is the youngest member ever inducted into the Radio Hall of Fame. We think Casey's Vegetable Soup rates in "Cooking's Top Forty."

   ³/₄   **pound fresh green beans or 1 box frozen green beans**
   1   **green pepper, chopped**
   ½   **large or 1 small head of cauliflower, cut into florets**
   6   **celery stalks, chopped**
   ¼   **cup chopped parsley or celery leaves**
2 to 4   **large yellow onions, sliced or chopped**
   1   **16-ounce can of peeled tomatoes without salt**
   1   **16-ounce can V-8 Juice**
   2   **teaspoons thyme**
   1   **package frozen okra (optional)**
   1   **cup water**

Mix all ingredients and simmer for 45 minutes. Keeps for 2 weeks in the refrigerator.

PER SERVING:
Calories: 108   Fat: <1 g (6% of calories)   Cholesterol: 23 mg   Protein: 4 g
                 Saturated Fat: <1 g   Sodium: 336 mg   Carbohydrate: 8 g

ૹઔ

Edward M. Kennedy's
Cape Cod Fish Chowder
8 servings

☆☆

Senator Edward Kennedy of Massachusetts, youngest brother of President John F. Kennedy, was first elected to the United States Senate in 1962. Ever since, he has been a leading crusader for civil rights, education, health and other causes. While conservatives might not like some of his political stands, everyone should love the senator's Cape Cod Fish Chowder.

- 2 **pounds fresh haddock**
- 2 **ounces salt pork, diced**
- 2 **medium onions, sliced**
- 1 **cup chopped celery**
- 4 **large potatoes**
- 1 **bay leaf, crumbled**
- 4 **cups 1% low-fat milk**
- 2 **tablespoons butter or margarine**
- 1 **teaspoon salt or salt substitute**
   freshly ground black pepper to taste

1. Simmer haddock in 2 cups of water for 15 minutes. Drain off and reserve the broth. Remove the skin and bones from the fish.
2. Sauté the diced pork in a large pot until crisp. Remove and discard the salt pork and sauté the onions in the pork fat until golden brown. Add fish, celery, potatoes and bay leaf. Measure reserved fish broth plus enough boiling water to make 3 cups liquid. Add to pot and simmer 40 minutes.
3. Add milk and butter and simmer for an additional 5 minutes, or until well heated. Season with salt and pepper.

PER SERVING:
Calories: 280   Fat: 9 g (31% of calories)   Cholesterol: 84 mg   Protein: 27 g
                 Saturated Fat: 4 g   Sodium: 527 mg   Carbohydrate: 21 g

ૹઔ

Frank Langella's
Pumpkin Soup
8 servings

☆ ☆

Halloween conjures up thoughts of pumpkins, black cats and vampires. What a perfect time to brew a pot of pumpkin soup! It seems fitting that this recipe comes to us from distinguished actor Frank Langella, who played Dracula in the 1979 film of that name. Frank has starred in many stage and film productions, including Dave, Amadeus *and* Diary of a Mad Housewife, *and received a Tony Award in 1975 for* Seascape. *This pumpkin soup contains stunning amounts of beta-carotene.*

3 cups chicken stock (see page 21) or low-sodium canned broth
4 pounds peeled, seeded fresh pumpkin (or 1½ one-pound cans
   unsweetened canned pumpkin purée)
2 cups water
2 cups skim milk
2 tablespoons packed brown sugar
1 tablespoon unsalted butter
   pinch ground ginger
   large pinch cinnamon
   salt and pepper (optional)
   optional garnishes: non-fat yogurt, chopped peanuts and parsley

1. Heat stock in medium saucepan over high heat to boiling. Boil until reduced to about 2 cups, about 15 to 20 minutes. Remove from heat and skim fat from surface.
2. Cut pumpkin into 1-inch chunks. Place in large heavy saucepan with 2 cups water, bring to a boil and simmer, covered, for 5 minutes. Drain and purée in a food processor.
3. Heat milk in a large heavy saucepan over medium heat until hot (do not boil). Stir in pumpkin purée, brown sugar and butter. Stir in stock. Add ginger, cinnamon and salt (adds sodium) and pepper to taste. Continue to cook, stirring until just heated (do not boil).
4. Soup can be prepared to this point and frozen or put into fridge for up to 2 days. Just before serving, gently reheat soup over low heat or in microwave, stirring to prevent scorching. Again, do not boil.
5. Serve with optional garnishes: non-fat yogurt, chopped peanuts and parsley.

PER SERVING:

Calories: 64	Fat: 1 g (21% of calories)	Cholesterol: 5 mg	Protein: 3 g
	Saturated Fat: 1 g	Sodium: 34 mg	Carbohydrate: 10 g

Abby Mandel's
Winter White Fennel Bisque
6 servings

☆☆

An expert on food for fast-paced, fat-conscious folks, Abby Mandel won the IACP/Seagram best-cookbook award in the quick-cooking category for More Taste Than Time. *She has authored several other cookbooks, writes for publications such as* Bon Appétit *and consults for the restaurant industry. If you aren't familiar with parsnips and fennel, this recipe will have you coming back for more. Her Strawberry Sherbet is on page 190.*

Abby says, "This milky-white soup is rich and soothing, as though it were amply endowed with cream. In truth, there's not a drop. Parsnips are used as a body builder, adding a velvety finish and a hint of sweetness to the delicately flavored fennel."

  1 **medium onion, peeled**
  1 **tablespoon unsalted butter**
  2 **large fennel bulbs (1¾ pounds total)**
  2 **small parsnips, peeled**
2½ to 3 **cups chicken stock (see page 21) or low-sodium canned broth**
     freshly ground white pepper

1. Cut the onion into very thin slices with the thin slicer of a food processor or by hand. Thinner slices will cook more quickly. Melt the butter in a 3-quart pan. Add the onion and cook gently until it is soft, about 10 minutes.
2. Trim about ¼ of the feathery greens from the fennel and reserve. Remove the slender stalks and the rest of the greens from the fennel, leaving only the bulb. Slice the fennel bulb and the parsnips as you did the onions.
3. Add the fennel and the parsnips to the pan along with 2½ cups stock or broth. Cover and bring to a boil. When the mixture is boiling, reduce the heat and simmer until all the vegetables are very soft, about 25 minutes.
4. Strain the vegetables from the liquid, reserving both. Purée the vegetables and the reserved fennel greens in the processor or in batches in a blender.
5. Stir the purée into the cooking liquid and thin with additional broth if the soup is too thick. Add salt and pepper to taste. The soup can be refrigerated up to 3 days, or frozen. Reheat gently and adjust the seasoning, if necessary, before serving.

PER SERVING:

Calories: 93	Fat: 2 g (21% of calories)	Cholesterol: 5 mg	Protein: 2 g
	Saturated Fat: 1 g	Sodium: 71 mg	Carbohydrate: 16 g

John and Mary McDougall's
Black Bean Soup

10 servings

☆☆☆☆☆☆ ☆☆☆☆☆☆☆☆☆ ☆☆☆☆☆☆☆ ☆☆☆☆☆☆☆☆☆☆☆☆☆☆☆

We need more doctors like John McDougall. Dr. McDougall focuses on the prevention and treatment of disease through diet, exercise and stress reduction. His ideas are explained in his book, The McDougall Plan, 12 Days to Dynamic Health, *and put into practice at St. Helena Hospital and Health Center in Deer Park, California, where he and his wife Mary run a crash course on health and fitness. Their Vegetarian Chili is on page 78.*

Dr. McDougall says, "This recipe used to be served at one of our favorite Mexican restaurants. Based on suspected ingredients, Mary invented her own version, and it's every bit as tasty and a lot healthier."

1	**pound black beans**
2	**quarts water**
1	**large onion, coarsely chopped**
1 to 2	**cloves of garlic, minced**
1	**16-ounce can chopped tomatoes**
1	**4-ounce can chopped green chilies**
1	**teaspoon cumin**
1	**teaspoon chili powder**
1	**teaspoon lemon juice**
¼	**teaspoon crushed red pepper**
¼	**cup chopped cilantro**
	salt (optional)

1. Soak beans overnight in the water.
2. Bring water and beans to a boil, cover and reduce heat. Simmer for 1 hour, then add remaining ingredients, except for the cilantro. Cook covered until beans are tender, about 2 hours.
3. Add cilantro (and salt to taste, if you want) just before serving, mixing well, and let rest, covered, for about 15 minutes. Serve hot.

Note: This is great to make in a slow-cooker. Put everything into the pot, except the cilantro, early in the morning. (No need to soak the beans first.) Turn the cooker to high heat, cover and let cook all day. Add cilantro just before serving.

PER SERVING:

Calories: 180	Fat 1 g (6% of calories)	Cholesterol: 0 mg	Protein: 11 g
	Saturated Fat: <1 g	Sodium: 173 mg	Carbohydrate: 33 g

Ross and Margot Perot's
Lentil and Brown Rice Soup
10 servings

☆☆☆☆☆☆☆☆☆☆☆☆☆☆☆☆☆☆☆☆☆☆☆☆☆☆☆☆☆☆☆☆☆☆☆☆☆☆

Ross and Margot Perot shot from relative obscurity to national prominence in 1992, when businessman Ross ran for the presidency and did better than any third-party candidate in seventy-five years. While people have mixed feelings about his venture into national politics, we think everyone will be enthusiastic about the Perots' classic Lentil and Brown Rice Soup and Black Bean Salad on page 44.

  5 cups chicken or vegetable stock (see page 21)
  3 cups water
 1½ cups lentils, picked over and rinsed
  1 cup brown rice
  2 1-pound cans tomatoes, drained and chopped, juice reserved
  3 carrots, halved lengthwise and cut crosswise into ¼-inch pieces
  1 onion, chopped
  1 stalk celery, chopped
  3 cloves of garlic, minced
 ½ teaspoon dried basil
 ½ teaspoon dried oregano
 ½ teaspoon dried thyme
  1 bay leaf
 ½ cup fresh parsley leaves, chopped
  2 tablespoons cider vinegar, or more to taste
    salt and pepper to taste (optional)

1. In a heavy kettle, combine the stock, water, lentils, rice, tomatoes, reserved juice, carrots, onion, celery, garlic, basil, oregano, thyme and bay leaf. Bring the liquid to a boil and simmer, covered, stirring occasionally, for 40 minutes. Add vinegar and cook for 5 more minutes or until the lentils and rice are tender.
2. Stir in the parsley, vinegar and salt and pepper (if desired). Remove bay leaf. The soup will be thick and will thicken as it stands. Thin the soup, if you want, with additional hot stock or water.

PER SERVING:
Calories: 170   Fat: 1 g (6% of calories)   Cholesterol: 0 mg   Protein: 11 g
                  Saturated Fat: <1 g   Sodium: 115 mg   Carbohydrate: 30 g

Sally Schneider's

Yellow Pepper and
White Bean Soup with Sage

8 servings

☆☆

Chef and cookbook writer Sally Schneider says her goal is to "lighten the wonderful foods of memory without compromising integrity or deliciousness." Sally is the author of The Art of Low-Calorie Cooking *and a contributing editor to* Food and Wine *magazine. Formerly, she cooked professionally in France and ran a catering business in New York.*

Sally says this soup is "a meal in itself...extremely rich, yet has all the healthful virtues of beans, which are low in calories and high in fiber and protein. This recipe began with the classic Italian Tuscan flavorings for white beans—garlic and sage—and evolved into a rustic soup, almost a stew, embellished with sweet bell pepper and tomato."

14 ounces navy or great northern white beans (2 cups), picked over to remove any grit
1 tablespoon plus 2 teaspoons olive oil
3 yellow bell peppers, seeded and cut into ½-inch dice (3 cups)
1 medium onion, chopped
4 large cloves of garlic, coarsely chopped
1 35-ounce can Italian peeled tomatoes and their liquid, seeded and coarsely chopped
1½ cups chicken stock (see page 21) or low-sodium canned broth
8 sage leaves, preferably fresh
¾ teaspoon salt
½ teaspoon sugar
1 teaspoon balsamic or red wine vinegar
   freshly ground black pepper

1. In a medium saucepan, soak the beans overnight in enough water to cover. Alternatively, in a medium saucepan, cover the beans with water and bring to a boil over moderately high heat. Cover, remove from the heat and let stand for 1 hour.
2. Drain the beans. Return to the saucepan and add enough cold water so the water line is at least 2 inches above beans. Bring to a boil, reduce the heat to a simmer and cook until the beans are tender but not mushy, about 1 hour. Drain the beans.
3. In a large heavy saucepan or flameproof casserole dish, combine the oil, bell peppers, onion and garlic. Cover and cook over low heat, stirring frequently, until the vegetables are soft but not brown, about 15 minutes.
4. Add the tomatoes and their liquid, the chicken stock, sage, salt, sugar and cooked beans. Simmer until the soup begins to thicken and the beans are soft, 30 to 45 minutes.

5. Stir in the vinegar. Season with black pepper to taste. This soup can be made ahead. Let cool, cover and refrigerate for up to 4 days or freeze for up to 3 months.

Variation: This soup also makes a superb sauce for pasta. For each serving, figure ½ portion (about ½ cup) of the soup per 2 ounces of dry pasta.

PER SERVING:
Calories: 248   Fat: 4 g (15% of calories)   Cholesterol: 0 mg   Protein: 13 g
                 Saturated Fat: <1 g   Sodium: 334 mg   Carbohydrate: 41 g

William Styron's
New England Clam Chowder
8 *servings*

☆☆☆ ☆☆☆☆☆☆☆☆☆☆☆ ☆☆☆☆☆ ☆☆☆☆☆☆☆☆☆☆☆☆☆☆☆☆☆☆☆☆☆☆☆☆

William Styron is probably best known for his book Sophie's Choice, *which won the American Book Award and became a 1982 Oscar-winning movie starring Meryl Streep and Kevin Kline. He also captured the Pulitzer Prize in 1968 for* The Confessions of Nat Turner. *Styron's recent book,* Darkness Visible, *describes his personal experience with depression. William's meticulously described chowder offers a good amount of iron, other minerals and vitamin C:*

New England clam chowder, if made properly, is one of the sublime products of American cuisine. Too often, however, the result is disappointing. Most clam chowders are overly creamy, starchy concoctions from which the tangy clam taste is muted or virtually missing. There is no need to overload a chowder with rich cream or milk. Another defect of many clam chowders is the unsatisfying consistency. This is the result, usually, of maintaining the tired practice of filling the chowder with little cubes of diced, peeled potatoes. A far more pleasant texture can be achieved by running the potatoes (unpeeled for the sake of both taste and nutrition) through a food processor equipped with a julienne blade. The potato strips can then be cut to shorter length with a sharp knife. Medium-sized Cherrystone clams make the best chowder, and the freshly opened clams can be chopped by hand or by the food processor's utility blade, care being taken to avoid a puréed effect. All clam juice should be carefully reserved. There is no need for added salt, the clams being pleasantly saline. I've been cooking this chowder for over a quarter century, both in Connecticut and at my summer place on Martha's Vineyard, where the clams are especially delicious and abundant. I serve it frequently, and am not displeased that the praise it receives often exceeds the few nice words I occasionally get for my writing.

5 dozen Cherrystone clams
1 2-inch cube of salt pork, or 4 slices bacon, chopped
1 large onion, chopped finely
5 medium potatoes, sliced by a food processor's julienne blade then
  chopped into 2-inch strips
  black pepper
3 cups low-fat milk

1. Open clams by hand, reserving juice, or steam them open by placing
   them in a pot along with 5 cups of water and letting boil for 10 minutes
   or until shells open. Reserve water and juice.
2. Chop clams by hand or, coarsely, in a food processor.
3. Fry salt pork or bacon in 4-quart saucepan. Add chopped onion and
   cook until it becomes transparent. Add chopped clams and juice.
4. Add potatoes. Season liberally with pepper. No salt is needed. Simmer
   on low heat for approximately 40 minutes, stirring occasionally.
5. Add low-fat milk that has been previously warmed. Do not allow to boil.
   Serve piping hot.

PER SERVING:
Calories: 260   Fat: 4 g (13% of calories)   Cholesterol: 32 mg   Protein: 16 g
                 Saturated Fat: 1 g   Sodium: 144 mg   Carbohydrate: 44 g

Dick Van Patten's
Paton e Fasool (Beans and Potato Soup)   *6 servings*

☆☆☆ ☆☆☆☆☆☆☆ ☆☆☆☆☆☆☆☆☆☆☆☆☆☆☆☆☆☆ ☆☆☆☆☆☆☆☆☆☆☆☆☆

*Perhaps you recall that struggling father raising eight kids in the television
series "Eight Is Enough." Now you'll remember Dick Van Patten as the creator of
this hearty, low-fat soup, the Eggplant Parmesan on page 89 and the Vegetable
Lasagna on page 122.*

½ tablespoon olive oil
½ tablespoon safflower oil
¼ cup onions, diced finely
6 medium potatoes, peeled and diced (leave 1 whole)
1 carrot, diced finely
1 stalk celery, diced finely
6 cups water
2 19-ounce cans great northern beans with liquid
½ cup fresh oregano
  sun-dried tomatoes, for garnish, plumped with water according to package

1. Put oil in 5-quart pot. Steam onions (don't let them brown). Add 5 peeled and diced potatoes and 1 whole potato (cut in half), carrot, celery and enough water to more than cover.
2. Let simmer for at least 1 hour. Take out whole potato, mash and return to pot. Add more water if necessary.
3. About 15 minutes before cooking ends, add beans (if desired, rinse and drain to reduce sodium) and oregano. Serve with cut up sun-dried tomatoes on the side.

PER SERVING:

Calories: 427	Fat: 4 g (9% of calories)	Cholesterol: 0 mg	Protein: 15 g
	Saturated Fat: <1 g	Sodium: 458 mg	Carbohydrate: 84 g

Anya von Bremzen's
Armenian Lentil and Apricot Soup   *6 servings*

☆☆☆☆☆ ☆☆☆☆☆☆☆☆☆ ☆☆☆☆☆☆☆☆☆ ☆☆☆☆☆☆☆☆☆☆☆☆☆☆☆☆☆☆☆

Moscow-born food writer Anya von Bremzen co-authored Please to the Table: The Russian Cookbook, *winner of the 1990 James Beard Award for the best international cookbook. One of the book's aims is to dispel the myth that foods of the former Soviet Union are all heavy, dairy rich and bland.*

Anya says, "I have a special fondness for the cuisines of the former Soviet Caucasian republics of Armenia, Georgia and Azerbaijan. In this soup the dried apricots blend beautifully in color and taste with the red lentils. When combined with the lemon juice, they impart a lovely sweet and tart flavor to this dish. This soup is so special that I like to serve it as a first course at a Thanksgiving meal."

- 2 tablespoons vegetable oil
- 1 large onion, finely chopped
- 2 teaspoons finely chopped garlic (about 4 cloves)
- 6 to 8 dried apricots, chopped
- 1½ cups dried split red lentils (available at Middle Eastern shops and health food stores), rinsed and thoroughly dried
- 5 cups chicken stock (see page 21) or low-sodium canned broth
- 6 medium plum tomatoes, peeled, seeded and chopped
- ½ teaspoon ground cumin
- ½ teaspoon dried thyme
  fresh lemon juice to taste
- ½ teaspoon salt
  black pepper to taste
  freshly chopped parsley for garnish

1. Heat the oil in a large soup pot. Add the onion, garlic and dried apricots. Sauté over medium heat until tender, about 15 minutes.
2. Add the lentils and the broth. Bring to a boil, reduce heat and cover. Simmer until the lentils are tender, about 30 minutes.
3. Stir in tomatoes, cumin, thyme, salt and pepper. Simmer for another 10 minutes.
4. Process half of the soup in a food processor fitted with a steel blade and return it to the pot. Add lemon juice, salt and pepper to taste and simmer, stirring, for 2 to 3 minutes. Serve garnished with parsley.

PER SERVING:
Calories: 201   Fat: 6 g (25% of calories)   Cholesterol: 0 mg   Protein: 15 g
                Saturated Fat: <1 g   Sodium: 190 mg   Carbohydrate: 24 g

Gene Wilder's
Turnip Soup with Thyme   *8 servings*

☆☆ ☆☆☆☆☆☆☆☆☆☆ ☆☆☆☆☆☆☆☆ ☆☆☆☆☆☆☆☆☆☆☆☆☆☆☆☆☆☆☆☆☆

When it comes to versatility as an actor, Gene Wilder has few peers. Children will remember him as Willy Wonka in Willy Wonka and the Chocolate Factory. *Their parents will recall his stellar performances in* Blazing Saddles *and* Young Frankenstein. *Besides starring in films for thirty years, Gene has played in Broadway productions and many television specials. When he is not writing, acting or directing, Gene whips up a big pot of turnip soup. Both the turnips and the greens are rich in vitamin C, while the greens are loaded with beta-carotene and calcium.*

    4 teaspoons olive oil
    2 medium onions, chopped
    3 large cloves of garlic, minced
 2½ pounds turnips, cut into ½-inch cubes
    2 medium red potatoes, cut into ½-inch cubes
  ¼ teaspoon salt
  ½ teaspoon freshly ground black pepper
    1 tablespoon fresh thyme
    3 cups chicken stock (see page 21) or low-sodium canned broth, mixed with 2 cups water, brought to a boil and set aside
  ¾ pound of turnip greens, washed and chopped coarsely, or 1 package frozen turnip greens, thawed
    2 tablespoons red wine vinegar

1. Heat olive oil in a soup kettle and add onions and garlic. Sauté over medium heat for about 5 minutes until soft. Add turnips, potatoes, salt, pepper and thyme. Cover and cook on low heat until turnips and

potatoes have softened slightly, about 15 minutes.

2. Add 3 cups warm broth, cover and simmer until vegetables are tender, about 20 minutes.

3. Add turnip greens and additional broth and simmer 5 to 10 minutes longer. Add red wine vinegar, adjust seasoning and if a thicker soup is desired, purée half and return to pot.

PER SERVING:

Calories: 98	Fat: 3 g (27% of calories)	Cholesterol: 0 mg	Protein: 3 g
	Saturated Fat: <1 g	Sodium: 144 mg	Carbohydrate: 18 g

SIDE SALADS AND DRESSINGS

Barbara Bach's
Green Salad
8 servings

☆ ☆☆☆☆☆☆☆ ☆☆☆☆☆☆☆☆ ☆☆☆☆☆☆☆☆☆☆☆☆☆☆☆☆☆☆☆☆☆☆☆☆☆☆☆

Besides being married to Ringo Starr, whose Chunky Fish recipe is on page 146, Barbara Bach is a celebrity in her own right. You may have seen her in The Spy Who Loved Me, Force 10 from Navarone *or other films in which she starred. Or you may have seen her on the cover of* Mademoiselle *or* Glamour *magazines. Barbara stays in such good shape by eating recipes like this nutritious green salad.*

- ½ **small head arugula lettuce**
- ½ **small head radicchio lettuce**
- ½ **small head iceberg lettuce**
- ½ **small head romaine lettuce**
- 2 **teaspoons sunflower seeds**
- 1 **ounce shredded Parmesan cheese**

VINAIGRETTE:
- ¾ **teaspoon smooth Dijon mustard**
   pinch of salt
- 1½ **tablespoons red wine vinegar**
- 1½ **tablespoons olive oil**
- ¾ **tablespoon water**

1. Tear or chop lettuces and mix in a bowl. Arrange on separate chilled plates.
2. Sprinkle each salad with 1 teaspoon sunflower seeds and ¼ of the Parmesan.
3. Place all the vinaigrette ingredients in a small jar. Cover tightly and shake until the ingredients are blended. Spoon over each salad.

PER SERVING:

Calories: 62	Fat: 5 g (66% of calories)	Cholesterol: 3 mg	Protein: 3 g
	Saturated Fat: 1 g	Sodium: 93 mg	Carbohydrate: 3 g

Pat Baird's
Almost No Fat Potato Salad
8 servings

☆☆ ☆☆☆☆☆☆☆ ☆☆☆☆☆☆☆☆ ☆☆☆☆☆☆☆☆☆☆☆☆☆☆☆☆☆☆☆☆☆☆☆☆☆☆

Pat Baird is the author of Quick Harvest: A Vegetarian's Guide to Microwave Cooking. *She has written articles for* Restaurant Business, Bon Appétit *and other publications and is a consultant for health organizations and corporations.*

Pat offers this Almost No Fat Potato Salad as a great alternative to the usual mayonnaise-drenched version. The sweet potatoes make this supercharged with beta-carotene and vitamin C. Use any of your favorite herbs—dill, chives or chervil—in place of the ones here. Pat has a stunning appetizer recipe using beets and tofu on page 50.

1¼ pounds small red new potatoes (about 12)
  1 pound sweet potatoes (2 medium)
  3 scallions, including green tops, thinly sliced
  ½ cup packed parsley, finely chopped
  ½ cup packed cilantro leaves, finely chopped
  ⅓ cup loosely packed mint leaves, finely chopped
  ½ cup non-fat yogurt
  ½ cup low-fat mayonnaise
  ¼ teaspoon Tabasco
    juice of 1 large lemon (about 3 tablespoons)
    salt and freshly ground pepper (optional)

1. Scrub potatoes. Bake at 375° until just tender. Let cool slightly and cut into 1-inch cubes, leaving skins on.
2. In a large mixing bowl, combine the potatoes, scallions and chopped herbs.
3. In a small bowl, combine the yogurt, mayonnaise, Tabasco and lemon juice until well blended. Stir the sauce into the potato mixture. Sprinkle with salt and pepper to taste and adjust other seasonings if desired.

PER SERVING:

Calories: 140	Fat: 3 g (20% of calories)	Cholesterol: 4 mg	Protein: 3 g
	Saturated Fat: <1 g	Sodium: 92 mg	Carbohydrate: 25 g

Mayim Bialik's
Carrot Raisin Salad
2 servings

☆☆ ☆☆ ☆☆ ☆☆ ☆ ☆☆ ☆☆ ☆☆ ☆ ☆☆ ☆☆ ☆☆ ☆☆ ☆☆ ☆☆ ☆☆ ☆☆ ☆☆ ☆☆ ☆☆ ☆☆ ☆

Mayim Bialik stars as the spunky, thoroughly modern teenager in the television sitcom "Blossom" and had a starring role in the movie Beaches. *Her distinctive voice has been used in cartoons and commercials, including the Peanuts character Peppermint Patty. Mayim has been active in causes ranging from the environment to animal rights to the homeless. Her salad provides plenty of beta-carotene and is quick and easy to prepare.*

  2 carrots, shredded
  4 tablespoons Miracle Whip Free Nonfat Dressing
  ½ cup raisins
  ⅛ cup chopped walnuts

Combine all ingredients and chill.

PER SERVING:

Calories: 227	Fat: 5 g (18% of calories)	Cholesterol: 0 mg	Protein: 3 g
	Saturated Fat: <1 g	Sodium: 30 mg	Carbohydrate: 47 g

Kenneth Cooper's
Creamy Dill Salad Dressing

27 servings

☆☆☆☆ ☆☆☆☆☆☆☆☆☆☆ ☆☆☆☆☆☆☆☆☆☆☆☆☆☆☆☆☆☆☆☆☆ ☆☆☆☆☆☆☆☆☆

Dr. Kenneth Cooper's revolutionary 1968 book Aerobics *spawned massive interest in jogging and catapulted him to the forefront of the physical-fitness movement. In 1970, he founded The Aerobics Center in Dallas to undertake exercise research, conduct wellness programs and provide consulting services. Among his other books are* Controlling Cholesterol *and* Kid Fitness. *Anyone who doesn't exercise regularly should put down this cookbook and run (or walk briskly!) directly to the bookstore or library to get one of Dr. Cooper's books.*

Dr. Cooper recommends this low-fat salad dressing that appeared in the Cooper Clinic Cook-It-Light Cookbook.

½ **cup low-fat cottage cheese**
½ **cup skim milk**
2 **tablespoons white wine vinegar**
1 **clove garlic, crushed (or ½ teaspoon minced garlic)**
  freshly ground black pepper to taste
½ **cup Miracle Whip Free Nonfat Dressing**
1 **tablespoon olive oil**
⅛ **teaspoon sugar**
1 **teaspoon dillweed**

Using a food processor, blend together all ingredients until smooth.

PER SERVING (1 TABLESPOON):

Calories: 16	Fat: 1 g (33% of calories)	Cholesterol: 0 mg	Protein: 1 g
	Saturated Fat: <1 g	Sodium: 20 mg	Carbohydrate: 2 g

Larry Gelbart's
Cooked Carrot Salad Moroccan
4 servings

☆☆☆☆ ☆☆☆☆☆☆☆☆☆☆ ☆☆☆☆☆☆☆☆☆☆☆☆☆☆☆☆ ☆☆☆☆☆☆☆☆☆☆

Lovers of the television show "M*A*S*H" have writer and producer Larry Gelbart to blame for their addiction. Larry has perfected the knack of making people laugh. Jack Paar, Jack Carson, Bob Hope, Red Buttons, Sid Caesar and Art Carney all used his material. His stage and screen credits include A Funny Thing Happened on the Way to the Forum *and* Tootsie. *Larry's two fat-free salads— no joke—are a culinary delight, tangy and thinning.*

1	**pound carrots**
1	**clove of garlic**
1	**teaspoon cumin**
1	**teaspoon chili powder**
2	**tablespoons white vinegar**
¼	**cup minced Italian parsley**
¼	**cup minced Chinese parsley**
1 to 4	**tablespoons tomato sauce**

1. Peel carrots and slice diagonally. Cook in boiling water (or steam) with the garlic clove until fork-tender. Drain.
2. Add remaining ingredients and mix gently. Chill. Remove garlic clove before serving.

PER SERVING:

Calories: 60	Fat: <1 g (6% of calories)	Cholesterol: 0 mg	Protein: 2 g
	Saturated Fat: 0 g	Sodium: 140 mg	Carbohydrate: 14 g

Larry Gelbart's
Cooked Eggplant Salad Moroccan
4 servings

☆☆☆☆ ☆☆☆☆☆☆☆☆☆☆ ☆☆☆☆☆☆☆☆☆☆☆☆☆☆☆☆ ☆☆☆☆☆☆☆☆☆☆

1	**pound eggplant**
1	**clove of garlic, minced or pressed**
1	**teaspoon chili powder**
1	**teaspoon cumin**
1	**teaspoon paprika**
2	**tablespoons mild vinegar**
4	**tablespoons tomato sauce**

1. Pierce eggplant in several places with skewer and roast in 400° oven until skin can be easily peeled (over 1 hour for large eggplant).
2. When cool, peel and cut into pieces or mash with fork. Add remaining ingredients. Mix well and chill.

Note: This is better the second day.

PER SERVING:

Calories: 41　　　Fat: <1 g (8% of calories)　　　Cholesterol: 0 mg　　　Protein: 2 g
　　　　　　　　　Saturated Fat: 0 g　　　　　　　Sodium: 103 mg　　　Carbohydrate: 10 g

Ross and Margot Perot's
Black Bean Salad
4 servings

☆☆☆☆ ☆☆☆☆☆☆☆☆☆☆☆ ☆☆☆☆☆☆☆☆☆☆☆☆☆☆☆☆☆☆ ☆☆☆☆☆☆☆☆☆

Though Ross and Margot Perot didn't get to the White House in 1992, this is one unusual, high-protein salad that can get into your house. Referring to this recipe and the Perots' Lentil and Brown Rice Soup on page 32, Margot says, "These have become family favorites over the years."

　1　19-ounce can Progresso black beans, drained and rinsed
　1　small can whole kernel corn, drained and rinsed
　1　large tomato, chopped
　½　bunch cilantro, chopped
　1　pickled jalapeño, chopped
　　　juice of 1 lime
　2　tablespoons olive oil
　1　tablespoon cumin
　2　cloves of garlic, minced
　　　salt and pepper, if desired

Mix all ingredients well and marinate overnight.

PER SERVING:

Calories: 209　　　Fat: 8 g (34% of calories)　　　Cholesterol: 0 mg　　　Protein: 9 g
　　　　　　　　　Saturated Fat: 1 g　　　　　　　Sodium: 259 mg　　　Carbohydrate: 27 g

Phyllis Richman's
Bob's Stay-at-Home Chickpea Salad *4 servings*

☆☆☆☆ ☆☆☆☆☆☆☆☆☆☆ ☆☆☆☆☆☆☆☆☆☆☆☆☆☆☆☆ ☆☆☆☆☆☆☆☆☆

Phyllis Richman has been a restaurant critic and food writer for the Washington Post *since the 1970s. Washington-area restaurateurs would kill to get a good review from her—and those who get skewered probably also have killing on their mind. Though taste has been her passion more than health, she combines both concerns in this chickpea salad. Phyllis says:*

As a restaurant critic getting my fill of rich food and formal settings, I really crave a simple meal at home. Bob Burton, the man I share my home with, would almost always prefer that simple at-home meal, and frequently makes this for me as an antidote for restaurant cooking. It is easy, nutritious and refreshing, as well as endlessly variable. If you need to watch your salt intake, you can cut the anchovies, but they are a remarkably good contrast to the chickpeas.

1 **19-ounce can chickpeas, drained and rinsed**
1 **small ripe tomato, (no tomato is preferable to a bad tomato), chopped**
1 **small red onion, chopped coarsely**
½ **2-ounce can flat anchovies, cut in quarters**
  several sprigs of fresh parsley, chopped finely
  olive oil (optional)
  balsamic vinegar to taste
  freshly ground black pepper to taste

In a large bowl, lightly mix chickpeas, tomato, onion, anchovies and parsley. Add ½ the oil from anchovy can and, if desired, an extra splash or 2 of olive oil. Add a goodly amount of vinegar and pepper to taste. Mix lightly.

Variations: Olives or red bell peppers are good additions. Scallions—or any other raw vegetables—can be added as well.

PER SERVING:

Calories: 169	Fat: 6 g (30% of calories)	Cholesterol: 0 mg	Protein: 10 g
	Saturated Fat: <1 g	Sodium: 426 mg	Carbohydrate: 20 g

Lorna J. Sass's
Red Bean Salad Olé *8 servings*

☆☆☆☆ ☆☆☆☆☆☆☆☆☆☆ ☆☆☆☆☆☆☆☆☆☆☆☆☆☆☆☆ ☆☆☆☆☆☆☆☆☆

From her home in New York City, Lorna Sass creates recipes that tread lightly on the heart and Earth. Her dishes in these pages are from Recipes from an

Ecological Kitchen, *which contains cost- and environmentally conscious vegan (no meat, dairy or eggs) dishes. Lorna also authored* Cooking Under Pressure, *which features quick, healthy cooking with a pressure cooker, and writes for publications such as the* New York Times, *the* Washington Post *and* Gourmet. *Two of this culinary historian's books,* To the Queen's Taste *and* Christmas Feasts from History, *have won the prestigious Tastemaker Award.*

Here is a bean and roasted pepper salad with a Spanish accent. Since the taste is optimum after the beans have had a chance to marinate, prepare this salad a few hours before serving. For a wonderful, healthful dessert, try Lorna's Lemon Poppyseed Cake on page 196.

2½ cups firm, cooked red beans, such as kidney beans or tolosanas
¼ cup finely chopped red (Spanish) onion or thinly sliced scallion greens
2 large red peppers, roasted (see page 116), seeded and cut into thin strips
1 cup thinly sliced celery
½ cup tightly packed minced fresh parsley
¼ cup tightly packed minced fresh coriander

DRESSING:
2 tablespoons olive oil
juice of 2 limes (about ⅓ cup)
3 to 5 tablespoons sherry wine or balsamic vinegar
1 teaspoon coarsely ground juniper berries
½ teaspoon paprika
½ teaspoon salt, or to taste
pinch of cayenne

1. In a salad bowl or storage container, combine the beans, onion, red peppers, celery, parsley and coriander.
2. In a jar, combine the oil, lime juice, 3 tablespoons vinegar, juniper berries, paprika, salt and cayenne. Shake well to blend. Pour over the beans and stir.
3. Add more salt, if needed, and sprinkle on enough additional vinegar to give the salad a distinctively pickled flavor. (The amount you add will depend upon your taste and the strength of the vinegar.)

Note: If you have a half cup or so of cooked grains in the house, they can be tossed in about an hour before serving to absorb the liquid released as the salad marinates. It's also fun to mix cooked Christmas limas or speckled butterbeans with the red beans for an unusually pretty salad.

PER SERVING:
Calories: 124   Fat: 4 g (27% of calories)   Cholesterol: 0 mg   Protein: 6 g
Saturated Fat: 1 g   Sodium: 150 mg   Carbohydrate: 18 g

Richard Simmons's
Classic Citrus Salad

1 serving

☆☆☆☆ ☆☆☆☆☆☆☆☆☆☆☆ ☆☆☆☆☆☆☆☆☆☆☆☆☆☆☆☆☆ ☆☆☆☆☆☆☆☆☆

For people a with weight problem, Richard Simmons is just short of being a god. With infectious good humor, a pile of great dance records and an empathy that comes from having been fat, Richard will do anything he possibly can to help people exercise and eat their way to fitness. Working out with Richard at his exercise salon in Beverly Hills is probably one of the most exhilarating things one can do in that city. Richard wrote The Never Say Diet Book *and an exercise book for the physically challenged. But it was his syndicated television show, "The Richard Simmons Show," that made him famous. More recently, his "Deal-a-Meal" weight-loss program has been featured in countless infomercials on late-night television, and his wonderful series of "Sweatin' to the Oldies" exercise videos has inspired millions of people to dance off the pounds.*

This salad is light on calories, but infused with gourmet flavor. And what with the spinach and orange, you'll get a nice dose of vitamin C and iron. Turn to page 198 for Richard's Pineapple Bavarian Creme—it sounds and tastes decadent, but still meets our healthful guidelines.

DRESSING:
  1 tablespoon natural rice vinegar
  ¼ teaspoon Dijon-style mustard
  ¼ teaspoon sugar
    dash each salt and pepper
  ½ teaspoon olive oil

SALAD:
  2 cups fresh spinach leaves, washed, dried, torn and chilled
  1 small orange, peeled and segmented
  2 tablespoons finely sliced red onion
  3 walnut halves, chopped coarsely

1. To make dressing, whisk together dressing ingredients in a small bowl.
2. To make salad, arrange salad ingredients in serving bowl. Pour dressing over salad and toss.

PER SERVING:
Calories: 160   Fat: 7 g (41% of calories)   Cholesterol: 0 mg   Protein: 6 g
                 Saturated Fat: <1 g   Sodium: 128 mg   Carbohydrate: 24 g

Ernst Wynder's
Creamy Oriental Cheese Dressing
4 servings

☆☆☆☆ ☆☆☆☆☆☆☆☆☆☆ ☆☆☆☆☆☆☆☆☆☆☆☆☆☆☆ ☆☆☆☆☆☆☆☆☆

Ernst Wynder, M.D., whose pioneering research demonstrated that smoking causes lung cancer, is one of America's leading health-promotion advocates. He preaches a diet low in fat and high in fiber, and this tangy salad dressing certainly fits in. Dr. Wynder founded the American Health Foundation, which not only does important research on diet and health, but also created a terrific program, "Know Your Body," that motivates school children to lead a healthy lifestyle. This Creamy Oriental Cheese Dressing is a piquant low-fat alternative to typical high-fat creamy dressings. His Apricot Tart is on page 200.

¼ **cup part-skim or non-fat ricotta cheese**
1 **tablespoon skim milk**
½ **tablespoon chopped fresh parsley**
1 **tablespoon vinegar**
½ **teaspoon ground cardamon seeds**
½ **teaspoon coriander seeds**
½ **teaspoon curry powder**
juice of ½ lemon
freshly ground black pepper to taste

Combine all ingredients in a blender and mix until smooth.

PER SERVING:

Calories: 25	Fat: 1 g (42% of calories)	Cholesterol: 5 mg	Protein: 2 g
	Saturated Fat: <1 g	Sodium: 23 mg	Carbohydrate: 2 g

APPETIZERS

Pat Baird's
Brilliant Tofu Beet Dip
6 servings

☆☆☆☆☆☆☆☆☆☆☆☆☆☆☆☆☆☆☆☆☆☆☆☆☆☆☆☆☆☆☆☆☆☆☆☆☆☆☆

When you can make delicious, healthy dips like this one from cookbook author Pat Baird, who needs fatty dips loaded with artery-clogging sour cream or cream cheese? For better nutrition, save the beet greens and boil for about twenty minutes; most of the vitamins in a beet plant are in the leaves. Pat's Almost No Fat Potato Salad is on page 40. About this recipe, Pat says:

The vibrant color of beets gives this low-calorie and almost fat-free dip a stunning look, and no one will guess that tofu is one of the ingredients. Using the microwave, beets cook up in just about ten minutes. Serve this dip in the center of steamed vegetables—like broccoli, mushrooms and green or yellow squash. The contrast of colors is dazzling. This dip also makes a great sauce for pasta or grains. Just add a bit of stock or broth to bring it to a thinner consistency.

4 **medium beets, scrubbed with stems, roots trimmed to about 1 inch**
4 **ounces soft tofu, drained**
2 **tablespoons apple cider vinegar**
2 **tablespoons minced shallots**
½ **teaspoon dried mustard**
½ **teaspoon dried thyme, crumbled**
½ **teaspoon dried tarragon, crumbled**
  salt to taste

1. Place beets in a shallow 1-quart glass casserole dish. Cover tightly with a lid or vented plastic wrap. Microwave on high for 10 to 12 minutes, or until the beets are tender (or cover with water in a pot and boil for 30 to 60 minutes). Let stand covered for 3 minutes.
2. Drain and cool the beets. Slip off the skins under cold running water. Slice off the top stem and root; cut beets into 1-inch chunks.
3. In the work bowl of a food processor, place the beets, tofu, vinegar, shallots, mustard, thyme and tarragon. Process until mixture is smooth, stopping occasionally to scrape down the sides of the bowl. Add salt, if desired.

PER SERVING:

Calories: 28	Fat: <1 g (29% of calories)	Cholesterol: 0 mg	Protein: 2 g
	Saturated Fat: <1 g	Sodium: 18 mg	Carbohydrate: 4 g

Jane Brody's
Intercontinental Chickpea Spread
8 servings

☆☆

Jane Brody is America's premier health teacher. Her weekly "Personal Health" column in the New York Times *(and more than 100 other newspapers) offers insights into new medical research and health controversies. Her* Jane Brody's Nutrition Book *and* Jane Brody's Good Food Book *are classics that provide a wealth of delicious recipes and health information and belong in every well-equipped kitchen.*

About this chickpea spread, Jane says, "This has been an incredible winner whenever and wherever I have served it. Should I be lucky enough to have leftovers, I eat it for lunch the next day."

1	19-ounce can chickpeas, drained and rinsed (or 1½ to 2 cups cooked chickpeas)
1	large clove of garlic
½	teaspoon salt (omit if using canned chickpeas)
½	cup plain non-fat or low-fat yogurt
⅓	cup salsa (without added salt), hot or mild to taste
1	small zucchini, coarsely shredded and squeezed (about ½ cup before squeezing)
3	plum tomatoes, halved lengthwise, seeds and pulp removed, turned cut side down on a paper towel to drain, then cut into small dice
2	tablespoons finely diced red onion
2 to 3	tablespoons shredded Parmesan
1	tablespoon chopped cilantro

1. In a food processor, combine the chickpeas, garlic, salt (if using) and yogurt. Process until the mixture forms a smooth paste. Transfer to a container, cover and chill.
2. Shortly before serving, spread the chickpea mixture on a platter. Gently spread the salsa over it. Then sprinkle on the zucchini, tomatoes, onion, Parmesan and cilantro.

PER SERVING:

Calories: 73	Fat: 5 g (12% of calories)	Cholesterol: 1 mg	Protein: 5 g
	Saturated Fat: <1 g	Sodium: 216 mg	Carbohydrate: 11 g

℘☙

Whoopi Goldberg's
Do You Dip?
8 servings

☆☆

Whoopi Goldberg's successful career in acting and comedy can be matched only by her tireless devotion to worthy causes, such as hosting the HBO "Comic Relief" benefits for the homeless. Whoopi rose to fame in 1985 with a starring role in The Color Purple *and later won an Academy Award for* Ghost. *She now stars in the television series "Star Trek: The Next Generation." As for culinary talents, her assistant says that "what Whoopi most likes to make is a reservation." But Whoopi did come up with what she calls a "versatile appetizer spread that works as a cocktail dip or a sandwich filling—great at picnics." We like this recipe because instead of using regular cream cheese, it has fat-free cream cheese—that cuts the fat per serving by almost ten grams.*

1 **7-ounce can tuna, packed in water, rinsed and drained**
1 **8-ounce package fat-free cream cheese**
½ **lemon, juiced**
1 **tablespoon fresh finely chopped dillweed**
2 **tablespoons sweet pickle relish**

Combine all ingredients. Spread on pumpernickel, crackers, etc.

PER SERVING:

| Calories: 66 | Fat: <1 g (4% of calories) | Cholesterol: 19 mg | Protein: 13 g |
| | Saturated Fat: <1 g | Sodium: 222 mg | Carbohydrate: 3g |

$\wp \partial$

Ellen Haas's
Red Peppers Ragout

6 servings

☆☆☆ ☆☆☆☆☆☆☆☆☆☆☆☆☆☆☆☆☆☆☆☆ ☆☆☆☆☆☆ ☆☆☆☆☆☆☆☆☆☆☆☆☆☆

Formerly, Ellen Haas worked from the outside (as executive director of Public Voice for Food and Health Policy) trying to improve the United States Department of Agriculture. Now, she can influence the department from the inside, as USDA assistant secretary for food and consumer services. At Public Voice, Ellen was a consummate lobbyist on food issues. This cookbook's senior editor (M.F.J.) says, "It was a marvel to watch her pressure government agencies, seek out industry allies and build consumer coalitions—always keeping her eyes on her goals." Ellen says:

Twenty years ago, Michael Jacobson and I were trying to put consumer health issues on the map and ignoring those who said nutrition wouldn't sell. Well, not only did we prove the naysayers wrong, but the close, working relationship of Public Voice and CSPI has been an integral part of bringing such critically important issues as nutrition, sustainable agriculture, school lunch and food safety to the forefront of public policy debate.

This dish proves that Ellen practices what she preaches. The Red Peppers Ragout gets its vitamin C from the bell peppers and beta-carotene from the paprika.

2 cloves of garlic, minced
1 large red onion, peeled and thinly sliced
1 tablespoon hot Hungarian paprika
3 pounds large sweet red bell peppers, washed, cored and cut into ¼-inch strips
  nonstick cooking spray or 1 teaspoon olive oil
  juice of 1 lemon
  freshly ground black pepper to taste

1. Spray or lightly coat a large, heavy pot with the oil, and add the garlic and onion. Place on medium heat and mix well. Cover and cook until soft, stirring once or twice (about 5 minutes). Add the paprika and stir. The onion will become tangled and pasty. Cover and cook for 1 minute.
2. Add the peppers and lemon juice, stirring to break up the clump of onions. Cover and cook about 15 minutes until tender and reduced down to about half the original volume, stirring occasionally.
3. Season with black pepper and cook uncovered for about another 15 minutes until most of the liquid has evaporated and a stew-like texture develops, stirring occasionally.

Note: Because there is no salt and virtually no fat in this ragout, the natural sweetness and rich fragrance of the red bell peppers come to life in this recipe. A little hot Hungarian paprika is used to add a shadow of warmth to the peppers, while lemon juice balances the sweet and hot flavors, and black pepper emphasizes the warm undertones. The peppers become soft as they stew, but never lose their fire-engine-red color. Sometimes I cut the peppers in ½-inch dice, instead of strips, turning this ragout into a spread that I use for moistening and flavoring sandwiches.

PER SERVING:

Calories: 52	Fat: <1 g (8% of calories)	Cholesterol: 0 mg	Protein: 2 g
	Saturated Fat: 0 g	Sodium: 7 mg	Carbohydrate: 11 g

Deborah Madison's
Tomatillo Salsa

16 servings

Deborah Madison serves up vegetables and other heart-healthy dishes at Cafe Escalera in Santa Fe, New Mexico. Her Salsa and Sabzee-Green Herb Sandwich (page 77) are from her award-winning vegetarian cookbook The Savory Way. *Deborah says:*

This versatile sauce can be used in many different ways—with potatoes and scrambled eggs, in quesadillas and tacos, or as a sauce for enchiladas or a dip for cubes of jicama and cucumbers. For a sauce that is both pleasantly tart and creamy textured, add an avocado. Those who like a hotter sauce can leave the jalapeños uncooked.

 8 tomatillos, husks removed
 1 medium-sized white or yellow onion, thickly sliced
 2 jalapeño peppers, halves and seeds removed
 4 cloves garlic, peeled
 1 avocado (optional)
 1 large bunch (about 1 cup) cilantro leaves
   lime juice to taste (1 or 2 limes)
 ¼ teaspoon salt

1. Bring several cups of water to boil in a small saucepan; add the tomatillos, onion, jalapeños and garlic and lower the heat to a simmer. Cook gently until the tomatillos have turned a dull shade of green, about 12 minutes.
2. Transfer the vegetables to a food processor or blender. Add the cilantro, and avocado if using, and process until everything is combined, but there is still a little texture. If the mixture is too thick, add a little of the cooking water and thin to the desired consistency.
3. Season with the lime juice and salt and chill. This will keep for a week in the refrigerator, but it's best used fresh.

PER SERVING (ABOUT 2 TABLESPOONS):

Calories: 14	Fat: 1 g (14% of calories)	Cholesterol: 0 mg	Protein: <1 g
	Saturated Fat: 0 g	Sodium: 34 mg	Carbohydrate: 3 g

Mark Miller's
Wild Mushroom and
Sun-Dried Tomato Salsa   *10 servings*

☆☆

If you like your food hot, you'll love Mark Miller's famous restaurants—The Coyote Cafe in Santa Fe, New Mexico, and the Red Sage Restaurant in Washington, D.C. Forbes magazine listed Coyote Cafe as one of America's top forty restaurants, and Time described Mark as "the nation's foremost champion of hot cuisine." Mark, an expert on chilies and the history of culinary traditions of the American Southwest, wrote the Coyote Cafe cookbook and The Great Chile Book. This recipe and his Jumpin' Jalapeño Beans (page 180) come from his latest book, Coyote's Pantry. Of this recipe, Mark says:

The woodsiness of the wild mushrooms mixed with the intense tones of the sun-dried tomatoes gives this dish wonderful depth and density of flavors. The mushrooms can be grilled and the tomatoes rehydrated ahead of time. If you enjoy the grilled flavor, you can also prepare the shallots the same way. For a spicy version, add ½ teaspoon chili caribe (dried red chili flakes with seeds). Serve at room temperature with grilled fish (tuna, halibut or sea bass), with grilled poultry or steaks, with pasta or on pizza. This salsa also makes an excellent relleno filling or, mixed with a little wild rice, a stuffing for quail.

8 ounces fresh chanterelles, oyster mushrooms or other wild mushrooms, washed
¼ teaspoon salt
4 tablespoons virgin olive oil
½ cup rehydrated sun-dried tomatoes (about 1 ounce dried)
4 shallots, peeled and minced (about 2 tablespoons)
2 tablespoons balsamic vinegar
¼ teaspoon brown sugar
1 tablespoon minced fresh basil leaves

1. Prepare the grill. Season the cleaned, still-damp mushrooms with salt. Pour 2 tablespoons of the olive oil in a bowl, add the seasoned mushrooms and toss well.
2. Grill the mushrooms evenly until lightly browned but not too soft. Brush with the remaining 2 tablespoons olive oil. Chop the mushrooms into ⅜-inch dice and transfer to a mixing bowl.
3. Combine with the sun-dried tomatoes, shallots, vinegar and sugar. Add the basil immediately before serving.

PER SERVING:

| Calories: 71 | Fat: 6 g (71% of calories) | Cholesterol: 0 mg | Protein: <1 g |
| | Saturated Fat: <1 g | Sodium: 113 mg | Carbohydrate: 5 g |

𝓎𝕒

Ralph and Rose Nader's
Baba Ghanoogh
12 servings

☆☆

When we requested a recipe from Ralph Nader (who attracted this cookbook's senior editor (M.F.J.) to Washington in 1970 with an unpaid summer internship), he confessed that he doesn't cook. But he said that his mother, Rose, can cook up a storm. This appetizer and a fabulous fish dish on page 139 are two of Ralph and Rose's favorites.

This recipe, from their native Lebanon, is a classic appetizer; it first appeared in her It Happened in the Kitchen: Recipes for Food and Thought, *a cookbook whose proceeds support causes of Ralph's late brother Shafeek. Rose says, "This appetizer can be a light meal in itself. It satisfies the palate and the eye. To keep the subtle flavor of the baba ghanoogh, serve lukewarm or cold, but not too cold. After the egg-*

plant is cooked and taken from its skin, you can freeze it for future use, having added the lemon juice to keep it from darkening. I prefer serving this recipe fresh."

      2 **medium eggplants**
      3 **cloves of garlic**
    ½ **teaspoon salt**
      3 **tablespoons tahini**
      3 **lemons (juice)**
6 to 8 **radishes**
         dash of paprika
3 to 4 **sprigs parsley, for garnish**
      6 **whole-wheat pita bread pockets**

1. Wash eggplants, score with a knife straight through to allow steam to escape when baking. Bake in a shallow pan in 400° oven until skin can be peeled off easily, about 40 minutes. Cool.
2. Remove eggplant from skin, mash well in a bowl by hand or in a food processor, which produces a smoother consistency.
3. Peel and pound garlic well with salt. Add tahini and mix. Add lemon juice and mix well. Additional lemon juice gives a tart taste to the baba ghanoogh. Pour dressing onto eggplant and mix well.
4. Serve on platter and decorate with radishes (fashioned into florets or cut into segments or minced) and sprigs of parsley at two ends of the platter. Sprinkle paprika on top for color and serve with toasted whole-wheat pita bread.

PER SERVING:
Calories: 115   Fat: 3 g (23% of calories)   Cholesterol: 0 mg   Protein: 5 g
                 Saturated Fat: 1 g   Sodium: 296 mg   Carbohydrate: 18 g

Sam and Colleen Nunn's
Garbanzo Dip   *12 servings*
☆☆☆

Senator Sam Nunn of Georgia is the powerful chairman of the Senate Armed Services Committee. Perhaps fortified by this easy-to-make dip from the Senator and his wife Colleen, whatever he says about defense policy usually carries the day. Garbanzos (also called chickpeas) are a great source of protein, complex carbohydrates, iron, potassium and a smattering of B vitamins.

    1 **19-ounce can garbanzo beans, drained and rinsed**
    1 **tablespoon olive oil**
  ½ **teaspoon sesame seeds**

freshly ground black pepper
1 large clove of garlic, minced
 juice of 1 lemon (or 3 tablespoons lemon juice)
6 whole-wheat pita pockets

Combine all ingredients in blender until creamy. Sprinkle with parsley and serve chilled as a spread for whole-wheat pita bread or as a dip for raw vegetables.

PER SERVING:

Calories: 122	Fat: 3 g (18% of calories)	Cholesterol: 0 mg	Protein: 6 g
	Saturated Fat: <1 g	Sodium: 236 mg	Carbohydrate: 19 g

ဢ

Harriet Roth's
Asparagus Dip

6 servings

☆ ☆ ☆☆☆☆☆☆☆☆☆☆☆ ☆☆☆☆☆☆☆☆ ☆☆☆☆☆☆☆☆☆☆☆☆☆☆☆☆☆

Who can predict where one's life will lead? Harriet Roth started out as a home economics teacher in a Pittsburgh public school. She went on to study French and Italian cooking, and taught classes in international cuisine. But then she discovered that her fatty sauces were compromising her husband's health. So Harriet switched to healthful cooking, helped provide guests at the Pritikin Longevity Center with tasty, low-fat meals and authored several popular cookbooks, including Deliciously Low *and* Harriet Roth's Complete Guide to Fat, Cholesterol and Calories. *The asparagus that is the basis of this dip not only tastes good, it's also a good source of vitamins A and C.*

1 pound fresh green or white asparagus, tough ends removed, cut into
 1-inch pieces
1 tablespoon fresh lemon juice
3 tablespoons red onion, chopped
1 teaspoon vegetable seasoning (Mrs. Dash's or another alternative to salt)
2 large cloves of garlic, minced
3 tablespoons non-fat yogurt
1 tablespoon grated Parmesan cheese, optional
1 large tomato, peeled, seeded and chopped

1. Steam asparagus for 4 to 5 minutes. Drain well and cool.
2. Place asparagus, lemon juice, onion, seasoning and garlic in blender or food processor. Process until puréed.
3. Add yogurt (and optional cheese for added flavor and a slightly grainy texture). Blend until smooth and chill.
4. Place in serving bowl and top with chopped tomato. Serve with toasted whole-wheat pita bread, crackers and/or assorted vegetables.

PER SERVING:

| Calories: 30 | Fat: <1 g (14% of calories) | Cholesterol: 1 mg | Protein: 2 g |
| | Saturated Fat: <1 g | Sodium: 25 mg | Carbohydrate: 4 g |

BREADS

Mel and Sheryl London's
Irish Brown Bread   *20 servings*

☆☆☆☆ ☆☆☆☆☆☆☆☆☆☆ ☆☆☆☆☆☆☆☆☆☆☆☆☆☆☆☆☆☆ ☆☆☆☆☆☆☆☆☆

Mel London has an unusual combination of talents: film making and food making. In 1963 he was nominated for an Academy Award for To Live Again, *a documentary on aging and chronic disease, and has won numerous film awards. He teaches in the Department of Film at New York University. In the food department, Mel is the author of the best-seller* Bread Winners, *which he wrote with his wife Sheryl. One of this cookbook's editors (M.F.J.) and thousands of other sometime bakers swear by that cookbook to help fill their homes with the smell of freshly baked bread. The Londons' latest cookbook is* The Versatile Grain and The Elegant Bean. *Both these bread recipes are made with whole-wheat flour, ensuring that you get all the vitamins, minerals and fiber that whole wheat is famous for. Mel says:*

This easy quick bread is a variation on the traditional Irish soda bread, only this one is made with whole-wheat flour. It uses no yeast, and it makes for a wonderfully delicious morning toast, covered with jam or marmalade. Just about one hour from start to finish—no kneading, no rising, no effort. It's the bread that I used for demonstrations when *Bread Winners* was published, and I did a coast-to-coast book tour. Television gives you very little time, so this recipe was perfect.

7 **cups stone-ground whole-wheat flour**
1 **teaspoon salt (optional)**
½ **teaspoon baking soda**
2 **tablespoons baking powder**
½ **cup white raisins**
½ **cup caraway seeds**
1 **tablespoon honey**
4 **cups buttermilk (room temperature)**

1. Preheat oven to 425°. In a large bowl, mix the flour, salt, baking soda and baking powder. Add the caraway seeds and stir. Add the raisins and stir to coat them thoroughly. Add the honey, then pour the buttermilk slowly into the bowl, mixing as you add it. The dough should be sticky, but easy to handle. However, if it feels too sticky, add more flour.
2. Using floured hands (or a wooden spoon if you don't like to get the dough between your fingers), mix thoroughly while still in the bowl. Divide the dough into 2 parts and form into oval, round or long shapes and place on a greased and floured cookie sheet. Cut deeply into the dough with a floured knife, making the shape of a cross on top. Then dust lightly with flour and blow off the excess.
3. Bake for 40 to 45 minutes in the preheated oven or until the breads test done when you tap them on the bottom. If they sound hollow, they're done. Cool them on a wire rack before slicing.

PER SERVING:

Calories: 184   Fat: 2 g (8% of calories)   Cholesterol: 2 mg   Protein: 8 g
                 Saturated Fat: <1 g   Sodium: 168 mg   Carbohydrate: 38 g

ℰ⅊

Mel and Sheryl London's
Pita

10 servings

☆☆☆☆ ☆☆☆☆☆☆☆☆☆☆☆☆☆☆☆☆☆☆☆☆ ☆☆☆☆☆☆☆☆ ☆☆☆☆☆☆☆☆☆

Mel says, "This bread is marvelously versatile. It originated in the Middle East and sometimes is known as `pocket bread.' The breads come out flat, but with a hollow center so they can be filled with all kinds of marvelous things. They're fun to make because they puff up in the oven as they're baking, giving everyone a great show through the oven window. I suppose that I was most flattered when one day, one of our Lebanese neighbors asked me to show her how to bake pita!"

  2 **packages dry yeast**
  2 **cups very warm water (about 130°)**
  ½ **teaspoon honey**
  ¼ **cup olive oil**
  1 **tablespoon salt (optional)**
5-6 **cups whole-wheat flour**
    cornmeal

1. Mix the yeast in ½ cup of the warm water, add the honey, stir and set aside to proof.
2. In a large mixing bowl, add the remaining 1½ cups of water, the oil, salt (omit to cut the sodium) and the yeast mixture. Then stir in 5 cups of the flour, a cup at a time, mixing vigorously with each addition. Turn out onto a lightly floured board and knead for 10 minutes, adding the additional cup of flour if the dough gets too sticky. When the kneading is finished, the dough should be smooth and elastic. Shape into a ball, place in a greased bowl, turning once to coat the top, cover and let rise to double in a warm spot for about 1½ to 2 hours.
3. Punch down on floured surface, let the dough rest for about 10 minutes and then divide it into 8 to 10 pieces, shaping each piece into a ball. Knead each ball for 1 to 2 minutes, cover and let rest for about 30 minutes.
4. Using a floured rolling pin, flatten each ball into a circle about 8 inches in diameter and about ⅛ inch thick. Dust 2 baking sheets with cornmeal, place 2 of the circles on each sheet, cover and let rest for about 30 minutes. Let the remaining circles stay on the floured surface—when you have baked the first breads and the cookie sheets are empty, you will

bake the remaining pita. Each time you place new breads on the cookie sheets, dust the sheets with cornmeal again.

5. The oven is set at 500°—very hot for these little breads, and therein lies the secret. Place 1 sheet on the lowest rack for 5 minutes. Do not open during this first baking. After 5 minutes, transfer the sheet to a higher shelf and let it bake for 3 to 5 more minutes. The breads will puff up and be lightly browned when they're ready.

6. When done, remove from oven, place the next tray on the bottom for its 5-minute, high-heat baking and remove the first ones to a wire rack to cool. Continue the process until all the breads are baked. Let them cool; rewarm them for serving or freeze them for future use.

PER SERVING:
Calories: 275   Fat: 7 g (23% of calories)   Cholesterol: 0 mg   Protein: 9 g
                 Saturated Fat: 1 g   Sodium: 3 mg   Carbohydrate: 48 g

Esther Peterson's
Quick and Easy Brown Bread
20 servings

☆☆☆☆ ☆☆☆☆☆☆ ☆☆☆☆☆☆☆ ☆☆☆☆☆☆☆☆ ☆☆☆☆☆☆ ☆☆☆☆☆☆☆☆☆☆☆☆

Esther Peterson, a leading national and international spokesperson on consumer, women's and labor issues, is trying to prevent baking from becoming a lost art by contributing this easy, no-yeast whole-wheat bread (and Utah Muffins on page 15). If you don't know what the word b-a-k-e on your stove means, pull out a mixing bowl and get cookin'!

  3 **cups whole-wheat flour**
  ½ **teaspoon salt**
1½ **teaspoons baking soda**
  1 **cup powdered non-fat milk**
  2 **cups water**
  1 **tablespoon vinegar**
  3 **tablespoons molasses**

Preheat oven to 350°. Combine all ingredients and bake for 1 hour. Best eaten when hot.

PER SERVING:
Calories: 79   Fat: <1 g (5% of calories)   Cholesterol: 1 mg   Protein: 4 g
                Saturated Fat: <1 g   Sodium: 138 mg   Carbohydrate: 16 g

Tracy Pikhart Ritter's
Sun-Dried Tomato Crostini   *12 servings*

☆☆☆☆ ☆☆☆☆☆☆☆☆☆☆☆☆☆☆☆☆☆☆☆ ☆☆☆☆☆☆☆☆ ☆☆☆☆☆☆☆☆☆

Tracy Pikhart Ritter is the executive chef at the Golden Door Fitness Resort in Escondido, California, a luxurious fitness spa that offers guests good-for-you gourmet meals. Tracy's "Vitality Cuisine" features low-sodium and low-fat ingredients, moderate amounts of protein, complex carbohydrates, seasonal certified organic fruits and vegetables, free-range poultry, farm-raised fish and Hawaiian seafood.

For a less expensive indulgence, treat yourself to these scrumptious little morsels—they make for a wonderful side dish. If Tracy's style impresses you, check out her Oatmeal-Crusted Chicken on page 161.

  1 tablespoon olive oil
  2 cloves of garlic, minced
  1 small loaf Italian or French bread
  2 ripe tomatoes, peeled and seeded
¼ red onion, minced
  2 teaspoons chopped fresh Italian parsley
  4 black olives, minced (optional)
½ teaspoon capers, chopped (optional)
  4 sun-dried tomatoes reconstituted in ¼ cup warm water with 2 tablespoons balsamic vinegar
    freshly ground black pepper
    grated mozzarella or Parmesan cheese (optional)

1. Blend olive oil and minced garlic in a small bowl.
2. Slice bread into circlets and allow to dry. Peel, seed and chop ripe tomatoes. Prepare onion, parsley, olives, capers; add to chopped ripe tomatoes. Drain sun-dried tomatoes and chop fine; add to tomato mixture.
3. Preheat oven to 350°. Toast bread for 5 minutes until dry. Remove and cool.
4. Brush bread with oil mixture. Place 1 to 2 tablespoons tomato mixture on top of toast circles. Return to oven and bake for 15 minutes or until cooked. Add freshly ground black pepper. Optional: Sprinkle with grated mozzarella or Parmesan cheese and return to oven until melted.
5. Remove and cool. Serve with roasted peppers or as a side dish.

PER SERVING:
Calories: 130   Fat: 1 g (11% of calories)   Cholesterol: 0 mg   Protein: 4 g
             Saturated Fat: <1 g   Sodium: 226 mg   Carbohydrate: 24 g

Paul and Jeanne Simon's
Honey Whole-Grain Bread
30 servings

☆☆☆☆ ☆☆☆☆☆☆☆☆☆☆☆☆☆☆☆☆☆☆☆☆☆ ☆☆☆☆☆☆☆☆☆ ☆☆☆☆☆☆☆☆

Paul Simon, a widely respected United States senator from Illinois, ran for the Democratic nomination for president in 1988. At the age of nineteen, several years before entering Illinois state politics, he dropped out of college to become a newspaper owner and built a chain of fifteen weekly papers. Senator Simon is already famous for his trademark bow ties—maybe now he will also become known for his baking skills. Of this recipe, the senator says, "Bread remains the most common course at the family dinner table, but it can also be a featured course in its own right." His wife Jeanne shares the credit for this recipe.

3 cups white flour
2 packages active dry yeast
1½ teaspoons salt
1 cup water
1 cup low-fat cottage cheese
4 tablespoons butter
½ cup honey
2 eggs
2½ cups whole-wheat flour
½ cup regular rolled oats
⅔ cup chopped walnuts or pecans

1. In a large bowl, combine 2 cups white flour with yeast and salt.
2. Heat water, cottage cheese, butter and honey until very warm (120 to 130°). Add warm liquid and eggs to flour mixture. Mix well.
3. Add whole-wheat flour, oats and nuts. Stir in remaining white flour (add more if necessary). Knead until smooth and elastic. Let rise in warm, draft-free place until double.
4. Punch down and place in 2 greased 5¼ x 9¼ x 3-inch pans. Cover and let rise about 1 hour. Preheat oven to 350°.
5. Bake for 35 to 40 minutes. Remove from pans onto cooling rack.

PER SERVING:

Calories: 144	Fat: 4 g (25% of calories)	Cholesterol: 19 mg	Protein: 5 g
	Saturated Fat: 1 g	Sodium: 158 mg	Carbohydrate: 23 g

Alan Thicke's
Irish Freckle Bread

40 servings

☆☆☆☆ ☆☆☆☆☆☆☆☆☆☆☆☆☆☆☆☆☆☆☆☆ ☆☆☆☆☆☆☆☆ ☆☆☆☆☆☆☆☆

Canadian-born Alan Thicke is best known to American audiences as host of his former late-night talk show "Thicke of the Night" and as the father in the popular sitcom "Growing Pains." But there's more. He has received six Emmy nominations for television writing. He's produced "The Bobby Vinton Show" and "The Cosby Show." He's even written the theme songs for a number of television shows, including "Different Strokes," "The Facts of Life" and "The Joker's Wild." You might say that he spreads himself thicke!

2½	cups whole-wheat flour
2½ to 3	cups white flour
½	cup sugar
2	packages rapid-rise yeast
¾	teaspoon salt
1	cup water
½	cup butter or margarine
2	eggs, room temperature
⅓	cup cooked mashed potatoes, room temperature
1	cup chopped dates

1. In large bowl, combine 1 cup whole-wheat flour, 1 cup white flour, sugar, undissolved yeast and salt.
2. Heat water and butter until very warm (125 to 130°). Gradually stir warm liquids into dry ingredients. Stir in eggs, mashed potatoes, dates and additional flours to make soft dough.
3. Knead on lightly floured surface until smooth and elastic, about 8 to 10 minutes. Cover and let rest on floured surface 10 minutes.
4. Divide dough into 4 equal pieces. Shape into 4 slender loaves, about 8½ inches long. Set 2 loaves side by side in each of 2 well-greased or sprayed 8½ x 4½-inch loaf pans. Cover and let rise in warm, draft-free place until doubled in size, about 1 hour. Preheat oven to 350°.
5. Bake for 35 minutes or until done. Remove from pans; cool on wire racks.

PER SERVING:

Calories: 112	Fat: 3 g (23% of calories)	Cholesterol: 14 mg	Protein: 2 g
	Saturated Fat: <1 g	Sodium: 77 mg	Carbohydrate: 20 g

VEGETARIAN MAIN COURSES

Steve Allen and Jayne Meadows's
Cajun Red Beans and Rice

4 servings

☆☆

Steve Allen and Jayne Meadows are consummate TV-movie-theater stars—and they can cook. You can put some spice in your life with this spicy vegetarian entree. A low-sodium spaghetti sauce works great in this recipe, because the hot pepper sauce ensures that this almost fat-free meal is high in flavor. Husband-wife team Allen and Meadows also contributed a Niçoise Tuna Salad (page 92).

> nonstick cooking spray
> 1 large onion, chopped
> 2 cloves of garlic, minced
> 1 medium green bell pepper, coarsely chopped
> 1 cup sliced celery
> 1 15-ounce can kidney or red beans, rinsed and drained
> 1 cup Pritikin Spaghetti Sauce, any flavor
> 1 teaspoon dried thyme
> ¾ teaspoon hot pepper sauce
> 3 cups hot cooked brown rice

1. Lightly spray a 10-inch skillet with nonstick cooking spray. Add onion and garlic; cook over medium-high heat 3 minutes or until tender, stirring frequently.
2. Add remaining ingredients except rice. Simmer uncovered over low heat for 15 minutes or until vegetables are crisp-tender, stirring occasionally. Serve over rice.

PER SERVING:

Calories: 304	Fat: <1 g (3% of calories)	Cholesterol: 0 mg	Protein: 12 g
	Saturated Fat: <1 g	Sodium: 125 mg	Carbohydrate: 62 g

ℱℨ

Anne Bancroft's
Garbanzo Stew

4 servings

☆☆

Anne Bancroft, one of America's greatest actresses, also contributed Tomato-Veggie Sauce (page 104) and Low-Calorie Seafood Stew (page 128). This stew is a great way of enjoying the fiber, protein and taste of garbanzo beans.

> 1 cup diced onion (about 1 medium onion)
> 1 teaspoon olive oil
> 1 cup eggplant, cubed, packed
> 1 cup zucchini, cubed, packed (about 1 medium squash)

5 medium tomatoes, peeled, chopped
3 ounces canned tomato paste (½ small can)
1 cup garbanzo beans, drained
¼ teaspoon allspice
¼ teaspoon cinnamon
¼ teaspoon oregano
¼ teaspoon turmeric
1½ cups water
  juice of ½ lemon (about 1½ tablespoons lemon juice)
2 cups cooked bulgur wheat or rice

1. Sauté onion in olive oil until translucent. Place in 15½ x 11-inch baking pan and add remaining ingredients, except for the lemon juice. Mix well.
2. Place pan uncovered in 350° oven for 2½ hours. Stir every half hour. Add lemon juice after 2 hours. Add water if stew looks like it is drying out. If too soupy, pour into pot and reduce liquid over medium-high heat. Serve over bulgur wheat or rice.

PER SERVING:
Calories: 213   Fat: 2 g (9% of calories)   Cholesterol: 0 mg   Protein: 9 g
                  Saturated Fat: <1 g   Sodium: 257 mg   Carbohydrate: 41 g

ℰࢇ

Ken Dryden's
Pizza Provençal
with Fresh Basil Pesto
10 servings

☆☆

Renaissance man Ken Dryden may go down in history as the only earthling who has been inducted into the Hockey Hall of Fame (Montreal Canadiens), produced television and radio programs, interned for Ralph Nader, earned a law degree, wrote two best-selling books (Home Game and The Game), served as a political appointee (Ontario Youth Commissioner) and created this wonderful recipe. Ken says: "There are so many bright and different colors, so many textures and flavors that it's inviting to look at, looks and feels healthy to eat and tastes great."

2 cups firmly packed fresh basil leaves, washed and dried
3 cloves of garlic
½ cup pine nuts
¾ cup freshly grated Parmesan cheese
¼ cup freshly grated Romano cheese
2½ tablespoons olive oil
1 large onion, sliced thinly

½ tablespoon olive oil
 2 red, green or yellow sweet peppers, thinly sliced
 1 medium-sized eggplant, unpeeled and cut into small cubes
10 whole-wheat pita pocket breads, large size, split in half
 1 8-ounce jar good-quality tomato sauce (no salt added)
 2 teaspoons dried herbes de provence
¼ cup freshly grated Parmesan cheese
¼ pound any good soft cheese—Gorgonzola, Brie, Saint André (optional)

1. Combine basil leaves, garlic and pine nuts in a blender or food processor and purée to desired smoothness (we like our pesto a bit chunky). Add Parmesan and Romano cheeses and blend briefly. With motor of blender or processor running, add olive oil and mix well. Set aside.
2. In skillet, gently sauté onion in ½ tablespoon of olive oil; add peppers and eggplant. Cook for 2 to 3 minutes.
3. Place split pita pockets on cookie sheets and toast at 450° for 2 to 4 minutes (until slightly crisp, but not browned). Remove pitas from oven.
4. Place small amount of tomato sauce on pita, followed by vegetable mixture. Then place 4 or 5 small teaspoons of pesto on each pita. Sprinkle Parmesan cheese and herbs over pita pizza, and if using, sprinkle chunks of cheese on top (adds fat, 3 grams per serving for Brie, *eds.*).
5. Return pizza to oven and cook for 5 minutes or until everything is hot and bubbling and cheeses have melted.

PER SERVING:

Calories: 372	Fat: 10 g (24% of calories)	Cholesterol: 9 mg	Protein: 16 g
	Saturated Fat: 3 g	Sodium: 528 mg	Carbohydrate: 53 g

Lynn Fischer's
Gnocchi
6 servings

☆☆

Lynn Fischer teaches people how to cook healthfully on the top-rated "The Low Cholesterol Gourmet" airing on The Discovery Channel and in her cookbook of the same name. This recipe (and a pasta recipe on page 108) are from her latest cookbook, The Quick Low Cholesterol Gourmet. *Lynn is a walking (and skiing, horseback-riding, bicycling, rollerblading) example of the wonderful benefits of healthful eating and exercise. In describing this recipe, Lynn says:*

Gnocchi—potato dumplings—are light, filling, comfort foods. This recipe is one of my favorites—it's very easy to make, contains no fat and not counting the potatoes (which are precooked), gnocchi and sauce can be on the table in 15 minutes. Serve it as you would pasta, with marinara sauce, a light cheese sauce, or plain with a little margarine or olive oil and chopped parsley. The potatoes for the gnocchi are cooked whole and unpeeled so they don't become watery.

3 **large russet potatoes, boiled unpeeled, then peeled**
2 **cups flour (may be more or less)**
  flour for the board
  low-fat, low-sodium sauce of your choice (see Tomato-Veggie Sauce on page 104)

1. Mash the cooked, peeled potatoes while they are hot. Add about half of the flour and knead, mixing it well into the potatoes, rolling it on a floured countertop or board for a few minutes. Add the other half of the flour and knead again for about 3 minutes. Add more flour if necessary. The dough should not be sticky and the amount is approximately the same as that of the potatoes—more flour makes the gnocchi harder; less flour, lighter and softer. Also, resist using a processor to mix the dough or mash the potatoes as the gnocchi will be tough and chewy.
2. Cut off baseball-size pieces of the dough. Roll them into several ropes ½ to ¾ inches thick by about 8 to 12 inches long. This takes a few minutes. Cut the ropes with a knife into 1-inch lengths. Press a depression into each of the gnocchi with your finger so more sauce gets on each piece. Let the cut gnocchi pieces dry about 5 minutes, separated on several plates, sprinkled very lightly with flour.
3. The gnocchi can now be frozen, or cooked fresh as follows: In a large pot, boil several quarts of water. Drop in the gnocchi and let them cook for 3 to 5 minutes or until each one rises to the top. With a slotted spoon, remove, let drain and serve hot with a sauce of your choice, with marinara being the most popular.

PER SERVING (SAUCE NOT INCLUDED):
Calories: 212   Fat: 1 g (2% of calories)   Cholesterol: 0 mg   Protein: 6 g
                  Saturated Fat: <1 g   Sodium: 3 mg   Carbohydrate: 45 g

ℒᴈ

Michael Foley's
Pot-au-Feu of Root Vegetables with Tortellini
6 servings

☆☆

Michael Foley is the co-designer, builder and joint operator of Printer's Row Restaurant in Chicago. Michael has won several culinary awards and written for the Chicago Sun-Times. *He says the sauces in this recipes are traditional in a bollito misto—a French stew that historically contained a mixture of fatty meats. His Sweet and Sour Cabbage can be found on page 172.*

```
2 carrots
2 celery ribs
1 large onion
½ small head of cabbage, shredded
2 parsnips
2 turnips
2 beets
2 leeks
3 baby bok choy
2 celery root
3 cloves of garlic, minced
4 bay leaves
1 sprig of thyme
1 sprig of tarragon
1 teaspoon salt
4 white peppercorns, crushed
1 pound tortellini
  Red Sauce (see following recipe)
  Green Sauce (see following recipe)
```

1. Cut vegetables into uniform shape for stewing. Combine first 14 ingredients in 8-quart pot. Add salt and peppercorns.
2. Bring to simmer and let cook for about 2 hours.
3. Remove some of the broth and simmer tortellini until tender. Pour tortellini and broth back into stew pot.
4. Serve in large bowls offering the 2 sauces on the side.

PER SERVING (WITHOUT SAUCES):

Calories: 347	Fat: 2 g (4% of calories)	Cholesterol: 6 mg	Protein: 12 g
	Saturated Fat: <1 g	Sodium: 424 mg	Carbohydrate: 71 g

RED SAUCE: *10 servings*

```
2 tablespoons vegetable oil
3 medium onions, sliced thin
1 red pepper, cored, seeded, sliced
1 cup canned Italian tomatoes with juice chopped
  cayenne to taste
  salt (optional)
```

1. Heat oil in a saucepan. Cook onions and pepper for 25 minutes until soft, but not browned.
2. Add tomatoes, cayenne and salt if desired. Simmer until mixture is sauce-like, about 20 minutes.

PER SERVING:

Calories: 54	Fat: 3 g (52% of calories)	Cholesterol: 0 mg	
Protein: 1 g	Saturated Fat: <1 g	Sodium: 41 mg	Carbohydrate: 6 g

GREEN SAUCE: *20 servings*

- 1 slice of Italian bread
- 2 tablespoons red wine vinegar
- 2 cups Italian parsley, packed down
- 2 cloves of garlic
- 4 flat anchovy fillets (optional)
- 1 tablespoon capers
  salt and pepper to taste
- ¼ cup olive oil

1. Cut crust from bread. Tear remaining bread into small pieces. Place in a bowl. Pour vinegar over bread. Set aside for 10 minutes.
2. Process bread, parsley, garlic, anchovies, capers and seasoning in food processor or blender.
3. With machine running, gradually add oil.

PER SERVING:

Calories: 30	Fat: 3 g (81% of calories)	Cholesterol: 0 mg	Protein: 0 g
	Saturated Fat: <1 g	Sodium: 10 mg	Carbohydrate: 1 g

Carol Tucker Foreman's
Black Beans
8 servings

☆☆☆

Carol Tucker Foreman, a Washington powerhouse who grew up in Arkansas and helped place women in jobs in the Clinton administration, is high on fiber. This black bean recipe is great for a main course and her bran muffin recipe on page 8 could be served for dessert.

- 1 1-pound package of black beans
- 2 teaspoons minced garlic
- ½ large onion, chopped
- ½ green pepper, cored, seeded and chopped
- 1½ ounces salsa
- 1 tablespoon cumin
- ½ teaspoon oregano
- ½ teaspoon freshly ground black pepper
- 2 bay leaves
- 1½ tablespoons red wine vinegar
- 5 cups cooked brown rice

1. Pick over beans for small stones and wash thoroughly. Cover with water, bring to a boil and boil for 2 or 3 minutes. Remove from heat, cover and let stand overnight.
2. Pour off soaking water. Add fresh water (about 6 cups) to cover well. Add all ingredients except the vinegar. Simmer partially covered until beans are tender (about 2½ hours).
3. Remove bay leaves. Use rotary beater to mash some of the beans until desired consistency. Add the vinegar. Reheat and serve over rice.

PER SERVING:

Calories: 310	Fat: 1 g (4% of calories)	Cholesterol: 0 mg	Protein: 14 g
	Saturated Fat: <1 g	Sodium: 39 mg	Carbohydrate: 62 g

৪৯

Joan Gussow's
Corn, Bean and Pumpkin Stew
8 servings

☆☆☆

Joan Dye Gussow, professor of nutrition and education at Columbia University's Teachers College, has inspired a generation of nutrition educators. Her book Chicken Little, Tomato Sauce and Agriculture *reflects her belief that just eating nutritiously isn't enough—we also need to eat in a way that protects the planet. Joan was inducted into Center for Science in the Public Interest's "Nutrition Hall of Fame" in 1991 for her groundbreaking work in the 1970s on junk-food advertising on children's TV and for training hundreds of students. This stew, adapted from Deborah Madison's* The Greens Cookbook, *is loaded with fiber, beta-carotene and vitamin C.*

 1 **teaspoon cumin seeds**
 1 **teaspoon oregano**
 1 **1-inch piece cinnamon stick**
 3 **whole cloves, ground to a powder in a spice mill or coffee grinder**
 2 **tablespoons corn oil, light olive oil or sesame oil**
 1 **large onion, diced**
 2 **cloves of garlic, minced**
 1 **tablespoon paprika**
 ½ **teaspoon salt**
1½ **cups reserved bean broth or vegetable or chicken stock (see page 21)**
 1 **pound fresh or canned tomatoes (no salt added), peeled, seeded and chopped (reserve juice)**
 3 **cups pumpkin, winter squash or sweet potatoes (my favorite), cut into 1-inch cubes**
 3 **ears worth of corn kernels (about 1½ cups corn)**
 2 **cups cooked pinto or pink beans (reserve 1½ cups of cooking broth)**

2 serrano chilies, seeded and chopped
   cilantro or parsley, chopped (optional garnish)

1. In a small, heavy skillet, toast cumin seeds until aromatic. Add oregano
   for 5 seconds. Quickly remove toasted spices to saucer. Combine with
   cinnamon stick and ground cloves.
2. Heat oil in a wide skillet and sauté onion. Add garlic, paprika, salt and
   spice mixture. Stir well to combine.
3. Add ½ cup reserved bean broth or stock and cook until onion is soft.
   Add tomatoes and cook for 5 minutes.
4. Add pumpkin, squash or sweet potato cubes plus another cup of bean
   broth or stock. Cook 20 to 30 minutes or until pumpkin is about half done.
5. Add corn (or accompany meal with corn bread or tortillas instead), beans,
   chilies and reserved tomato juice. Cook until pumpkin is tender.
   Garnish with chopped cilantro or parsley. Devour.

PER SERVING:

Calories: 179	Fat: 5 g (23% of calories)	Cholesterol: 0 mg	Protein: 7 g
	Saturated Fat: <1 g	Sodium: 156 mg	Carbohydrate: 30 g

Arlyn Hackett's
Vegetables with Thai Marinade   *4 servings*

☆☆☆

*Arlyn Hackett hosts the "Health Smart Gourmet Cooking" program on public
television. He provided a terrific borscht recipe (see page 23), and now offers this vegetable dish. Arlyn says, "Asian cuisine offers a diversity of low-fat vegetable prepara-
tions. Unfortunately, many of these dishes are extremely high in sodium. I developed
Thai Marinade to provide an accent of Asian flavor without the excessive sodium."*

1 cup yellow crookneck squash, sliced
1 small red pepper, cut into slivers
1 medium carrot, thinly sliced
2 cups cauliflower florets

THAI MARINADE:
⅓ cup rice vinegar
⅓ cup water
2 teaspoons reduced-sodium soy sauce
2 cloves of garlic, finely minced
1 tablespoon fresh ginger, finely minced
2 tablespoons unsweetened frozen orange juice concentrate
¼ teaspoon hot pepper sauce (e.g., Tabasco), optional

1. Mix together all of the ingredients for the marinade. It can be stored in the refrigerator for 1 week.
2. In a saucepan, simmer the vegetables with the marinade for 4 minutes. Although they can be served immediately, the vegetables will have a richer flavor if allowed to marinate for 1 hour. Reheat or serve at room temperature.

PER SERVING:

Calories: 53	Fat: <1 g (7% of calories)	Cholesterol: 0 mg	Protein: 2 g
	Saturated Fat: 0 g	Sodium: 117 mg	Carbohydrate: 13 g

Belle Jacobson's
Eggplant Delight Sandwich
1 serving

☆☆

Getting one of the nation's least-known great cooks into print is among the editor's greatest pleasures. Sure, she's Michael Jacobson's mother, but that doesn't mean that Belle doesn't make everything from dynamite soups to to-kill-for casseroles. While she grew up in the butter-schmaltz-chopped liver tradition of high-cholesterol Jewish cooking, her husband Larry's adoption of a low-fat diet spurred her to develop numerous heart-healthy recipes. This recipe doesn't reveal her skillful preparation of fancy dishes, but it's a quick, healthy, vegetarian sandwich that will delight every eggplant lover's heart.

1 large ¾-inch-thick slice eggplant, peeled
   nonstick cooking spray
2 slices whole-wheat bread
1 large slice tomato
½ ounce part-skim mozzarella (approximately ½ slice) or 1 ounce
   reduced-fat mozzarella
¼ cup alfalfa sprouts (or romaine or red leaf lettuce)

1. Place eggplant slice on a hot grill or pan lightly coated with nonstick cooking spray. Grill until lightly browned and tender. Meanwhile, lightly toast the bread.
2. Place the eggplant, tomato and cheese on one of the pieces of toast and broil in a toaster oven until the cheese is melted. Add the alfalfa sprouts (or lettuce) and top with the second piece of bread.

PER SERVING:

Calories: 200	Fat: 5 g (20% of calories)	Cholesterol: 8 mg	Protein: 11 g
	Saturated Fat: 2 g	Sodium: 439 mg	Carbohydrate: 31 g

Deborah Madison's
Sabzee–Green Herb Sandwich

2 servings

☆☆

Deborah Madison is the founding chef of The Greens *restaurant in San Francisco and the author of* The Greens Cookbook. *She won two International Association of Culinary Professionals awards for her vegetarian cookbook,* The Savory Way, *from which she chose this recipe and one for Tomatillo Salsa (page 53). Deborah says:*

Sabzee is a simple, vigorous dish from Afghanistan—pungent greens and spicy yogurt tucked inside of whole-wheat pita bread. The tastes are very distinct—the tart, cool yogurt, the nutty presence of wheat in the bread and the complex, strong flavors of the herbs. The mixture comes completely alive in the mouth. The sandwich filling can be made of many things—arugula leaves, spinach, cilantro, watercress, dandelion leaves, dill and scallions. A few mint or lovage leaves would be delicious, too. The measurements given are approximate. Compose the salad mixture to your own taste and toss it with just a bit of oil to moisten the leaves.

FOR 2 SANDWICHES:

  large handful of tender greens (spinach, watercress, lettuce, arugula, etc.), washed and dried
½ bunch of cilantro
10 large parsley branches
10 dill branches
 2 scallions, chopped
  salt to taste (one shake used in nutritional analysis)
  olive oil or sunflower seed oil to taste (about 1 teaspoon)
 2 whole-wheat pita breads, sliced in half
½ cup plain non-fat yogurt, seasoned with a pinch of cayenne pepper

1. Gather the greens, cilantro, parsley and dill together and roughly chop them. Toss them with the scallions, a little salt and just enough oil to barely coat the leaves.
2. Line each half of the pita bread with the seasoned yogurt and then stuff in the greens. If there is extra yogurt, serve it on the side and dip your sandwich in it as you eat.

PER SERVING:
Calories: 219   Fat: 5 g (19% of calories)   Cholesterol: 1 mg   Protein: 12 g
                Saturated Fat: 1 g   Sodium: 492 mg   Carbohydrate: 33 g

John and Mary McDougall's
Vegetarian Chili

8 servings

☆ ☆

Dr. John McDougall—who "cures" his patients' penchant for fatty foods and sedentary, stressed-out lifestyles—also hosts radio and television programs on health. His wife Mary creates the recipes for the plan, including this hearty vegetarian chili. The McDougalls say, "This recipe was easily modified from a typical meat chili recipe—the beans and spicy taste give it all the flavor it needs. You should consider this one for family members who haven't quite made the step to cutting down on their meat dishes." Another McDougall recipe to try (Black Bean Soup) is on page 31.

1	28-ounce can chopped tomatoes
¾	cup bulgur
1	onion, coarsely chopped
3	celery stalks, coarsely chopped
2	carrots, peeled and chopped
5	tablespoons chili powder
2 to 4	cloves of garlic, minced
1	tablespoon lemon juice
1	teaspoon freshly ground pepper
1	teaspoon cumin
1	teaspoon basil
½	teaspoon oregano
1½	cups coarsely chopped green pepper
3	cups cooked red kidney beans
1½	cups cooked garbanzo beans
2	cups tomato juice

1. Drain tomatoes, reserving liquid. Bring 1 cup of reserved liquid to boil in medium saucepan over medium heat. Remove pan from heat. Stir in bulgur. Cover and let stand while cooking vegetables.
2. Cook onion in ½ cup water until translucent, stirring frequently. Add drained tomatoes, celery, carrots, chili powder, garlic, lemon juice, pepper, cumin, basil and oregano and cook until vegetables are almost tender, stirring frequently, about 15 minutes. Add green pepper and cook until tender, about 10 minutes.
3. Add the soaked bulgur, kidney beans, garbanzo beans and the tomato juice. Mix well. Reduce heat to low and simmer for 30 minutes, stirring occasionally. If it seems too thick, add the remaining tomato liquid or some water to thin it to the proper consistency.

Note: This can be prepared ahead: It reheats well over low heat.

PER SERVING:

Calories: 268	Fat: 3 g (9% of calories)	Cholesterol: 0 mg	Protein: 13 g
	Saturated Fat: <1 g	Sodium: 468 mg	Carbohydrate: 50 g

Moosewood Restaurant's
Polenta Cutlets

6 servings

☆☆

Moosewood Restaurant in Ithaca, New York, was made famous by Mollie Katzen's Moosewood Cookbook, *which introduced a generation of Americans to earthy, gourmet vegetarian cooking. The recipes in the* 15th Anniversary Moosewood Cookbook *are just as tasty as in the original, but many have much less fat. While Mollie has gone on to other cookbooks, the restaurant remains in Ithaca, churning out delicious, natural meals and its own cookbook,* Sundays at Moosewood Restaurant.*

- ½ teaspoon salt
- 6 cups boiling water
- 2½ cups cornmeal
- 1 cup grated sharp cheese, pecorino recommended
  nonstick cooking spray
- 2 cups toasted, unsalted whole-wheat bread crumbs
- ½ cup fresh parsley (or 1½ tablespoons dried)
- 2 tablespoons fresh basil, finely chopped
  salt and pepper (optional)
- ½ cup all-purpose flour or corn flour
- 3 egg whites, lightly whisked

1. Place salt into the boiling water. Using a whip, stir in cornmeal. Then mix in cheese.
2. Pour mixture into 2 sprayed 10-inch pie plates or cookie sheet. Set aside until cool, about 2 to 3 hours.
3. Toss together bread crumbs, parsley and basil. Set aside.
4. Preheat oven to 350°. Cut polenta into cutlets or other shapes.
5. Set up assembly line: cutlets, flour, egg wash, herbed bread crumbs, well-sprayed pan. Cover cutlet with flour, dip in egg wash, cover with bread crumbs and place into pan or onto sheet. Bake in oven for 30 minutes, turning after 20 minutes.

Serving suggestion: For Cutlets Parmesan, top the baked cutlets with tomato sauce and mozzarella cheese and return them to the oven for an additional 10 minutes. Polenta Cutlets also have a special affinity for Moosewood's Roasted Red Pepper Sauce (see page 115).

Note: To make whole-wheat bread crumbs, oven dry whole-wheat bread at 250° to 300° until crisp. Whirl in a food processor or place in a bag and roll with a rolling pin. Bread crumbs can be stored in an airtight jar for several weeks.

PER SERVING:

Calories: 434	Fat: 10 g (23% of calories)	Cholesterol: 22 mg	Protein: 16 g
	Saturated Fat: 5 g	Sodium: 566 mg	Carbohydrate: 70 g

*Reprinted with permission from *Sundays at Moosewood Restaurant* by the Moosewood Collective (Simon & Schuster, Inc.).

Marion Nestle's
Root Vegetable Medley
8 servings

☆☆

Marion Nestle chairs the Department of Nutrition, Food, and Hotel Management at New York University and is one of the most respected and widely quoted nutritionists in the country. Before moving to New York, she spent several years in Washington where, because their apartments were two floors apart, she and one of the editors (M.F.J.) often enjoyed a Saturday morning cup of tea together. Marion was the managing editor of the 1988 Surgeon General's Report on Nutrition and Health. *She says people don't eat enough parsnips, so here's a great way to enjoy them. Parsnips have vitamin C, but no beta-carotene; the yams and carrots in this recipe more than make up for that deficiency. Her Baked Pears recipe is on page 194.*

- 2 medium sweet potatoes (about 1 pound)
- 1 pound large carrots, scraped and cut into chunks
- 1 pound large parsnips, peeled and cut into chunks
- 1½ tablespoons unsalted butter
- ¼ cup maple syrup
- salt (optional) and freshly ground black pepper
- ½ teaspoon ground cumin seed
- ¼ cup Marsala
- ½ cup chopped parsley

1. Bake sweet potatoes until soft, about 45 minutes; set aside to cool. Meanwhile, in a separate pot, steam carrots and parsnips until tender, about 5 minutes, and set aside.
2. Peel sweet potatoes and put through a ricer or food mill to make a fine purée. Add ½ tablespoon butter and the maple syrup, season with salt (optional) and pepper and set aside. Pass carrots through a ricer or food mill and add ½ tablespoon butter, the cumin, salt and pepper and set aside. Pass parsnips through a ricer or food mill and add remaining ½ tablespoon butter, the Marsala, salt and pepper; set aside.
3. Preheat oven to 450°. Arrange the puréed vegetables in alternating strips in a glass baking dish. Bake in oven until hot, 30 to 45 minutes. Decorate border with parsley and serve.

PER SERVING:

Calories: 145	Fat: 2 g (14% of calories)	Cholesterol: 6 mg	Protein: 2 g
	Saturated Fat: 1 g	Sodium: 70 mg	Carbohydrate: 29 g

Dean Ornish's
Black Bean Burritos *6 servings*

☆ ☆

Dr. Dean Ornish's program emphasizing diet, exercise and stress reduction has catapulted him into celebrity status. Dr. Ornish's program grew out of his study that proved once and for all that a diet low in saturated fat and cholesterol decreases the amount of cholesterol plaque in arteries and actually reverses heart disease. Dr. Ornish is the director of the Preventive Medicine Research Institute at the University of California, San Francisco, and also is the author of Dr. Dean Ornish's Program for Reversing Heart Disease. *The book delivers largely vegetarian dietary advice, plus numerous recipes, including this one (by chef Mark Hall) and* Vegetable Cakes with Red Pepper Coulis *on page 83.*

Dr. Ornish's book recommends serving "this crowd pleaser with a tossed green salad and a bowl of chopped jalapeños on the side. If you have the black beans already made, this is a very quick meal to pull together. The 'guacamole' is a surprise for those who have given up avocados because of their fat content."

1½ **cups dry black beans**
6 **cups water**
4 **bay leaves**
1 **cup chopped onions**
½ **cup dry white wine**
2 **teaspoons freshly minced garlic**
2 **teaspoons ground cumin**
¼ **teaspoon freshly ground black pepper**
¼ **cup orange juice**
⅛ **teaspoon cayenne pepper**
 salt (optional)
 green pea "guacamole" for garnish (see following recipe)
 salsa cruda for garnish (see following recipe)
 chopped lettuce, scallions or tomatoes for garnish (optional)
6 **oil-free tortillas**
 cilantro for garnish

1. For the filling, sort and rinse the beans, then soak overnight in plenty of water. Drain and rinse. Cook the beans in a separate pot with the 6 cups of water and bay leaves for about 1 hour.
2. In another pot, braise the onions in ½ cup white wine with the garlic, cumin and black pepper. When the black beans are cooked, remove the bay leaves and drain, leaving about ¾ cup of liquid in the beans. Add the beans to the onions and stir. Add the orange juice and cayenne to the beans. Then add salt to taste, if you wish.
3. To assemble the burrito, place about ½ cup of the black beans, an equal amount of "guacamole" and ¼ cup of the salsa in the center of the tortillas.

Fold the opposite ends of the tortilla inward and roll. You can also add some chopped lettuce, scallions, tomatoes or cilantro before rolling the tortilla. Ladle some salsa over the tortilla, garnish with whole cilantro sprigs or chopped leaves and serve.

PER SERVING (WITHOUT GUACAMOLE AND SALSA):
Calories: 275　　Fat: 2 g (6% of calories)　　Cholesterol: 0 mg　　Protein: 14 g
　　　　　　　　　　Saturated Fat: <1 g　　　　Sodium: 21 mg　　　Carbohydrate: 50 g

GREEN PEA "GUACAMOLE":　　　　　　　　　　　　　　　　*12 servings*
　3　cups green peas, fresh or frozen
　2　tablespoons lemon juice
　1　cup chopped red onions
　2　teaspoons freshly minced garlic
　1　teaspoon cumin
　¼　teaspoon freshly ground black pepper
　⅛　teaspoon cayenne
　　　salt (optional)

1. Steam the peas if fresh. Do not overcook. They should still have their bright green color. If using frozen peas, just defrost them.
2. Purée the peas in a blender or food processor with the lemon juice, onions, garlic, cumin and black pepper. Add cayenne and salt to taste.

PER SERVING:
Calories: 40　　Fat: <1 g (4% of calories)　　Cholesterol: 0 mg　　Protein: 2 g
　　　　　　　　　Saturated Fat: 0 g　　　　Sodium: 35 mg　　　Carbohydrate: 7 g

SALSA CRUDA:　　　　　　　　　　　　　　　　　　　　　*6 servings*
　2　cups tomatoes, seeded and diced
　½　cup cucumber, peeled and diced
　½　cup onion, diced
　½　cup green bell pepper, diced
　1　teaspoon freshly minced garlic
　1　teaspoon rice wine vinegar
　2　tablespoons cilantro, freshly chopped
　1　teaspoon fresh lime juice
　⅛　teaspoon cayenne
　　　salt (optional)

1. Mix the tomatoes with the cucumber, onion, green pepper and garlic.
2. Season with vinegar, cilantro, lime juice and cayenne. Salt to taste and serve. Makes about 4 cups of salsa.

PER SERVING:
Calories: 25　　Fat: <1 g (13% of calories)　　Cholesterol: 0 mg　　Protein: 1 g
　　　　　　　　　Saturated Fat: 0 g　　　　Sodium: 11 mg　　　Carbohydrate: 5 g

Dean Ornish's
Vegetable Cakes
with Red Pepper Coulis

6 servings

☆☆☆

Dr. Dean Ornish's latest book, Eat More, Weigh Less, *shows people how to lose weight safely while eating abundantly. It includes some 250 healthful gourmet recipes. This vitamin-packed recipe comes from his previous book (as do his Black Bean Burritos on page 81) and was cooked up by the well-known California chef Wolfgang Puck.*

  1 **pound baking potatoes (2 medium)**
  1 **cup diced celery**
  1 **cup diced carrots**
  1 **cup diced onions**
  1 **medium peeled, seeded and diced tomato**
      vegetable stock (page 21) or low-sodium broth, if necessary
  1 **cup fresh peas**
  3 **tablespoons chopped fresh parsley**
  1 **teaspoon ground cumin**
 ½ **teaspoon turmeric**
      pinch of red pepper flakes
  3 **large egg whites**
  3 **tablespoons non-fat milk**
  1 **cup whole-wheat dried bread crumbs (page 79)**
      red pepper coulis (see following recipe)

1. Bake the potatoes until tender.
2. In a large nonstick skillet, slowly sauté the celery, carrots, onions and tomato until the vegetables are tender, 10 to 15 minutes. If the tomatoes are not juicy, add a little vegetable stock. Transfer to a large mixing bowl. Add the peas, parsley, cumin, turmeric and red pepper flakes. Set aside to cool.
3. Scrape the potato from the shell into a mixing bowl and mash. In a small bowl mix together the egg whites and the milk. Stir into the mashed potatoes until smooth. Add to the vegetables and combine thoroughly. Form into 12 patties, about 2 ounces each.
4. Pour the dried bread crumbs onto a large plate and lightly coat both sides of each patty. For firmer patties, stir the crumbs into the potato-milk mix until distributed evenly.
5. Spray 1 or 2 large skillets with a vegetable oil spray and sauté the patties until browned, about 5 minutes per side.

Presentation: Pour a layer of coulis on each of 6 plates and set 2 vegetable cakes on the sauce. Serve immediately.

PER SERVING (WITHOUT COULIS):

Calories: 140   Fat: <1 g (5% of calories)   Cholesterol: 0 mg   Protein: 7 g
                 Saturated Fat: <1 g   Sodium: 172 mg   Carbohydrate: 28 g

RED PEPPER COULIS: *10 servings*

  ½ **pound (2 small) cored, seeded and diced red peppers**
  1 **medium peeled, seeded and diced tomato**
  ½ **large onion, diced**
1¾ **cups vegetable stock (see page 21) or low-sodium canned broth**
  ¼ **cup chopped basil**
     pinch of thyme

1. In a medium skillet, combine the red peppers, tomato, onion and vegetable stock and cook until the vegetables are tender, 10 to 15 minutes.
   Stir in the basil and thyme.
2. Purée in a blender and pour back into a clean skillet. Reduce until about
   1½ cups remain.

PER SERVING:

Calories: 15   Fat:<1 g (11% of calories)   Cholesterol: 0 mg   Protein: 1 g
                Saturated Fat: 0 g   Sodium: 37 mg   Carbohydrate: 3 g

$$\wp\partial$$

Robert Pritikin's
Black Bean Chili   *8 servings*

☆☆☆

*As director of the Pritikin Longevity Centers, Robert Pritikin is carrying on his
father Nathan's commitment to saving lives by radically changing people's diets and
exercise habits. Robert, as easygoing as his father was intense, is (like his father)
largely self-trained but extraordinarily knowledgeable about nutrition. When he
was 24, he helped his father and a cardiologist at the San Diego Veterans
Administration hospital conduct a landmark study indicating that a low-fat diet
could undo the damage wrought by a lifetime of fatty foods.*

*Robert gave us a most appropriate recipe, since beans are one of nature's most
perfect foods. Like other legumes, beans are fat-free and provide protein, iron, potassium and a variety of other minerals and vitamins. For more Pritikin cuisine, try
Robert's Warm Chicken Salad on page 100.*

  1 **medium onion, chopped**
  1 **medium green bell pepper, chopped**
  2 **14½-ounce cans no-salt-added tomatoes, drained and chopped**
     (reserve liquid)

3 cups cooked black beans or two 15-ounce cans, rinsed and drained
1 cup Pritikin Spaghetti Sauce
1 tablespoon chili powder
2 teaspoons ground cumin
¼ teaspoon cayenne pepper

1. Lightly spray large saucepan or Dutch oven with nonstick cooking spray. Cook onion and green pepper over medium-high heat 3 to 4 minutes or until peppers are crisp-tender, stirring frequently.
2. Stir in remaining ingredients including reserved tomato liquid. Bring to a boil; reduce heat to low. Cover and simmer 25 to 30 minutes.

PER SERVING (1 CUP):

Calories: 137	Fat: 1 g (7% of calories)	Cholesterol: 0 mg	Protein: 8 g
	Saturated Fat: <1 g	Sodium: 31 mg	Carbohydrate: 25 g

વ્ટ

Carl and Estelle Reiner's
Cabbage Casserole

6 servings

☆☆

Carl Reiner has been giving Americans laughing fits since the 1950s. That's when he got his first big opportunity—working on "Your Show of Shows" and "Caesar's Hour" with the incomparable Sid Caesar. Since then, he has written, acted and directed Broadway plays, television shows and films, including Dead Men Don't Wear Plaid *and* Oh, God! *Carl may be best remembered, though, for writing and producing "The Dick Van Dyke Show." Luckily, he has received ample recognition for his talents, having won eleven Emmy awards so far. This recipe, created by his wife Estelle, a singer in her own right, is a real winner, too.*

1 head cabbage, shredded
1 onion, chopped
1 pint non-fat yogurt
1½ teaspoons turmeric
1 tablespoon coriander
1 teaspoon cumin
½ teaspoon salt
¼ teaspoon ginger, ground
3 to 4 medium potatoes, skinned, boiled and sliced
¼ cup Post Grape-Nuts cereal
1 tablespoon margarine

1. Steam the cabbage and onion until almost done. While they are steaming, combine the next 6 ingredients in a small bowl.
2. Preheat oven to 350°. Add spices to cabbage mixture. Layer the bottom of a casserole dish with the cabbage mixture. Next, layer the sliced potatoes, and continue alternating layers until ingredients are used. Top with Grape-Nuts and dot with margarine.
3. Bake covered for 30 minutes. Remove cover and bake for an additional 30 minutes.

PER SERVING:

| Calories: 223 | Fat: 2 g (9% of calories) | Cholesterol: 1 mg | Protein: 9 g |
| | Saturated Fat: <1 g | Sodium: 407 mg | Carbohydrate: 44 g |

Bill Rodgers's
Buckwheat Groats Loaf   *6 servings*

☆☆

Bill Rodgers has been winning marathons for twenty years and was ranked number one in the world by Track and Field News *in 1975 and 1979. He says, "This is one of our favorite recipes, especially before a marathon. We've had it for years and can't remember where we got it." This nutritious, delicious dish provides a real energy boost. It must—Bill has finished in first place in nineteen of thirty-one races.*

½ **cup raw buckwheat groats (whole)**
1 **egg white**
2 **cups brown rice, cooked**
3 **cups steamed, diced vegetables (such as carrots, potatoes, green pepper)**
  freshly ground black pepper
2 **cups reduced-fat cheddar cheese, shredded**
¾ **teaspoon salt**
  nonstick cooking spray

1. Preheat oven to 325°.
2. Mix ½ cup of groats with 1 egg white. Stir over medium heat in a heavy pan until groats are toasted. Add groats to 2 cups of boiling water. Cook until groats are tender, but not mushy.
3. Combine the groats, rice, vegetables, pepper, 1 cup of cheese and salt in a bowl. Mix well.
4. Turn into a sprayed casserole dish or ovenproof bowl. Bake for 20 minutes. Remove, sprinkle on remaining cheese, and return for 10 more minutes or until cheese is melted.

PER SERVING:

Calories: 300	Fat: 8 g (23% of calories)	Cholesterol: 27 mg	Protein: 16 g
	Saturated Fat: 4 g	Sodium: 573 mg	Carbohydrate: 42 g

৪৯

Bernd Schmitt's
Vegetable Strudel
with Red Pepper Coulis
8 servings

☆☆

You will simply dazzle your guests with this colorful, delicious recipe from Bernd Schmitt, executive chef at the posh Canyon Ranch in Tuscon, Arizona. Bernd's strudel is saturated with vitamins, but not with fat. His other sophisticated recipes include Salmon with Poached Leeks, Capers and Chive Vinaigrette on page 145 and Bread Pudding on page 197.

3 **cups minced broccoli**
2 **cups minced asparagus**
2 **cups carrots, julienne-cut (matchstick)**
4 **cups shredded savoy cabbage**
2 **cups red bell pepper, julienne-cut**
2 **cups yellow squash, julienne-cut**
¼ **cup chopped red onion**
3 **cups sliced shiitake mushrooms**
5 **phyllo pastry sheets**
   nonstick cooking spray
¾ **cup red pepper coulis (see following recipe)**

1. In a large pot, bring 2 cups of water to a boil over high heat. Add vegetables, lower heat, cover pot and allow to steam 2 to 3 minutes. Remove from heat, pour vegetables into a large bowl of ice water. This stops the cooking process and helps to maintain the color and texture of vegetables. Remove vegetables after 30 seconds, and place in a colander to drain.

2. Preheat oven to 350°. Layer 5 sheets of phyllo on work surface, spraying each layer with nonstick vegetable spray. Arrange well-drained vegetables lengthwise along one long edge of phyllo sheets, leaving about 1½ inches on each end. Fold the 1½-inch sides in, overlapping the vegetables to enclose ends of the filling. Roll the phyllo and filling over itself to form a strudel roll. Transfer seam down to a baking sheet, and spray the strudel roll lightly with nonstick spray.

3. Bake 25 minutes or until golden brown. While strudel is baking, make the red pepper coulis. Allow strudel to stand out of oven for 5 minutes

before slicing and serving. Cut strudel roll into 4 equal portions. Spread 2 tablespoons coulis on the bottom of each serving plate and arrange strudel roll on top of the coulis.

PER SERVING (WITHOUT COULIS):

Calories: 285   Fat: 1 g (4% of calories)   Cholesterol: 2 mg   Protein: 9 g
                  Saturated Fat: 0 g   Sodium: 237 mg   Carbohydrate: 74 g

RED PEPPER COULIS: *8 servings*

   2 **cups diced red bell peppers**
   ½ **cup diced onions**
1½ **cups vegetable stock (see page 21) or use low-sodium canned broth**
   4 **drops Tabasco sauce**
   2 **drops Worchestershire sauce**
   1 **pinch white pepper**
   1 **teaspoon minced fresh mint**

In a medium pan, combine red bell peppers, onion and vegetable stock. Bring to a boil, lower heat and simmer. Remove from heat and cool slightly, for 5 minutes. Place in a blender and process until puréed, then strain through a sieve. Add remaining ingredients and mix well. Serve warm.

PER SERVING:

Calories: 10   Fat:<1 g (11% of calories)   Cholesterol: 0 mg   Protein: <1 g
                  Saturated Fat: 0 g   Sodium: 2 mg   Carbohydrate: 2 g

ℛ

Kathy Smith's
Bean Stew   *4 servings*

☆☆

   Sports Illustrated *said it best: "Kathy Smith is fitness in America." As an athlete and world-renowned fitness guru, she has reported for NBC-TV's "Today Show," made award-winning videos, released albums and books and owns a high-tech fitness complex in Los Angeles. Since legumes have become a mainstay in many of Kathy's recipes, she simply adds a salad and bread to this bean stew and it becomes a favorite meal for her husband and daughter. Kathy says, "Beans can take a few hours to cook, so I like to prepare them first thing in the morning. If you like spicier food, you may want to add 1 teaspoon of crushed red pepper. Serve with a salad and crusty French bread."*

   1 **pound plum tomatoes (if using canned, use no-salt-added)**
   1 **cup dry kidney beans, cooked according to directions**

1 medium onion, chopped finely
4 cloves of garlic, chopped finely
½ cup red pepper, chopped
½ cup green pepper, chopped
8 ounces elbow macaroni, cooked
1 tablespoon olive oil
2 tablespoons chopped fresh basil (or substitute 1 teaspoon dried basil)
  pinch of pepper and oregano
½ teaspoon salt

1. Boil tomatoes, peel the skins and chop. Sauté the onions, garlic and peppers in the olive oil. Add the tomatoes. Add spices, cover and cook for 5 minutes until boiling.
2. Add cooked beans, water and macaroni and stir. Cover and let steam for 10 minutes.

PER SERVING:

Calories: 449	Fat: 6 g (12% of calories)	Cholesterol: 0 mg	Protein: 20 g
	Saturated Fat: <1 g	Sodium: 290 mg	Carbohydrate: 82 g

Dick Van Patten's
Eggplant Parmesan

4 servings

☆☆☆

Actor Dick Van Patten is keeping busy these days appearing in benefit performances of The Odd Couple *and cooking up scrumptious vegetarian cuisine. If you like this dish, try Dick's recipes for Beans and Potato Soup (page 35) and Vegetable Lasagna (page 122).*

1 large eggplant, sliced into medium pieces
  nonstick cooking spray
4 cups Tomato-Veggie Sauce (see page 104)
2 ounces reduced-fat mozzarella cheese
2 tablespoons grated Parmesan cheese to taste

1. Coat a pan with nonstick cooking spray, spread unpeeled eggplant on pan and lightly spray the top of the eggplant. Broil until brown.
2. Preheat oven to 350°. In baking dish, layer tomato-veggie sauce, eggplant, mozzarella, sauce, eggplant, mozzarella, sauce and sprinkle with grated Parmesan. Bake covered for 30 to 40 minutes.

PER SERVING:

| Calories: 176 | Fat: 5 g (23% of calories) | Cholesterol: 17 mg | Protein: 15 g |
| | Saturated Fat: 3 g | Sodium: 425 mg | Carbohydrate: 21 g |

MAIN-COURSE SALADS

Steve Allen and Jayne Meadows's
Niçoise Tuna Salad

4 servings

☆☆☆☆☆☆☆☆☆☆☆☆ ☆☆☆☆☆☆ ☆☆☆☆☆☆☆☆☆☆☆ ☆☆☆☆☆☆☆☆☆☆☆

You can put some spice in your life with this tangy entree from entertainers Steve Allen and Jayne Meadows. A low-sodium spaghetti sauce works great in the recipe, because the hot pepper sauce ensures that this almost fat-free meal is high in flavor. This extraordinarily talented husband/wife team also contributed the Cajun Red Beans and Rice recipe on page 68.

   6 cups torn mixed greens (such as spinach, romaine, red leaf and Boston lettuce)
   1 6½-ounce can white tuna in water, rinsed and drained
   4 small red potatoes, cooked and sliced
   1 cup fresh or frozen green beans, cooked, but still crisp
   2 plum tomatoes, quartered
   2 tablespoons chopped fresh tarragon, basil or Italian parsley (optional)
  ¼ cup Pritikin Italian dressing
    lemon wedges
    freshly ground black pepper to taste

1. Arrange greens on serving platter. Break tuna into chunks and arrange over lettuce with potatoes, green beans, tomatoes and tarragon.
2. Drizzle dressing over salad; serve with lemon wedges and freshly ground black pepper.

PER SERVING:

Calories: 224	Fat: 1 g (3% of calories)	Cholesterol: 26 mg	Protein: 23 g
	Saturated Fat: 0 g	Sodium: 122 mg	Carbohydrate: 34 g

Chris Evert's
Chicken Salad

4 servings

☆☆☆☆☆☆☆☆☆☆☆☆ ☆☆☆☆☆☆☆ ☆☆☆☆☆☆☆☆☆☆ ☆☆☆☆☆☆☆☆☆☆

Chris Evert won eighteen Grand Slam titles, including multiple wins at Wimbledon, the French Open, Australian Open and U.S. Open, in her remarkable seventeen-year pro-tennis career. In 1989, Chris retired from tennis and established Evert Enterprises/International Management Group in Boca Raton, Florida. At Chris's baby shower in 1991, her sister served this dish, which Chris says is now her favorite luncheon recipe. The pineapple, chutney and curry convert commonplace chicken into a wonderful salad.

  2 cups shredded boneless, skinless chicken, trimmed of fat (about 4 half
    breasts)
    nonstick cooking spray
  ½ cup pineapple chunks, unsweetened
  ½ cup celery, chopped
  ¼ cup scallions, chopped
  2 tablespoons dry-roasted unsalted peanuts
  ¼ teaspoon salt
  1 tablespoon chutney
  1 tablespoon lemon juice
  1 teaspoon lemon rind, grated
  ¼ teaspoon curry powder
  ⅓ cup Miracle Whip Free Nonfat Dressing or non-fat mayonnaise

1. Coat nonstick pan with cooking spray. Arrange chicken in 1 layer on pan
   and cook covered on medium heat until cooked through (about 7 minutes).
   Chicken should be turned once. Shred chicken.
2. Combine all ingredients and mix well. Refrigerate and serve.

PER SERVING:
Calories: 227   Fat: 7 g (28% of calories)   Cholesterol: 73 mg   Protein: 29 g
                 Saturated Fat: 1 g   Sodium: 210 mg   Carbohydrate: 12 g

David Horowitz's
Fight Back! Salad
4 servings

☆☆☆☆☆☆☆☆☆☆☆☆☆☆ ☆☆☆☆☆☆☆☆☆ ☆☆☆☆☆☆☆☆☆☆☆ ☆☆☆☆☆☆☆☆☆☆

*Consumer reporter David Horowitz's Fight Back! Salad was served in the com-
missary at NBC studios (where he worked for many years before moving to KCBS-
TV in 1993) in Burbank, California. If you want to fight back some more, try
David's Fight Back! Chicken on page 155. David says of this recipe,*

No salad dressing is added, although a topping of light vinaigrette is
optional. By chopping all ingredients to small bite-sized bits, natural
juiciness is released, creating a kind of silky texture. Surprisingly,
even those who normally dote on richly dressed salads find this dish
appealing. Oil in the garlic-flavored croutons plus the fat in Swiss
cheese do lend calories—but far fewer than if you heaped on added
dressing. You can vary the amounts to suit your taste and according
to the number of diners.

  1 large head romaine or iceberg lettuce, shredded (about 5 to 6 cups)
  1 red or mild white onion, chopped
  1 carrot, grated

1 large tomato, diced
2 cups finely shredded red cabbage
  garlic-flavored croutons (see directions below)
6 ounces roasted turkey breast, diced
2 ounces Swiss cheese, diced or julienne-cut (matchstick strips)
  light vinaigrette dressing (optional)

Wash and chop lettuce into bite-sized pieces. Place all ingredients in a bowl. Toss thoroughly to combine.

Note: To make garlic croutons, take 6 slices whole-wheat bread and cut into cubes. In 1 tablespoon of olive oil, saute two cloves of minced garlic for 1 minute. Add bread cubes and cook, stirring often, until bread starts to crisp and brown.

PER SERVING:

Calories: 318	Fat: 10 g (27% of calories)	Cholesterol: 59 mg	Protein: 28 g
	Saturated Fat: 4 g	Sodium: 361 mg	Carbohydrate: 31 g

ℰ∂

Nancy Harmon Jenkins's
Corn, Pepper, Rice and Crab Salad   *4 servings*

☆☆☆☆☆☆☆☆☆☆☆☆ ☆☆☆☆☆☆ ☆☆☆☆☆☆☆☆☆☆☆☆ ☆☆☆☆☆☆☆☆☆

Nancy Harmon Jenkins is a nationally known food writer, whose work has appeared in such publications as the New York Times, Food & Wine *and* Eating Well. *Nancy is the author of* The Mediterranean Diet *and is writing a book on American ethnic and immigrant foods. She describes these recipes as modern ways to use traditional Native American foods. You'll love the way this salad overflows with a cornucopia of flavors and colors.*

1 cup brown rice, uncooked
2 cups water
2 cups cooked corn (4 ears)
½ medium green pepper, seeded and sliced
1 small jalapeño pepper, seeded and diced (use gloves if fresh)
½ medium red or yellow pepper, seeded and sliced
2 ripe tomatoes, peeled, seeded and diced
6 scallions, including about 2 inches of green tops
½ pound fresh cooked crab meat
2 tablespoons extra-virgin olive oil
⅓ cup fresh strained lemon juice
¼ cup chopped fresh green herbs (basil, cilantro, dill, tarragon and/or thyme)
  salt and freshly ground black pepper to taste

1. Cook the rice in boiling water until tender (about 45 minutes).
2. While rice is cooking, slice corn kernels off the cooked ears and mix with peppers and tomatoes in a salad bowl. Slice scallions and add. Pick over crab meat, discarding any cartilage, and add to the salad bowl.
3. Mix together olive oil and lemon juice, blending with a fork. Add to vegetables and mix well. Add the green herbs and mix again. When rice is done, drain if necessary and add hot rice to the salad. Mix well and taste, adding salt and pepper as desired. Set aside to let flavors blend for about 20 minutes. Serve at room temperature. If necessary to refrigerate, return to room temperature before serving. May be served on a bed of greens.

PER SERVING:

Calories: 403	Fat: 10 g (22% of calories)	Cholesterol: 57 mg	Protein: 19 g
	Saturated Fat: 1 g	Sodium: 208 mg	Carbohydrate: 62 g

✿⳺

Nancy Harmon Jenkins's
Spiced Quinoa Salad

8 servings

☆☆☆☆☆☆☆☆☆☆☆☆☆☆ ☆☆☆☆☆☆ ☆☆☆☆☆☆☆☆☆☆☆☆☆ ☆☆☆☆☆☆☆☆☆☆☆☆

In addition to its spectacular taste, this salad provides lots of protein (from the shrimp and quinoa) and vitamin A (from the apricots).

- 1 cup quinoa
- 2 cups boiling water
- 1 cup seedless green grapes, or ½ cup raisins soaked in hot water to plump
- 4 fresh apricots, or 4 dried apricots soaked in hot water to plump
- 1 teaspoon ground coriander
- ⅛ teaspoon freshly ground nutmeg
  freshly ground black pepper to taste
- 1 piece fresh ginger root (about 1½ inches long), peeled and minced
- 4 large scallions with about 2 inches green tops
- ⅓ cup toasted almonds, coarsely chopped
- 2 tablespoons extra-virgin olive oil
  juice of half a lemon, strained (about 1½ tablespoons)
- 1 pound steamed shrimp

1. Rinse quinoa. Steam in boiling water until grains are fluffy (about 15 minutes). Remove from heat and drain if necessary.
2. Rinse grapes and cut in half lengthwise. Peel apricots and cut in pieces about the same size as the grapes. Gently toss quinoa in a salad bowl with the two fruits. Add seasonings (coriander, nutmeg, pepper and ginger) and stir to mix well. Slice scallions and add to the salad with almonds.

Mix together the olive oil and lemon juice, blending with a fork. Pour over the salad and toss gently to mix well.

3. Peel steamed shrimp and cut in half lengthwise, removing the vein. Toss with the salad just before serving. Taste and adjust seasoning. Serve on a bed of greens.

PER SERVING:

Calories: 389	Fat: 11 g (26% of calories)	Cholesterol: 111 mg	Protein: 23 g
	Saturated Fat: 2 g	Sodium: 130 mg	Carbohydrate: 52 g

Larry King's
King Tuna Health Salad
4 servings

☆☆☆☆☆☆☆☆☆☆☆☆☆ ☆☆☆☆☆☆☆ ☆☆☆☆☆☆☆☆☆☆☆☆ ☆☆☆☆☆☆☆☆☆☆☆☆

Larry King is indeed the king of talk radio and television. His nightly interview show on CNN catapulted to fame when Ross Perot announced on the show that he might run for president. Larry was once a big smoker and was totally uninterested in nutrition. His heart attack cured him of both problems. Larry made up this recipe with the help of Washington restaurateur Duke Zeibert, illustrating one of the best ways to dress up an ordinary tuna salad sandwich.

2 6½-ounce cans water-packed tuna, rinsed and drained
2 tablespoons diced sweet onions
2 tablespoons diced green pepper
2 tablespoons diced celery
2 tablespoons diced tomato
1 tablespoon Miracle Whip Free Nonfat Dressing
1 tablespoon corn oil
4 tablespoons vinegar
  bermuda onion, sliced, optional
  tomato, sliced, optional

Combine all except optional ingredients in a bowl and mix gently. Serve on a bed of lettuce and garnish with slices of Bermuda onion and tomato. Serve chilled.

PER SERVING:

Calories: 189	Fat: 5 g (22% of calories)	Cholesterol: 52 mg	Protein: 33 g
	Saturated Fat: <1 g	Sodium: 95 mg	Carbohydrate: 4 g

Steve Largent's
Fruited Chicken Salad

8 servings

☆☆☆☆☆☆☆☆☆☆☆☆☆☆ ☆☆☆☆☆☆☆☆ ☆☆☆☆☆☆☆☆☆☆ ☆☆☆☆☆☆☆☆☆☆☆☆

Steve Largent holds the National Football League record for most seasons with at least fifty catches, and ranks as the second leading receiver in NFL history. This Seattle Seahawks star caught 471 passes and sixty touchdowns over eight seasons and in 1986 broke a league record by catching at least one pass in over 128 consecutive games. In 1975 and 1976, Largent topped the nation in touchdown receptions while at Tulsa University. This fruity salad ought to light up the scoreboard in your home.

4 cups shredded boneless, skinless chicken breasts, trimmed of fat
(about 8 half breasts)
nonstick cooking spray
2 cups seedless green grapes, halved (or 15-ounce can drained pineapple chunks)
1 cup chopped celery
1 11-ounce can drained mandarin orange sections
2 tablespoons grated onion
1 cup Miracle Whip Free Nonfat Dressing
1 tablespoon prepared mustard
1 5-ounce can chow mein noodles
lettuce leaves for decoration

1. Coat nonstick pan with cooking spray. Arrange chicken in 1 layer on pan and cook covered on medium heat until cooked through (about 7 minutes). Chicken should be turned once. Shred chicken.
2. In a large bowl, combine chicken, grapes (or pineapple chunks), celery, oranges and onion. Blend in dressing and mustard; toss gently with chicken mixture. Cover and chill several hours.
3. Just before serving, mix in chow mein noodles; turn salad into a lettuce-lined serving bowl.

PER SERVING:
Calories: 324   Fat: 8 g (21% of calories)   Cholesterol: 75 mg   Protein: 30 g
                 Saturated Fat: 2 g   Sodium: 276 mg   Carbohydrate: 34 g

Patrick and Marcelle Leahy's
Curried Chicken and Rice Salad   *4 servings*

☆☆☆☆☆☆☆☆☆☆☆☆☆☆ ☆☆☆☆☆☆ ☆☆☆☆☆☆☆☆☆☆☆ ☆☆☆☆☆☆☆☆☆☆

As head of the Senate Agriculture Committee, Senator Patrick Leahy has used his power to promote environmentally sound agriculture. In 1990 he led the effort to pass a law defining organically grown food, which had been one of the Center for Science in the Public Interest's goals for several years. This spicy chicken salad is perfect for a summer lunch.

1¼ cups long-grain brown rice
1 teaspoon salt
3 cups cold water
½ teaspoon minced fresh ginger root
1 cup cooked, diced skinless, boneless chicken
1 cup cooked peas or green beans
½ cup chopped celery
¼ cup sliced scallions
¼ cup chopped parsley
½ cup chopped green pepper
½ cup raisins
½ cup reduced-calorie mayonnaise
½ cup plain non-fat yogurt
2 teaspoons honey
1 tablespoon lemon juice
2 tablespoons curry powder
   salad greens
¼ cup toasted peanuts
¼ cup toasted shredded coconut

1. Combine rice, salt (use less or omit to reduce sodium), water and ginger in heavy saucepan. Bring to a boil, then stir with a fork. Cover, reduce heat and simmer about 15 minutes or until rice is tender and water is absorbed. Cool.
2. Combine cooled rice, chicken, cooked and raw vegetables and raisins. Combine mayonnaise, yogurt, honey, lemon juice and curry powder; beat until blended. Pour over rice salad and mix very well. Chill.
3. Serve in bowls lined with salad greens and garnished with peanuts and coconut.

PER SERVING:
Calories: 463   Fat: 8 g (15% of calories)   Cholesterol: 47 mg   Protein: 20 g
                 Saturated Fat: 3 g   Sodium: 642 mg   Carbohydrate: 79 g

Walter Mondale's
Shrimp Salad in Papaya
with Fresh Fruit
4 servings

☆☆☆☆☆☆☆☆☆☆☆☆☆☆ ☆☆☆☆☆☆☆☆ ☆☆☆☆☆☆☆☆☆☆☆☆ ☆☆☆☆☆☆☆☆☆☆☆

We like this recipe from former Vice President Walter Mondale because papaya has so much vitamin A, but because shrimp is so high in cholesterol, we suggest you save this dish for an occasional treat or use fewer shrimp. He also has a chicken recipe on page 159.

1½ pounds large shrimp, raw
⅓ cup non-fat mayonnaise
½ teaspoon curry powder
1 tablespoon lemon juice
2 ripe papayas
1 head Boston or Bibb lettuce
1 bunch watercress
1 pineapple, peeled, cored and cut into fingers
2 kiwi, sliced

BROTH FOR COOKING SHRIMP:
2 quarts water
1 stalk celery
½ bay leaf
10 peppercorns
1 teaspoon salt
3 tablespoons lemon juice

1. To prepare broth, simmer the broth ingredients for 30 minutes. Slowly add the shrimp so that the broth remains at a simmer. After 5 minutes, remove from the heat and let stand for 10 minutes. Drain the shrimp in a colander and run under cold water. Peel, devein and chill the shrimp.

2. Slice each shrimp in half by placing it flat on a cutting board and cutting carefully with the knife parallel to the board. Each shrimp half should remain a crescent shape. Place the shrimp halves in a bowl. Season the mayonnaise with curry powder and fresh lemon juice to taste. Toss the shrimp in the seasoned mayonnaise until well coated and let marinate for 30 minutes; add more mayonnaise if the shrimp seem dry.

3. Prepare the papayas by peeling, halving and scooping out the seeds. Place each half on a plate covered with lettuce leaves, fill with shrimp salad and garnish with watercress, pineapple and kiwi (or any other ripe fresh fruit).

PER SERVING:
Calories: 241   Fat: 3 g (10% of calories)   Cholesterol: 261 mg   Protein: 32 g
             Saturated Fat: 1 g   Sodium: 415 mg   Carbohydrate: 27 g

Robert Pritikin's
Warm Chicken Salad
4 servings

☆☆☆☆☆☆☆☆☆☆☆☆☆☆ ☆☆☆☆☆☆ ☆☆☆☆☆☆☆☆☆☆☆ ☆☆☆☆☆☆☆☆☆☆

This recipe from Robert Pritikin (director of the Pritikin Longevity Centers) shows how easy it is to make a low-fat chicken dish. Robert also contributed Black Bean Chili on page 84.

4 boneless, skinless chicken breast halves (about 3½ ounces each)
½ cup Pritikin Italian dressing
¼ cup Pritikin chicken broth
1 clove garlic, minced
4 cups torn mixed greens (such as spinach, romaine and red leaf lettuce)
1 medium tomato, chopped
¼ cup fresh basil (optional)
   freshly ground black pepper

1. Place chicken in glass dish or plastic bag. Add dressing, broth and garlic; turn to coat. Cover and refrigerate at least 30 minutes or up to 24 hours.
2. Place chicken on rack of broiler pan; reserve dressing. Broil about 5 to 7 minutes or until cooked through, turning once. Combine greens and tomato on serving platter. Slice chicken crosswise into ½-inch strips and arrange over greens.
3. Heat remaining dressing to boiling; drizzle over salad and top with basil. Serve with freshly ground black pepper.

PER SERVING:

Calories: 183	Fat: 3 g (17% of calories)	Cholesterol: 73 mg	Protein: 29 g
	Saturated Fat: <1 g	Sodium: 102 mg	Carbohydrate: 9 g

ｆる

Steve Sax's
Clubhouse Chicken Salad
with Honey Mustard Dressing
4 servings

☆☆☆☆☆☆☆☆☆☆☆☆☆☆ ☆☆☆☆☆☆ ☆☆☆☆☆☆☆☆☆☆☆ ☆☆☆☆☆☆☆☆☆☆

Chicago White Sox outfielder Steve Sax is personally devoted to both nutrition and fitness. The brown rice is a little richer in nutrients and fiber than white rice, and the bell pepper adds vitamin C. In addition to this all-star recipe, Steve has a Brown Rice & Shiitake Pilaf on page 122.

SALAD:

- 1 tablespoon olive oil
- 1 pound boneless, skinless chicken breasts
- 3 cups hot cooked brown rice (if desired, cook in chicken stock–see page 21 or use low-sodium canned broth)
- ½ cup sliced red onion
- 1 medium green or red pepper, chopped
- 1 14-ounce can artichoke hearts, drained and quartered
- ¼ teaspoon ground black pepper

DRESSING:

- 2 tablespoons olive oil
- 3 tablespoons cider vinegar
- 1 tablespoon honey
- 1 teaspoon Dijon mustard
- ¼ teaspoon ground black pepper
- ¼ teaspoon salt

1. Heat oil in large skillet over medium-high heat. Cook chicken in hot oil until lightly browned, about 5 minutes. Let cool and cut into chunks. Combine chicken, rice, onion, pepper, artichoke hearts and pepper in large bowl.
2. Combine dressing ingredients in small saucepan. Heat to just boiling and toss with salad.

PER SERVING:

Calories: 454	Fat: 15 g (29% of calories)	Cholesterol: 68 mg	Protein: 32 g
	Saturated Fat: 3 g	Sodium: 429 mg	Carbohydrate: 48 g

ℛ

Rebecca Wood's
Quinoa, Black Bean and Corn Salad with Tomato
4 servings

☆☆☆☆☆☆☆☆☆☆☆☆☆☆ ☆☆☆☆☆☆☆☆☆☆☆☆☆☆☆☆ ☆☆☆☆☆☆☆☆☆☆

Rebecca Wood is the author of the Whole Foods Encyclopedia, *which ABC-TV's "Good Morning America" praised as one of the top food books of 1988. She also wrote* Art of Grain Cookery *and* Quinoa the Supergrain *(from which this recipe is taken). Rebecca says:*

Quinoa, the newly introduced high-protein grain from South America, is rapidly becoming popular not only among the fitness-conscious, but also among all people who enjoy fine foods. Quick-cooking quinoa is light in texture and has a pleasing flavor. This versatile grain is available in some supermarkets and in natural-foods stores. Here, quinoa makes a great flavor and texture addition to a salad; substitute it freely in most recipes calling for rice, barley, bulgur, couscous and buckwheat.

2 **tablespoons lemon juice**
2 **tablespoons olive oil**
2 **tablespoons minced cilantro**
¼ **teaspoon salt or salt substitute**
1 **cup fresh or frozen corn, simmered until tender, ½ cup cooking
   liquid reserved**
¼ **cup quinoa, rinsed thoroughly**
¼ **teaspoon cumin seeds**
½ **cup cooked black beans, rinsed**
1 **medium tomato, diced into small pieces**
2 **tablespoons minced red onions**

1. Mix lemon juice, olive oil, cilantro and salt in a small non-reactive bowl; set aside.
2. Bring reserved corn liquid to a boil in a small saucepan. Add quinoa and cumin; cover and simmer until quinoa absorbs the liquid and is tender, about 10 minutes. Transfer quinoa to a large nonmetal bowl; cool slightly. Then add corn, remaining ingredients and dressing; toss to combine and chill. Can be covered and refrigerated up to 4 hours before serving.

PER SERVING:

| Calories: 294 | Fat: 10 g (29% of calories) | Cholesterol: 0 mg | Protein: 9 g |
| | Saturated Fat: 1 g | Sodium: 140 mg | Carbohydrate: 45 g |

PASTA, RICE AND OTHER GRAINS

Alan Alda's
Che-Cha
5 servings

☆☆☆☆☆☆☆☆☆☆ ☆☆☆☆☆☆☆☆☆☆ ☆☆☆☆☆☆☆☆☆☆ ☆☆☆☆☆☆☆☆☆☆

Alan Alda chops garlic with the skill of an accomplished surgeon. Eleven years starring as the irreverent combat surgeon "Hawkeye" in the television series "M*A*S*H," which captured five Emmy awards, gave him practice with the knife. Among his other achievements as writer, actor and director are the Broadway shows The Owl and the Pussycat *and* The Apple Tree *and such films as* California Suite *and* Crimes and Misdemeanors. *Alan, an ardent feminist, doesn't mind donning an apron to prepare this tasty, low-fat tomato and cheese dish.*

> 14 good-sized Italian plum tomatoes
> 2 handfuls fresh basil leaves, chopped
> 1 clove garlic, minced
> ⅓ pound reduced-fat mozzarella, shredded
> 1 tablespoon olive oil
> 10 ounces fusilli (corkscrew macaroni)

1. Fill a pot with enough water to cover tomatoes. Bring to a boil. Drop tomatoes in. Remove after about 10 seconds. Peel and chop tomatoes.
2. Mix the tomatoes, basil, garlic and cheese with the olive oil. Let stand in covered bowl at room temperature for at least 3 hours.
3. Cook fusilli. Drain. Add tomato sauce to hot fusilli. Mix well. Serve warm.

PER SERVING:

Calories: 436	Fat: 9 g (18% of calories)	Cholesterol: 15 mg	Protein: 24 g
	Saturated Fat: 3 g	Sodium: 235 mg	Carbohydrate: 64 g

Anne Bancroft's
Tomato-Veggie Sauce
8 servings

☆☆☆☆☆☆☆☆☆☆ ☆☆☆☆☆☆☆☆☆☆ ☆☆☆☆☆☆☆☆☆☆ ☆☆☆☆☆☆☆☆☆☆

Actress extraordinaire Anne Bancroft contributed this pasta sauce, as well as Garbanzo Stew *(page 68) and* Low-Calorie Seafood Stew *(page 128). Her recipe could become your standby anytime you want a delicious homemade pasta dinner.*

> ½ cup water
> 2 to 3 celery ribs
> 1 to 2 green peppers
> 1 to 2 large onions
> 1 to 2 cloves of garlic

1 to 2 large zucchini
1 to 2 carrots
1 to 2 18-ounce cans of tomatoes (no salt added)
1 to 2 8-ounce cans tomato sauce
1 to 2 6-ounce cans tomato paste (no salt added)
   1 teaspoon parsley
   1 teaspoon oregano
     fresh basil
   2 cups water
   1 pound pasta, cooked

1. Bring water to a boil in a large skillet. Mince celery, peppers, onions, garlic, zucchini and carrots in food processor or with a knife. Add vegetables to skillet and steam covered for 5 to 7 minutes.
2. Add remaining ingredients and simmer covered for 1 to 1½ hours. Serve over pasta.

PER SERVING (SMALLER INGREDIENT AMOUNTS USED):

Calories: 274	Fat: 2 g (6% of calories)	Cholesterol: 0 mg	Protein: 10 g
	Saturated Fat: <1 g	Sodium: 224 mg	Carbohydrate: 57 g

ℬℬ

Stan and Jan Berenstain's
Green Noodle Lasagna

8 servings

☆☆☆☆☆☆☆☆☆☆ ☆☆☆☆☆☆☆☆☆☆ ☆☆☆☆☆☆☆☆☆☆ ☆☆☆☆☆☆☆☆☆☆

Best-selling authors Stan and Jan Berenstain are the creators of over ninety-five children's books featuring The Berenstain Bears, including Too Much Junk Food. *They created* Good Housekeeping *magazine's "It's All in the Family" cartoon feature. Stan and Jan say this recipe is "low-cal, delicious and good for the whole family—even Papa Bear!"*

SAUCE:
   3 tablespoons margarine
   6 tablespoons flour
  ¼ teaspoon salt
  ¼ teaspoon black pepper
   4 cups skim milk
   2 teaspoons Worcestershire sauce
   1 tablespoon minced fresh parsley or 1 teaspoon dried parsley

LASAGNA:
   8 ounces spinach lasagna noodles (12 noodles)
   4 boneless, skinless chicken breast halves, steamed until tender, then chopped
  ¾ cup mushrooms, sliced

1 16-ounce package 1% fat cottage cheese
1 6-ounce package part-skim mozzarella, grated
¼ cup grated Parmesan cheese (optional, adds sodium and fat)

1. To make sauce, begin by melting margarine in saucepan. Remove from heat and blend in flour, salt and pepper. Add milk gradually to blend in smoothly, then return to heat and cook, stirring constantly until thickened. Remove from heat and stir in Worcestershire sauce and ⅓ of the parsley.
2. Cook noodles according to instructions on package. In a 9 x 13-inch baking dish—with a couple of spoons of sauce in the bottom to start—alternate layers of noodles, chicken, mushrooms, large dots of cottage cheese, sprinkles of grated and broken mozzarella and sauce, ending with sauce. Sprinkle the top with Parmesan cheese (if desired) and the rest of the parsley.
3. Bake in oven at 350° for 45 to 50 minutes. Remove and let stand for 15 minutes to set before cutting.

Note: May be baked in advance and reheated, covered with foil, in 350° oven for 30 minutes.

PER SERVING:36

Calories: 357	Fat: 9 g (23% of calories)	Cholesterol: 53 mg	Protein: 36 g
	Saturated Fat: 4 g	Sodium: 554 mg	Carbohydrate: 31 g

৪৯

Peter Burwash's
Spinach Lasagna
6 servings

☆☆☆☆☆☆☆☆☆☆☆ ☆☆☆☆☆☆☆☆☆☆ ☆☆☆☆☆☆☆☆☆☆ ☆☆☆☆☆☆☆☆☆☆☆

Peter Burwash is a former Canadian Tennis Champion and Davis Cup star. He is founder and president of Peter Burwash International, an international tennis-management firm. Peter wrote Tennis for Life, Total Tennis *and other books, including* Vegetarian Primer. *This meatless lasagna dish proves he can cook as well as he can play tennis. The spinach and tomato sauce serves up plenty of vitamins A and C.*

2 bunches spinach, chopped, or 1 package frozen chopped spinach
½ pound cooked whole-wheat or spinach lasagna noodles
¼ pound mushrooms, sliced
1 tablespoon oil
4 cups tomato sauce (no salt added)
¼ cup low-fat cottage cheese or ricotta cheese
½ pound part-skim mozzarella cheese, shredded

1. Steam fresh spinach until tender or defrost frozen spinach until it can be broken apart. Cook lasagna noodles until tender and drain. Separate and lay out lasagna sheets so they don't stick while you prepare the other ingredients.

2. Brown mushrooms in oil and add tomato sauce (if adding spices to canned sauce, let this simmer).

3. In a large roasting pot or casserole, arrange in layers: lasagna noodles, spinach, cottage cheese and mozzarella. Cover with tomato sauce and mushrooms, seeing that the sauce also reaches the sides of the casserole. Bake at 375° for 45 minutes.

PER SERVING:

Calories: 310	Fat: 10 g (29% of calories)	Cholesterol: 21 mg	Protein: 19 g
	Saturated Fat: 5 g	Sodium: 310 mg	Carbohydrate: 38 g

ß૱

Nancy Clark's
Tortilla Lasagna   *5 servings*

☆☆☆☆☆☆☆☆☆☆☆ ☆☆☆☆☆☆☆☆☆☆ ☆☆☆☆☆☆☆☆☆☆☆☆☆ ☆☆☆☆☆☆☆☆☆☆☆☆

Nancy Clark is the author of The Athlete's Kitchen *and* Nancy Clark's Sports Nutrition Guidebook. *Nancy, a registered dietitian with additional training in exercise physiology, is the director of nutrition services for Sportsmedicine Brookline, an athletic-injury clinic. She lectures widely and writes for publications such as* Runner's World. *Needless to say, Nancy is no couch potato—she is an avid runner and bicyclist and has trekked in the Himalayas.*

As for this recipe, Nancy says, "Tortillas are an easy, precooked alternative to lasagna noodles, and they taste wonderful." The beans in this spicy lasagna will help supply your daily quota of fiber.

- 1 pound cottage cheese, 2% low-fat
- 1 15-ounce can pinto or kidney beans, drained and rinsed
- 1 tablespoon flour
- ¼ teaspoon dried red pepper or ⅛ teaspoon cayenne
  salt, pepper and garlic powder if desired
- 1 tablespoon chili powder
- 1 10-ounce package frozen chopped spinach
- 6 tortillas, corn or flour

(Optional mix-ins: 1 cup chopped broccoli or other vegetables;
1 cup corn; 1 pound lean ground beef or turkey, browned and drained)

SAUCE:
- 1 32-ounce can crushed tomatoes (no salt added)
- 2 tablespoons chili powder
- ¼ teaspoon red pepper flakes
- 1 tablespoon molasses

1. Mix the cottage cheese, beans, flour, seasonings and spinach plus any optional mix-ins.
2. Make sauce by combining the tomatoes and seasonings. Preheat oven to 375°.
3. In a 9 x 9-inch casserole dish, alternate layers of cheese mixture, tortillas and sauce. Top with the sauce. Bake covered for 30 minutes. Let stand about 5 minutes before cutting into squares.

PER SERVING:

Calories: 297	Fat: 5 g (14% of calories)	Cholesterol: 8 mg	Protein: 21 g
	Saturated Fat: 2 g	Sodium: 560 mg	Carbohydrate: 44 g

$\mathcal{R}$

Lynn Fischer's
Quick-Stuffed Manicotti
8 servings

☆☆☆☆☆☆☆☆☆☆ ☆☆☆☆☆☆☆☆☆☆ ☆☆☆☆☆☆☆☆☆☆ ☆☆☆☆☆☆☆☆☆☆

You can watch Lynn Fischer on The Discovery Channel as host of the popular "Low Cholesterol Gourmet" cooking program or if you're ever in Washington, D.C., you can catch Lynn (along with one of this cookbook's editors (J.C.D.)) on the treadmill or lifting weights at her favorite health club. Like many of us, Lynn's always on the move—that's why she gave us this fine recipe (and one for Gnocchi on page 70) from her latest cookbook, The Quick Low Cholesterol Gourmet:

You'll need some premade sauce for this if you want to have dinner on the table in under 20 minutes. However, homemade marinara doesn't take very long to make. Served with a salad and a good bread, this is a great, quick, cold-weather dinner. The manicotti noodles take about 12 to 15 minutes, so begin cooking them as soon as possible (water comes to a boil more quickly in a lidded pot). Be sure to use a very big pot and carefully stir the noodles occasionally because they can stick together. Defrost the spinach in the microwave (in its package), while the manicotti is boiling. Stuffed manicotti can be made ahead of time and reheated in a microwave, and the recipe can be doubled. Even though ricotta is often labeled "part skim," the percentages of skim milk differ widely, so purchase the one with the lowest amount of fat. If you make your own sauce, you don't have to add the extra onions, mushrooms and green bell peppers unless you want more vegetables. They are definitely needed, however, to freshen a prepared sauce.

1 **pound manicotti or 8 large noodles for stuffing**
1 **package frozen chopped spinach, defrosted**
½ **cup chopped onion (if using prepared sauce)**
1 **6-ounce can sliced mushrooms (if using prepared sauce)**
½ **cup chopped green bell pepper (if using prepared sauce)**

1 15-ounce container part-skim ricotta
¼ teaspoon ground nutmeg
1 pint commercial meatless spaghetti sauce (no salt added) or Tomato-
   Veggie Sauce (see page 104)
2 tablespoons chopped parsley

1. Preheat oven to 400°. Cook the manicotti in boiling water for 12 to 15
   minutes until al dente. Drain and rinse in cold water. Separate and place
   on wax paper or kitchen towels. Meanwhile, squeeze the spinach completely dry with your hands. In a large nonstick skillet, simmer the
   onion, mushrooms and pepper in a small amount of water until soft,
   about 5 minutes, adding more water when necessary.
2. Mix the nutmeg and the spinach into the cheese by hand. To stuff the
   manicotti easily, divide the cheese mixture into 8 portions and form each
   into a roll like a short, skinny hot dog. Hold the manicotti in the palm of
   one hand with your thumb in the opening. With the other hand, slide
   the cheese roll in. In an ovenproof dish, arrange manicotti in rows side
   by side, with cheese ends pressed together.
3. Add the sauce to the onion, mushrooms and pepper and heat for 1
   minute on high, stirring constantly. Pour over the top of the stuffed
   manicotti. Bake for 15 minutes, or heat in a microwave for 5 minutes on
   high or until bubbly. Serve hot.

PER SERVING:

Calories: 340	Fat: 6 g (15% of calories)	Cholesterol: 19 mg	Protein: 17 g
	Saturated Fat: 3 g	Sodium: 186 mg	Carbohydrate: 55 g

Joyce Goldstein's
Linguine with Tuna, Potatoes, Arugula and Green Beans

4 servings

☆☆☆☆☆☆☆☆☆☆ ☆☆☆☆☆☆☆☆☆☆ ☆☆☆☆☆☆☆☆☆☆ ☆☆☆☆☆☆☆☆☆☆

*Joyce Goldstein contributed two of the best and healthiest pasta dishes from Square
One, her renowned restaurant in San Francisco. Formerly, Goldstein served as chef and
manager at another famous Bay-area eatery, Chez Panisse Cafe in Berkeley. In 1993 she
won the International Association of Culinary Professionals best general cookbook award
for* Back to Square One: Old-World Food in a New-World Kitchen. *Joyce also
authored* The Mediterranean Kitchen *and writes for several publications. She says
these dishes can be prepared with whole-wheat pasta, but are best with semolina pasta from
Italy. In addition to being ultra-sophisticated and ultra-tasty, these pasta dishes give your
body lots of nutrients, including good amounts of low-fat protein, fiber and vitamin C.*

6 to 8 small new potatoes
    4 tablespoons mild olive oil
      6-ounce slice of yellowfin tuna
      salt (if desired) and pepper to taste
    8 ounces linguine or spaghetti
  ½ cup green beans, cut in 2-inch lengths, blanched
    4 cups arugula
    2 teaspoons finely minced garlic (2 large cloves)
    1 teaspoon hot pepper flakes

1. Preheat oven to 400°. Place the potatoes in a small baking pan. Rub lightly with olive oil and sprinkle with salt (if desired) and pepper. Bake about 25 minutes, or until done but firm. Set aside.
2. Preheat the broiler, brush the tuna with 1 tablespoon olive oil and sprinkle with salt and pepper. Broil about 2 to 4 minutes per side, until medium-rare. Set the tuna aside.
3. Bring a large pot of water to a boil. Drop in the pasta and cook until al dente. Cut the potatoes into ¾-inch chunks. Cut the tuna into 1½-inch chunks. In a large sauté pan over high heat, add 3 tablespoons olive oil. Drop in the potato chunks and turn them until lightly browned. Add the green beans, arugula, garlic and hot pepper and stir often until the arugula is wilted. Add the tuna and warm through. Season to taste.
4. Drain the pasta and toss with the sauce. This pasta would be good with scallops, too.

PER SERVING:

Calories: 560	Fat: 16 g (25% of calories)	Cholesterol: 19 mg	Protein: 24 g
	Saturated Fat: 2 g	Sodium: 69 mg	Carbohydrate: 84 g

Joyce Goldstein's
Orecchiette with Broccoli, Chickpeas, Onions and Tomatoes

4 servings

☆☆☆☆☆☆☆☆☆☆ ☆☆☆☆☆☆☆☆☆☆ ☆☆☆☆☆☆☆☆☆☆ ☆☆☆☆☆☆☆☆☆☆

  ½ cup dried chickpeas (or 1¼ cups cooked)
    3 tablespoons fruity olive oil
    1 large head of broccoli, trimmed into small florets (about 3 cups)
    1 small red onion, diced
    2 tablespoons finely minced garlic
    2 cups diced, canned plum tomatoes
      salt and freshly ground black pepper to taste (if desired)

½ pound orecchiette (may substitute rigatoni or bow-tie noodles)
¼ cup grated pecorino cheese (optional)

1. Soak the dried chickpeas in 2½ cups of cold water and refrigerate overnight. The next day, drain and rinse the chickpeas. Transfer them to a small saucepan and cover them with fresh, lightly salted water. Bring the chickpeas to a boil over moderate heat, then reduce the heat and simmer covered until they are tender but not mushy, about an hour. Drain the chickpeas and transfer them to a bowl. Dress them with a tablespoon of olive oil. Set aside to cool. (You can use canned chickpeas, drained and rinsed, but cooking them yourself means the texture will be firmer.)
2. Blanch the broccoli florets in water and refresh in ice water. Bring a large pot of salted water to a boil. Drop in the orecchiette and cook until al dente, about 12 minutes. While the pasta is cooking, heat the remaining olive oil in a large sauté pan over medium heat. Add the onion and cook until tender. Add the chickpeas and garlic and warm through. Add the tomatoes and broccoli and warm all. Season with salt (if desired) and pepper and then toss with the drained pasta. Sprinkle with pecorino cheese, if desired.

Note: You may spice this up by adding a pinch of red pepper flakes to the sauteed onions or you may add some chopped sun-dried tomatoes to the final sauce. White beans can also be used instead of chickpeas.

PER SERVING:

Calories: 560	Fat: 16 g (25% of calories)	Cholesterol: 0 mg	Protein: 24 g
	Saturated Fat: 2 g	Sodium: 73 mg	Carbohydrate: 84 g

℘ℨ

Gael Greene's
Mock Linguine Carbonara *6 servings*

☆☆☆☆☆☆☆☆ ☆☆☆☆☆☆☆☆ ☆☆☆☆☆☆☆☆ ☆☆☆☆☆☆☆☆

New York *magazine restaurant critic Gael Greene was called "our foremost food critic" by the late food authority James Beard. And* Cuisine *magazine says Gael "conveys—and exudes—the sheer joy of eating a fine meal." Gael has also written several books, including* Delicious Sex, *and won awards for her investigative journalism. She says, "This linguine sauce tastes faintly smoky, eggy. And it's convincingly yellow."* What's more, since egg substitutes are used—it has hardly any cholesterol!*

1 tablespoon olive oil
1 medium red onion, chopped
3 slices turkey ham, cut into 1 x ⅓-inch strips
⅔ cup dry white wine

    1 8-ounce package of Egg Beaters (or another egg substitute)
    4 tablespoons chopped Italian parsley
      freshly ground black pepper to taste
  1/3 cup grated Parmesan cheese
    1 pound cooked linguine (cooked al dente and drained of all but 1/2 cup
      cooking liquid)

1. Heat oil in a nonstick skillet; add onion and sauté until soft. Toss in
   turkey ham; pour on wine and simmer until almost evaporated. Remove
   from heat and keep warm.
2. Meanwhile, beat Egg Beaters with parsley, pepper and half of Parmesan.
   Combine with onion mixture; toss with linguine and 1/2 cup of its liquid.
   Serve with remaining cheese and a pepper mill.

PER SERVING:

Calories: 390	Fat: 6 g (14% of calories)	Cholesterol: 12 mg	Protein: 19 g
	Saturated Fat: 2 g	Sodium: 301 mg	Carbohydrate: 61 g

*Recipe and quote Copyright ©1990 by Gael Greene.

Sharon Pratt Kelly's
Linguine with
Marinara Sauce and Clams
6 servings

☆☆☆☆☆☆☆☆☆☆ ☆☆☆☆☆☆☆☆☆ ☆☆☆☆☆☆☆☆☆☆ ☆☆☆☆☆☆☆☆☆☆

Washington, D.C. Mayor Sharon Pratt Kelly is the first African-American woman to serve as mayor of a major city. She helped rescue Washington from the drugs-and-sex scandal caused by her predecessor, Marion Barry. She has been Washington's Democratic National Committeewoman from 1977 to the present. Mayor Kelly received the Ebony Magazine Achievement Award and Glamour Magazine's Award for the "Top Ten Women of 1991." We think her low-fat, vitamin C-rich (from the tomatoes) Linguine with Marinara Sauce and Clams deserves an award, too!

    4 cloves of garlic
    1 medium onion, chopped
 1 1/2 tablespoons olive oil
    2 28-ounce cans of Italian tomatoes, chopped or processed
    2 tablespoons fresh basil, chopped (or 2 teaspoons dried)
    2 tablespoons fresh oregano, chopped (or 2 teaspoons dried)
  1/2 teaspoon freshly ground black pepper
  1/4 teaspoon dried red pepper
    1 6-ounce can minced clams and liquid
    1 can tomato paste (no salt added)

1 pound cooked linguine
grated Parmesan (optional)

1. Sauté garlic and onion in olive oil until onion is translucent. Add tomatoes, basil, oregano and both peppers. Simmer for 45 minutes, adding
   water if sauce is too thick. Stir in can of minced clams, the juice of the
   clams and tomato paste. Simmer for another 45 minutes.
2. Serve over linguini with grated Parmesan on the side, if desired.

PER SERVING:

| Calories: 405 | Fat: 6 g (14% of calories) | Cholesterol: 1 mg | Protein: 14 g |
| | Saturated Fat: <1 g | Sodium: 476 mg | Carbohydrate: 77 g |

Phil and Jill Lesh's
Risotto with Asparagus
and Shiitake Mushrooms   *4 servings*

☆☆☆☆☆☆☆☆☆☆ ☆☆☆☆☆☆☆☆☆☆ ☆☆☆☆☆☆☆☆☆☆ ☆☆☆☆☆☆☆☆☆☆

*One of this cookbook's editors (J.C.D.) was late for a Grateful Dead show because
testing this recipe from band member Phil Lesh took longer than anticipated. The
recipe is worth the wait though—especially for deadheads. Phil and Jill sent Center
for Science in the Public Interest a nice letter that said, "We are firm believers that
good nutrition is essential to good health. It's difficult to maintain a healthy diet
when on the road but thanks to organizations like yours, it's getting easier." They
have a recipe for Broccoli-Stuffed Potatoes on page 178.*

½ pound shiitake mushrooms, sliced
½ pound thin asparagus, sliced into 1-inch pieces
3 teaspoon margarine
1 shallot, peeled and chopped
1 large ripe tomato, chopped
½ teaspoon salt
  freshly ground black pepper
2 cups Arborio rice (risotto)
6 cups low-sodium vegetable stock (see page 21) or low-sodium
  canned broth
½ cup freshly grated Parmesan cheese

FOR GARNISH:
8 asparagus spears
  Parmesan cheese shavings

1. Steam mushrooms and asparagus until mushrooms are soft and asparagus is tender but not mushy.
2. In a nonstick skillet, melt 1 teaspoon margarine, add shallot and sauté until soft. Add mushrooms and asparagus and cook for 3 minutes. Add tomatoes, salt and pepper, stir gently and cook for 1 minute. Turn off heat.
3. In a medium saucepan, melt 2 teaspoons margarine, add the rice and stir to coat. Cook the rice for 1 minute over low heat. Add the stock 1 cup at a time, waiting for the liquid to be absorbed before adding the next cup. When all the stock is absorbed and risotto is creamy, add the vegetables and grated cheese, stirring gently to combine.
4. To serve, divide the risotto among 4 plates and top each plate with 2 asparagus spears and Parmesan shavings. (To make shavings, grate on the thickest or widest part of a hand grater, or use a vegetable peeler or very sharp small knife). Serve with a fresh salad and enjoy!

PER SERVING:

Calories: 387	Fat: 9 g (21% of calories)	Cholesterol: 7 mg	Protein: 11 g
	Saturated Fat: 3 g	Sodium: 407 mg	Carbohydrate: 66 g

Meredith McCarty's
Pasta with Red Lentil Sauce   *6 servings*

☆☆☆☆☆☆☆☆☆☆ ☆☆☆☆☆☆☆☆☆☆ ☆☆☆☆☆☆☆☆☆☆ ☆☆☆☆☆☆☆☆☆☆

Meredith McCarty is the co-director of the East West Center for Natural Health Education in Eureka, California. She specializes in creative macrobiotic cooking and is the author of two cookbooks, FRESH from a vegetarian kitchen *and* American Macrobiotic Cuisine. *Between the whole-grain pasta and the red lentils, this dish provides well-balanced nutrition, including plenty of fiber. McCarty suggests serving the pasta with a side dish of green vegetables and carrots or a salad. Her fruit compotes are on pages 191-2.*

      2 tablespoons sesame oil or extra-virgin olive oil
      2 onions, diced finely
      2 cloves of garlic, minced
      2 cups red lentils
   1½ quarts water
      1 6-inch piece kombu sea vegetable
      1 bay leaf
      1 tablespoon thyme
      1 tablespoon cumin
     ½ teaspoon sea salt
2 to 4 tablespoons miso (less of barley miso, more of white miso)

1 pound whole-grain pasta
chives or parsley, finely sliced or minced, for garnish

1. In a 4-quart pot, heat oil and briefly sauté onions and garlic. Sort through, rinse and drain lentils. Add them to the pot with the water, kombu, bay leaf and herbs. Bring to boil, then turn heat down to slow boil until lentils are tender, about 15 minutes. Stir or whisk in salt and miso. (Kombu will soften and expand.)
2. Meanwhile, bring a pot of water to boil for pasta. Add pasta and cook until tender, 8 to 15 minutes average. (Whole-wheat spaghetti takes longer, about 20 minutes.) Drain. Serve immediately or immerse in cold water to reserve for later use. Pour sauce over individual servings of pasta and garnish to serve.

Note: Kombu is a dry kelp that is high in minerals and trace elements. Kombu helps to soften beans and make them more digestible. Miso is a fermented soy bean paste used like bouillon to season soups and stews. Both are available in natural foods stores.

PER SERVING:

Calories: 505	Fat: 6 g (11% of calories)	Cholesterol: 0 mg	Protein: 30 g
	Saturated Fat: 1 g	Sodium: 578 mg	Carbohydrate: 80 g

Moosewood Restaurant's
Roasted Red Pepper Sauce   *6 servings*

☆☆☆☆☆☆☆☆☆☆ ☆☆☆☆☆☆☆☆☆☆ ☆☆☆☆☆☆☆☆☆☆ ☆☆☆☆☆☆☆☆☆☆

If you're tired of that same old commercial spaghetti sauce, try this scrumptious creation from the Sundays at Moosewood *cookbook. The chefs at the famous Moosewood restaurant in Ithaca, New York, also gave us a superb recipe for Polenta Cutlets (page 79). Sweet peppers not only taste great, but also give you a big vitamin C bonus. From* Sundays at Moosewood Restaurant:*

During fall and winter months, when tomatoes are not at their best, ripe red peppers are usually available, and here they are used in a light but surprisingly full and rich-tasting sauce. A combination of red, yellow and green peppers is festive, but the red peppers should predominate. We recommend serving this sauce over a short and thick pasta such as penne, ziti, spirals, or rigatoni. Undercook the pasta, drain it and put it into the pot of hot sauce to finish cooking with the sauce for 2 to 3 minutes. Pass grated pecorino or Parmesan at the table. Roasted Red Pepper Sauce will keep nicely in the refrigerator in a covered sterilized jar for a couple of weeks.

6 huge or 9 medium red bell peppers
1 onion, chopped
1½ tablespoons olive oil
3 garlic cloves
3 fresh tomatoes, finely chopped (or 6 canned whole Italian plum tomatoes—no salt added, with enough juice to make 1½ cups)
2 tablespoons chopped fresh basil (1 teaspoon dried)
   freshly ground black pepper to taste
¼ cup chopped fresh parsley
12 ounces dry pasta, cooked (best: penne, ziti, spirals, rigatoni)
   grated pecorino or Parmesan cheese (optional)

1. Place the peppers directly on the racks in a preheated 500° oven for about 20 minutes, turning 2 or 3 times to get all sides evenly charred. Cover the bottom of the oven with aluminum foil to catch any drips in case a pepper splits open. Peppers should be roasted until their skins are charred (black and blistered). When the peppers are all charred, put them immediately into a covered bowl. Allowing the peppers to cool down in their own steam makes them easy to peel.
2. When the peppers are cool enough to handle comfortably, peel off the skins. They should flake off in large pieces. Don't worry about removing every little fleck of blackened skin though, and do not wash the peppers or you will lose much of the special roasted flavor. Remove the stems, thick inner membranes and seeds. Slice into thin strips. Cut the long strips in half lengthwise. You should have at least 2 cups. Set aside.
3. In a large skillet, sauté the onion in the olive oil for a few minutes. Add the garlic and sauté a few minutes more. When the onions are translucent, add the tomatoes, basil and black pepper. Stir in the red pepper strips and cook for a few minutes.
4. Purée about ⅓ of the sauce in a blender or food processor and then return it to the pan. Add the parsley. Serve hot over pasta.

PER SERVING:

Calories: 300	Fat: 5 g (15% of calories)	Cholesterol: 0 mg	Protein: 10 g
	Saturated Fat: <1 g	Sodium: 14 mg	Carbohydrate: 55 g

*Reprinted with permission from *Sundays at Moosewood Restaurant* by the Moosewood Collective (Simon & Schuster Inc., 1990).

Martina Navratilova's
Pesto à la Martina
4-6 servings

☆☆☆☆☆☆☆☆☆☆ ☆☆☆☆☆☆☆☆☆☆ ☆☆☆☆☆☆☆☆☆☆ ☆☆☆☆☆☆☆☆☆☆

Martina Navratilova's résumé includes Wimbledon championships, the U.S. Open and a Grand Slam victory. After nineteen-year-old Navratilova defected from Czechoslovakia in 1975, her weight jumped to 167 pounds from overindulgence on American junk foods and desserts. She became known as "The Great Wide Hope," but she changed her diet and took up fitness training after losing the 1983 French open to a number 33-ranked player. She proceeded to win the tennis Grand Slam (Australian, French and U.S. Opens, followed by Wimbledon). Martina calls this recipe "Pesto à la Martina (in other words—wing it)" and says, "I developed this recipe about ten years ago when I became more conscious of eating correctly. I make it for myself as well as for company." We think the dish is simple and wonderful. The parsley adds some beta-carotene and vitamin C.

¼ **cup olive oil**
¼ **cup water**
½ **cup fresh basil**
 2 **cloves of garlic**
¼ **teaspoon black pepper**
¼ **teaspoon salt**
 2 **tablespoons pine nuts (or walnuts)**
¼ **cup fresh parsley**
¼ **cup grated Parmesan cheese**
 1 **pound pasta, cooked**

1. Mix olive oil, water, basil and garlic in a blender at high speed and let stand for 15 minutes. Add pepper, salt and pine nuts and blend at a lower speed.
2. Add parsley and cheese and mix again. Serve pesto over pasta as needed. Enjoy!

PER SERVING (6 SERVINGS):

Calories: 384	Fat: 12 g (28% of calories)	Cholesterol: 3 mg	Protein: 12 g
	Saturated Fat: 2 g	Sodium: 169 mg	Carbohydrate: 58 g

৪৯

Joseph Piscatella's
Calamari with Linguine
6 servings

☆☆☆☆☆☆☆☆☆☆ ☆☆☆☆☆☆☆☆☆☆ ☆☆☆☆☆☆☆☆☆☆ ☆☆☆☆☆☆☆☆☆☆

As the author of heart-healthy cookbooks, Joe Piscatella has helped untold numbers of people make transitions to better diets. He was kind enough to give us two recipes from his Controlling Your Fat Tooth *cookbook—this pasta dish and*

Southwest Jambalaya on page 142. Joe says these recipes "represent for me the cardinal rule for healthy eating in the real world: Food should be tasty and have eye appeal as well as be low in fat." We couldn't agree more.

 1 28-ounce can Italian plum tomatoes, puréed in a blender or food
   processor
1½ tablespoons plus ½ teaspoon olive oil
 ¼ cup dry white wine (Soave Bolla is good)
 2 6½-ounce cans chopped clams, drained
 1 tablespoon tomato paste (no salt added)
 ½ teaspoon oregano
 ½ teaspoon basil
 ½ teaspoon salt
 ½ teaspoon black pepper
 1 14-ounce can water-packed artichoke hearts, drained
 3 cloves of garlic, minced
 1 pound squid tubes, cleaned and cut into ¼-inch rings
 1 pound fresh linguine, cooked al dente
 3 tablespoons chopped fresh parsley
 ½ teaspoon crushed red pepper

1. In a large saucepan, combine puréed tomatoes, 1½ tablespoons olive oil, wine, clams, tomato paste, oregano, basil, salt and pepper. Heat just to boiling, reduce heat and simmer 20 to 30 minutes. Add artichokes.
2. In a nonstick skillet, heat the remaining ½ teaspoon olive oil. Add garlic and squid tubes, and sauté 3 to 4 minutes or until done. Drain. Add to tomato sauce. Divide pasta into bowls. Ladle sauce over top. Sprinkle with parsley and crushed red pepper.

PER SERVING:

Calories: 416	Fat: 7 g (15 % of calories)	Cholesterol: 102 mg	Protein: 21 g
	Saturated Fat: 1 g	Sodium: 497 mg	Carbohydrate: 67 g

Ilene Pritikin
Thai Pasta
8 servings

☆☆☆☆☆☆☆☆☆☆ ☆☆☆☆☆☆☆☆☆☆ ☆☆☆☆☆☆☆☆☆☆ ☆☆☆☆☆☆☆☆☆☆

Nathan Pritikin, who created a dietary revolution by advocating an almost fat-free diet, was nurtured along by his wife Ilene Pritikin. This cookbook's senior editor (M.F.J.) first encountered the Pritikin name in the early 1970s, when Nathan had sent him an enormous and brilliant manuscript that summarized his analysis of scientific studies on diet and health. Nathan subsequently became the most avid salesperson ever for reducing the risks of diabetes, heart disease, stroke and cancer by eat-

ing a low-fat, low-cholesterol diet. Ilene's recipe combines Thai spices with Italian pasta and California health consciousness to create sensational taste. Ilene says:

In recent years, I've done relatively little cooking, but some good recipes have come out of my kitchen nevertheless, thanks mostly to the creative genius of Esther Taylor. Esther is a cooking natural who helped us invent recipes for the early Pritikin program cookbooks. These days I'm lucky enough to have her putter around inventing new dishes for me. Here's one she developed, with a little inspirational input from me, which she named Thai pasta, because of the exotic seasoning. You can use any kind of pasta you wish. I like to use a no-egg pasta, De Boles Substitute Fettucine (called "substitute" because it contains Jerusalem artichoke flour, not standard for fettuccine), using one package of spinach fettuccine and one plain. The two colors of noodles add extra flavor and color interest. For special occasions, I vary the recipe by adding a small amount of fresh seafood or fish to the vegetable-sauce mixture, as explained below.

1 13¾-ounce Pritikin brand low-sodium fat-free chicken broth
3 stalks celery, cut into 1-inch diagonal slices
2 medium onions, chopped
2 cups mushrooms, chopped
1 green pepper, coarsely chopped
2 red peppers, coarsely chopped
1 bunch green onions, cut into 1-inch lengths
½ cup chopped fresh basil
7 ounces canned green chili salsa, mild or hot to taste
1 8-ounce can sliced bamboo shoots
1 tablespoon finely chopped fresh ginger
2 tablespoons fresh chopped garlic
2 tablespoons Dijon mustard (or more for hotter pasta)
2 tablespoons reduced-sodium soy sauce
2 teaspoons curry powder
1 tablespoon herb-spice blend (like Mrs. Dash's)
2 tablespoons arrowroot
2 8-ounce packages De Boles Substitute Fettucine (made with Jerusalem artichoke flour) or other pasta
1 cup fresh white fish or seafood—crab, shrimp, lobster (optional)

1. Heat a small amount of the chicken broth in the bottom of a large skillet or wok and stir-fry the celery, onions, mushrooms, green pepper, red peppers, green onions and basil over medium heat. When the vegetables are partially cooked, remove from pan. (There should be about 8 cups of vegetables.)
2. Combine the salsa, bamboo shoots and all the seasonings in a large saucepan. Add the rest of the chicken stock. Make a paste of the arrowroot with a little water and stir into the pan. Bring the mixture to a boil, turn down heat and let simmer until the sauce is thickened.

3. Stir in the partially cooked vegetables. (If desired, at this point you could also stir in about 1 cup bite-size chunks of fresh white fish or seafood, such as crab, shrimp, lobster, etc.)
4. Cook the fettuccine noodles in boiling water according to the instructions. Drain well and combine with the sauce mixture. Serve hot.

PER SERVING:
Calories: 275   Fat: 2 g (7% of calories)   Cholesterol: 0 mg   Protein: 11 g
         Saturated Fat: <1 g   Sodium: 323 mg   Carbohydrate: 55 g

John Robbins's
Robbins's Rice
6 servings

John Robbins's book Diet for a New America *is a powerful indictment of how a meat-based diet harms the environment, results in cruelty to animals and undermines our health. The book helped convince one of this cookbook's editors (J.C.D.) to become a vegetarian, and she frequently lends it to friends who are deciding whether to kick the meat habit. John's sequel,* May All Be Fed, *examines the powerful forces that influence our food choices and provides lots of vegetarian recipes. John, whose father and uncle founded the Baskin-Robbins ice-cream chain, himself founded the EarthSave foundation, which advocates more healthful and environmentally sound diets.*

  6 **cups water**
  2 **cups wild rice**
  2 **large onions, diced**
  4 **tablespoons miso**
  6 **tablespoons tahini**
  2 **teaspoons chili powder**

1. In a heavy pot, cook water, rice and onions for 35 minutes.
2. Blend together the miso, tahini, chili powder and extra water as needed to blend. Mix together cooked wild rice and miso-tahini sauce.

PER SERVING:
Calories: 330   Fat: 9 g (25% of calories)   Cholesterol: 0 mg   Protein: 13 g
         Saturated Fat: 1 g   Sodium: 358 mg   Carbohydrate: 52 g

Richard Sax's
Pasta with Marinated Tomatoes
and Four Cheeses
6 servings

☆☆☆☆☆☆☆☆☆☆ ☆☆☆☆☆☆☆☆☆ ☆☆☆☆☆☆☆☆☆☆☆ ☆☆☆☆☆☆☆☆☆☆

Richard Sax co-writes a monthly column called "Cooking for Health" for Bon
Appétit *magazine and contributes to other major publications. Richard has written
several cookbooks, including* From the Farmers' Market *and* Cooking Great Meals
Every Day. *Richard admonishes you to "make this only with perfectly ripe tomatoes and freshly made ricotta and mozzarella cheese, if at all possible. Both are found
in cheese shops and at Italian markets."*

2½ to 3 pounds ripe tomatoes, cored, seeded and cut into ¾-inch dice
  ½ cup shredded fresh basil
  1 large clove of garlic, minced
  1 cup part-skim ricotta cheese, room temperature
  2 tablespoons 1% low-fat milk or as needed
     freshly ground black pepper to taste
     freshly grated nutmeg
  2 ounces Italian Fontina cheese, cut into ¼-inch dice
  2 ounces fresh, part-skim mozzarella cheese, cut into ¼-inch dice
  1 pound rotelle (wheels), penne, ziti or other short pasta
  2 tablespoons good olive oil
  ¼ cup freshly grated Parmesan cheese

1. Combine the tomatoes, basil and garlic in a mixing bowl. Let stand at
   room temperature 1 to 2 hours, stirring occasionally.
2. Fluff the ricotta with a fork in a medium mixing bowl. Season with pepper and nutmeg. Stir in the diced Fontina and mozzarella; let stand at
   room temperature while cooking pasta.
3. Drain most of the liquid from the tomatoes, leaving just enough to keep
   them moist. Cook the pasta in a large pot of boiling water until al dente.
   Drain well and place in a heated bowl, tossing with the olive oil.
4. Place the cheese mixture over the top, tossing together at the table.
   Sprinkle each serving with some of the Parmesan; pass the remaining
   Parmesan and a pepper mill at the table.

PER SERVING:
Calories: 512   Fat: 15 g (28% of calories)   Cholesterol: 32 mg   Protein: 23 g
                Saturated Fat: 7 g   Sodium: 205 mg   Carbohydrate: 69 g

Steve Sax's
Brown Rice and Shiitake Pilaf   *6 servings*

☆☆☆☆☆☆☆☆☆☆ ☆☆☆☆☆☆☆☆☆ ☆☆☆☆☆☆☆☆☆☆☆ ☆☆☆☆☆☆☆☆☆☆

Steve Sax says he eats healthful food like this dish (and his Clubhouse Chicken Salad on page 100) to remain in top condition for his job as an outfielder for the Chicago White Sox:

To stay strong for a 162-game season, I have to watch my diet more than anything. The key to eating for peak performance is fueling up on complex carbohydrates. Rice, an excellent source, provides a variety of vitamins and minerals and is particularly popular with basball players who need to control their weight yet maintain high energy levels.

1 cup (about 2 ounces) sliced fresh shiitake mushrooms
1 cup asparagus spears, cut into 1-inch pieces
1 clove of garlic, minced
1 tablespoon olive oil
3 cups cooked long-grain brown rice
¼ cup toasted pine nuts
¼ cup sliced green onions
1 tablespoon grated lemon peel
½ teaspoon salt
½ teaspoon ground black pepper

In large skillet, sauté mushrooms, asparagus and garlic in oil over medium-high heat until tender, about 1 to 2 minutes. Add rice, pine nuts, green onions, lemon peel, salt and pepper; heat thoroughly.

PER SERVING:

Calories: 170	Fat: 4 g (18% of calories)	Cholesterol: 0 mg	Protein: 4 g
	Saturated Fat: 1 g	Sodium: 181 mg	Carbohydrate: 31 g

Dick Van Patten's
Vegetable Lasagna   *8 servings*

☆☆☆☆☆☆☆☆☆☆ ☆☆☆☆☆☆☆☆☆ ☆☆☆☆☆☆☆☆☆☆☆ ☆☆☆☆☆☆☆☆☆☆

Actor Dick Van Patten is good friends with another celebrity associated with this cookbook, Mel Brooks. Dick has appeared in several movies directed by Mel, including Robin Hood: Men in Tights *and* High Anxiety. *Dick's Beans and Potato Soup is on page 35, and his Eggplant Parmesan is on page 89.*

12 ounces whole-wheat lasagna noodles
1 pound part-skim ricotta cheese

nonstick cooking spray
½ teaspoon cinnamon
1 tablespoon minced fresh mint, or 1 teaspoon dried mint
1 egg white
3 cups Tomato-Veggie Sauce (see page 104)
1 pound fresh spinach (makes 1 cup cooked and drained)
1 cup shredded part-skim mozzarella (about 4 ounces)
¼ cup Parmesan cheese

1. Cook noodles in boiling water; rinse and drain.
2. Mix ricotta with cinnamon, mint and egg white.
3. In lightly sprayed 13 x 9-inch baking dish, layer ⅓ noodles, ⅓ sauce, ½ spinach, ½ ricotta mixture and ½ mozzarella. Repeat until all ingredients are used. Bake at 350° for 40 to 50 minutes.

PER SERVING:

| Calories: 370 | Fat: 10 g (22% of calories) | Cholesterol: 29 mg | Protein: 23 g |
| | Saturated Fat: 5 g | Sodium: 461 mg | Carbohydrate: 53 g |

℘ఎ

Lindsay Wagner's
Couscous with
Tomato-Eggplant Sauce
6 servings

☆☆☆☆☆☆☆☆☆☆☆ ☆☆☆☆☆☆☆☆☆☆ ☆☆☆☆☆☆☆☆☆☆☆ ☆☆☆☆☆☆☆☆☆☆

For many of us, Lindsay Wagner will always be the "bionic woman"—Lindsay's character in the television series of the same name, which one of this cookbook's editors (J.C.D.) watched with alarming regularity while growing up in the 1970s. Lindsay also has extraordinary powers when it comes to culinary matters. The following recipes are taken from her book for people moving toward a vegetarian diet, The High Road to Health.* They offer good amounts of vitamin C and fiber.

1 teaspoon cold-pressed olive oil
1 medium onion, chopped
2 large cloves of garlic, minced
1 eggplant, unpeeled, cut into ½-inch cubes
1 green pepper, finely sliced
2 cups fresh or canned tomatoes (no salt added), peeled and chopped
½ teaspoon salt
½ teaspoon pepper
¼ teaspoon paprika
¼ teaspoon rosemary
¼ cup finely chopped parsley

    ¼ teaspoon oregano
    ¼ teaspoon basil
    1 cup water
    1 pound whole-wheat couscous, cooked according to package directions

1. Heat the olive oil in a large skillet. Add the onion and sauté until golden. Add the garlic and cook for 1 minute. Add the eggplant and green pepper and cook for 10 minutes. Add the tomatoes, salt, pepper, paprika, rosemary, parsley, oregano, basil and water.

2. Cook covered for 30 minutes. Stir often to prevent sticking. Mash the eggplant with a fork or hand masher (or leave as chunks) and cook covered for 30 minutes more. Serve over cooked couscous.

PER SERVING:

Calories: 328   Fat: 1 g (4% of calories)   Cholesterol: 0 mg   Protein: 11 g
                 Saturated Fat: <1 g   Sodium: 195 mg   Carbohydrate: 66 g

*Reprinted from *The High Road To Health*, Lindsay Wagner & Oriane Spade, Copyright ©1990. Used by permission of the publisher, Prentice Hall Press/A Division of Simon & Schuster, New York.

ℰ𝔞

Lindsay Wagner's
Risotto with Tomatoes and Garbanzo Beans

6 servings

☆☆☆☆☆☆☆☆☆☆ ☆☆☆☆☆☆☆☆☆☆ ☆☆☆☆☆☆☆☆☆☆ ☆☆☆☆☆☆☆☆☆☆

    2 cups vegetable stock (see page 21) or low-sodium canned broth
    ½ cup white wine (or substitute ⅓ cup water, 1 tablespoon apple juice and 1 tablespoon white vinegar)
    1 cup long-grain brown rice

SAUCE:

    2 teaspoons cold-pressed olive oil
    1 small onion, finely chopped
    5 sprigs of parsley, chopped
    2 cloves of garlic, chopped
    4 cups fresh tomatoes, chopped (or substitute canned tomatoes, no salt added)
      salt to taste
      black pepper to taste
    1 cup cooked garbanzo beans, drained

1. Bring the broth and the wine to a boil and very slowly add the brown rice so that the water continues to boil. Turn down the heat, cover and cook for 45 to 50 minutes.

2. To start the sauce, heat the olive oil in a large skillet. Add the onion and cook slowly until translucent. Onions that are cooked slowly and are not allowed to burn become very sweet.

3. Combine the chopped parsley and garlic and add to the onion. Cook for 3 minutes. Add the tomatoes with their liquid, salt (omit to keep sodium low) and pepper. Bring to a boil and cook for 30 minutes. Add the garbanzo beans and cook for 10 minutes more.

4. If the liquid is not completely absorbed by the time the rice is tender, raise the heat and cook uncovered a few minutes more. Fluff with a fork and serve with the tomato garbanzo sauce on top.

PER SERVING:

Calories: 205	Fat: 3 g (12% of calories)	Cholesterol: 0 mg	Protein: 6 g
	Saturated Fat: <1 g	Sodium: 13 mg	Carbohydrate: 37 g

*Reprinted from *The High Road To Health*, Lindsay Wagner & Oriane Spade, Copyright ©1990. Used by permission of the publisher, Prentice Hall Press/A Division of Simon & Schuster, New York.

ℒℐ

Bill Walton's
Paglia E Fieno
4 servings

☆☆☆☆☆☆☆☆☆☆ ☆☆☆☆☆☆☆☆☆☆☆☆☆☆☆☆ ☆☆☆☆☆☆☆☆☆☆☆☆

Bill Walton led several basketball teams to championships, starting with UCLA, where he averaged over twenty points per game in his three-year college career. In 1976-77, he helped the Portland Trailblazers capture its first NBA championship, then took the Boston Celtics to the championship in 1985-86. Apart from his stupendous feats on the court, Bill also leads the pack when it comes to nutrition. He was probably one of the best-known vegetarians in professional sports, but even the most ardent meat eaters should love his Paglia E Fieno.

  1 **cup yellow summer squash, cut in narrow lengthwise strips**
  1 **cup zucchini, cut in narrow lengthwise strips**
  1 **cup chopped fresh tomato**
½ **cup chopped onion**
  3 **cloves of garlic, minced**
  1 **cup spinach noodles, cooked**
  1 **cup egg noodles, cooked**
½ **cup part skim ricotta cheese**
  1 **tablespoon olive oil**
  1 **tablespoon fresh basil**
    freshly ground black pepper to taste

1. Steam the squash briefly. Add the tomato, onion and garlic and continue steaming until all the vegetables are just heated through.
2. Gently mix the hot noodles with the ricotta. Combine the noodles and vegetables. Toss with the olive oil and basil. Season with freshly ground black pepper and serve hot.

PER SERVING:

Calories: 210	Fat: 7 g (30% of calories)	Cholesterol: 22 mg	Protein: 9 g
	Saturated Fat: 2 g	Sodium: 45 mg	Carbohydrate: 29 g

FISH AND SEAFOOD

Ed Asner's
Tuna Toast
8 servings

☆☆☆☆☆☆☆☆☆☆☆☆☆☆☆☆ ☆☆☆☆☆☆☆☆☆☆☆☆☆☆☆☆ ☆☆☆☆☆☆☆☆☆☆☆

In the 1970s, Edward Asner entered American homes every week as the crusty yet lovable journalist Lou Grant in "The Mary Tyler Moore Show." He won three Emmys for that role, two for "Lou Grant" and two more for "Rich, Man, Poor Man" and "Roots." Recently, Ed appeared in the film JFK. *He has served as president of the Screen Actors Guild and is active in many humanitarian and political organizations. Ed says this mayonnaise-less tuna sandwich is "fast, healthy and easy."*

   8 slices whole-grain bread, homemade if possible
   1 12¼-ounce can of albacore "dolphin-safe" tuna in spring water, rinsed and drained
   ½ cup black olives, chopped
   ½ cup low-fat cottage cheese

1. Take sliced whole-grain bread and toast for 3 minutes in an oven at 350°.
2. While the bread is toasting, open tuna, rinse and drain. Mix tuna with olives and cottage cheese.
3. Spread the mix on the toast and toast for another 5 minutes at 300°. Cut into small pieces for a fun party snack or eat by the slice.

PER SERVING:

Calories: 169	Fat: 4 g (22% of calories)	Cholesterol: 25 mg	Protein: 20 g
	Saturated Fat: 1 g	Sodium: 364 mg	Carbohydrate: 13 g

Anne Bancroft's
Low-Calorie Seafood Stew
4 servings

☆☆☆☆☆☆☆☆☆☆☆☆☆☆☆☆ ☆☆☆☆☆☆☆☆☆☆☆☆☆☆☆☆ ☆☆☆☆☆☆☆☆☆☆☆

Here's to you, Anne Bancroft! Anne, a member of Center for Science in the Public Interest's board of directors, is passionately concerned about safe food and nutrition. She not only contributed this recipe, along with Garbanzo Stew on page 68 and Tomato-Veggie Sauce on page 104, she also solicited recipes from many of her famous friends. Anne has acted on television and in numerous motion pictures, including the films Charing Cross Road *and* Honeymoon in Vegas. *Her most famous role was probably in* The Graduate *as the notorious Mrs. Robinson, who was immortalized in the Simon and Garfunkel song, "Mrs. Robinson." You won't become immortal with Anne's stew, but your life will certainly be more enjoyable!*

1 tablespoon olive oil
1 large onion, sliced
2 large cloves of garlic, minced
2 cups eggplant, cubed (about ½ an eggplant)
1½ cups zucchini, sliced (1 large)
1 green pepper, cut into 1-inch segments
1 cup V-8 juice
¼ cup parsley, minced
1 tablespoon crushed dried thyme
1 small bay leaf
1 teaspoon cumin
1 pound monkfish, lingcod, tru cod or any dense fish, cut into chunks
¼ cup lime juice

1. In 4- or 5-quart saucepan, sauté onion and garlic in olive oil until transparent.
2. Add eggplant, zucchini and green pepper and cook gently until just tender.
3. Add V-8, parsley, thyme, bay leaf and cumin. Heat until bubbling. Reduce to simmer. Don't cook long enough for the vegetables to get soggy.
4. Add fish and lime juice and simmer for 10 or 15 minutes.
5. Serve hot or cold on a bed of rice.

PER SERVING:

Calories: 200	Fat: 5 g (22% of calories)	Cholesterol: 48 mg	Protein: 23 g
	Saturated Fat: <1 g	Sodium: 289 mg	Carbohydrate: 17 g

Ed Bradley's
Shrimp Creole   *6 servings*

☆☆☆☆☆☆☆☆☆☆☆☆☆☆ ☆☆☆☆☆☆ ☆☆☆☆☆☆☆☆☆☆☆☆ ☆☆☆☆☆☆☆☆☆☆

Since 1981, Ed Bradley has co-anchored "60 Minutes," CBS News's immensely popular news magazine. Winner of several Emmy awards, Bradley served as CBS White House correspondent for several years. His Shrimp Creole is definitely for those who like their food hot!

4 tablespoons margarine
2½ cups finely chopped onions
2 teaspoons finely minced garlic (about 3 cloves)
1 cup chopped celery (2 to 3 stalks)
3 green peppers, seeded and chopped into ¾-inch pieces
2 jalapeño peppers, seeded and minced (use gloves)
salt (optional) and freshly ground black pepper to taste
4 cups cubed tomatoes (about 4 medium)

> 4 tablespoons finely chopped parsley
> 1 bay leaf
> 3 tablespoons Matouk's hot sauce (or substitute 1 teaspoon Tabasco or 1 teaspoon chili sauce)
> 1¼ pounds medium-sized raw shrimp, peeled and deveined
> 6 cups cooked brown rice
> 6 lemon wedges

1. Heat 2 tablespoons of the margarine in a saucepan over medium heat and sauté the onions and garlic for 5 minutes. Do not brown.
2. Add the celery, green peppers and jalapeño peppers to the pan and season with salt and pepper to taste. Cook for about 4 minutes, stirring often. Do not let the vegetables become soggy; they should remain crisp.
3. Add the tomatoes, parsley and bay leaf. Cover and bring to a boil. Simmer for 10 minutes and stir in the Matouk's sauce. Remove bay leaf.
4. Heat the remaining 2 tablespoons of margarine in a frying pan over high heat and sauté the shrimp for 2 to 3 minutes. Pour the tomato mixture over the shrimp, stir well and bring just to a boil. Remove from heat and serve with rice and lemon wedges.

Note: Matouk's hot sauce, a fiery blend of papaya and hot peppers from Trinidad, is available in some West Indian and Indian shops.

PER SERVING:

Calories: 439	Fat: 10 g (19% of calories)	Cholesterol: 145 mg	Protein: 24 g
	Saturated Fat: 3 g	Sodium: 292 mg	Carbohydrate: 64 g

ℰᕲ

Grandma Kate's (Mel Brooks's mother)
Gefilte Fish
30 servings

☆☆☆☆☆☆☆☆☆☆☆☆ ☆☆☆☆☆☆☆☆ ☆☆☆☆☆☆☆☆☆☆☆ ☆☆☆☆☆☆☆☆☆☆☆☆

Truth be told, Grandma Kate is no celebrity, but her son Mel is so famous that we thought we'd accept his mother's recipe. Mel Brooks, husband of Anne Bancroft, is one of the funniest men on earth. His credits include co-writing, directing and starring in such films as Blazing Saddles, High Anxiety *and* Spaceballs. *Besides his work in the film industry, Mel created the TV series, "Get Smart." Mel has probably done so well because he was raised on this traditional dish from his mom, affectionately known as Grandma Kate. Most people buy gefilte fish in a jar, but this is the way it's really done. For some of us, gefilte fish is just an excuse to have horseradish.*

4 pounds ground whitefish (fish heads and bones wrapped separately)
4 pounds ground yellow pike (fish heads and bones wrapped separately)
1 onion, grated
3 large eggs
· white pepper (to taste)
2 large onions, sliced
4 carrots, sliced
2 stalks celery, cut into 4 pieces
2 to 2½ quarts water

1. Mix grated onion, eggs and white pepper into ground fish.
2. Line the bottom of an 8- to 10-quart pot with onions, half the sliced carrots, celery, fish heads and bones and water. Simmer on medium heat.
3. Make balls with the chopped fish mixture and flatten into patties. Add the patties to the water as it simmers. Put the rest of the carrots on top. Bring to a boil and then simmer covered for 2 to 2½ hours. Let cool. Serve with the carrots, a little of the broth, whole-wheat matzo and red horseradish.

PER SERVING:

Calories: 150	Fat: 5 g (28% of calories)	Cholesterol: 81 mg	Protein: 24 g
	Saturated Fat: 1 g	Sodium: 74 mg	Carbohydrate: 2 g

ℰᔡ

Ellen Brown's
Baked Grouper in Herb Crust
6 servings

☆☆☆☆☆☆☆☆☆☆☆☆☆ ☆☆☆☆☆☆ ☆☆☆☆☆☆☆☆☆☆☆ ☆☆☆☆☆☆☆☆☆

Ellen Brown is author of the International Association of Culinary Professionals/ Seagram Award-winning Gourmet Gazelle Cookbook *and other cookbooks. She is a food consultant and food writer who regularly contributes to the* Washington Post *and other newspapers and was the founding food editor of* USA Today. *Ellen has run a gourmet carryout and a catering service and taught cooking at the University of Cincinnati. She has two recipes in the desserts chapter, Apricot Souffle on page 186 and Dried Fruit Bars on page 187.*

Ellen says, "This incredibly easy recipe can be done with any fish fillet. The mustard and herbs form an interesting coating that does not hide the delicacy of the fish." She created the recipe for the Cuisine Vitale program of The Lancaster Group of hotels.

6 grouper fillets (about 4 ounces each)
2 tablespoons Dijon mustard
3 Italian tomatoes, sliced
1 cup whole-wheat bread crumbs (see page x)
1 teaspoon fresh thyme

1 tablespoon chopped fresh basil
2 teaspoons chopped fresh tarragon
¼ teaspoon white pepper
¼ teaspoon salt
2 tablespoons olive oil

1. Heat oven to 425°. Spread mustard on fish and top with tomato slices.
2. Mix remaining ingredients and spread on top of fish. Bake for 7 to 10 minutes, according to thickness.

PER SERVING:

| Calories: 365 | Fat: 9 g (22% of calories) | Cholesterol: 96 mg | Protein: 53 g |
| | Saturated Fat: 1 g | Sodium: 389 mg | Carbohydrate: 15 g |

Marian Burros's
Tuna with Tomatoes and Capers
3 servings

☆☆☆☆☆☆☆☆☆☆☆☆☆☆ ☆☆☆☆☆ ☆☆☆☆☆☆☆☆☆☆☆☆ ☆☆☆☆☆☆☆☆☆☆☆

Marian Burros was well known to us at the Center for Science in the Public Interest long before she became the New York Times's *star food writer. She had covered CSPI's work for years as the food editor of the* Washington Post *and a consumer reporter on WRC-TV in Washington. She is the rare food writer who delves into the most complex food-policy issues one day, then offers the most mouth-watering recipes the next. Among Marian's cookbooks are* 20 Minute Menus *and* Keep It Simple. *Try this recipe anytime you are in a hurry and want a delicious, wonderful, low-fat, high-protein meal. Marian says it's especially nice in the summertime. Her Warm Potatoes Vinaigrette is on page 170.*

18 ounces fresh tuna
½ teaspoon olive oil
1½ tablespoons capers, rinsed
1½ cups chopped ripe tomatoes (2 large)
3 tablespoons chopped fresh basil, plus a few additional leaves for garnish
½ teaspoon dried oregano
   freshly ground black pepper to taste

1. Preheat broiler. Lightly rub tuna with about ½ teaspoon olive oil on both sides.
2. Combine capers, tomatoes, basil, oregano and pepper. Cook until tomatoes have softened.
3. Prepare stove top grill (if using) and either broil or grill tuna, using the Canadian rule: Measure tuna at thickest point and cook 10 minutes per inch.

PER SERVING:

| Calories: 186 | Fat: 4 g (19% of calories) | Cholesterol: 56 mg | Protein: 32 g |
| | Saturated Fat: <1 g | Sodium: 100 mg | Carbohydrate: 4 g |

ℬ

Anne Fletcher's
Broiled Honey-Lime Salmon   *4 servings*

☆☆☆☆☆☆☆☆☆☆☆☆☆ ☆☆☆☆☆☆ ☆☆☆☆☆☆☆☆☆☆ ☆☆☆☆☆☆☆☆☆☆☆

Anne Fletcher wants you to eat more fish! If you make these dishes, that will be an easy and pleasurable task. The recipes come from Anne's snappily titled book Eat Fish, Live Better: How to Put More Fish and Omega-3 Fish Oils into Your Diet for a Longer, Healthier Life. *Anne, a registered dietitian with a master's degree in nutrition science, is a nutrition consultant/writer and the former editor and chief writer of the* Tufts University Diet & Nutrition Letter.*

Salmon, whose flavor is brought out in this recipe with Dijon mustard, is higher in fat than most fish, but the omega-3 fatty acids in the fat may help reduce the risk of heart disease. Serve the fish with fresh lime wedges. Fish trade-offs: mako shark, swordfish, bluefish, tuna, pompano, freshwater trout, mahi mahi, sable or whitefish.

2	tablespoon Dijon mustard
	juice of 1 freshly squeezed lime
2	teaspoon olive oil
1	tablespoon honey
1½	teaspoons dried tarragon
2	tablespoon dry or semidry sherry
¼	teaspoon salt
1¼ to 1⅓	pounds salmon fillets, ½ to ⅝ inch thick
	nonstick cooking spray

1. To make the marinade, thoroughly combine the first 7 ingredients.
2. Place the salmon fillets in a shallow, nonmetal dish and top with the marinade. Turn to coat the other side. Marinate in the refrigerator for about an hour, turning once or twice.
3. Preheat the broiler. Coat the broiler pan-rack with the nonstick spray. Place the salmon on the rack, skin side down. Spoon the marinade over the fish.
4. Broil the fish 4 to 6 inches from the heating element for 5 to 6 minutes or until the fish is done. (No need to turn.)

PER SERVING:

| Calories: 246 | Fat: 10 g (36% of calories) | Cholesterol: 80 mg | Protein: 29 g |
| | Saturated Fat: 2 g | Sodium: 305 mg | Carbohydrate: 7 g |

Anne Fletcher's
Grilled Tuna in
Tomato-Basil-Mint Sauce
4 servings

☆☆☆☆☆☆☆☆☆☆☆☆☆☆ ☆☆☆☆☆☆☆☆ ☆☆☆☆☆☆☆☆☆☆☆ ☆☆☆☆☆☆☆☆☆☆

Fresh basil and mint are musts for this savory, yet easy, tomato sauce. Serve with any type of pasta, a curly-leaf lettuce salad and broiled eggplant slices.

1	16-ounce can of stewed tomatoes, drained of excess juice (no salt added)
1	medium clove of garlic
¼	cup whole basil leaves (about 20 good-sized leaves)
10	large mint leaves
	generous grinding of black pepper
1	tablespoon olive oil
2	tablespoons dry or semidry sherry
1¼ to 1⅓	pounds fresh tuna steaks, ¾ to 1 inch thick

1. In a blender, blend the stewed tomatoes and garlic for 20 to 30 seconds—until fine and frothy. Add the basil and mint and blend another 10 seconds (not too fine).
2. Pour the tomato-herb mixture into a medium-size saucepan. Add the pepper and oil. Bring to a boil. Reduce the heat and simmer uncovered for 20 to 25 minutes. At the end of that time, stir in the sherry.
3. While the sauce is simmering, start a charcoal fire or preheat a gas grill. When the coals are ready, grease the grill rack well. Then preheat it over the hot coals.
4. Blot the fish well with a paper towel. Spread a coating of sauce on 1 side of the fish and place it on the preheated grill, sauce side down. Grill for 5 to 7 minutes.
5. Blot the side of the fish facing up and spread with a coating of sauce. (Keep the remaining sauce warm in the pan.) Turn the fish and grill for another 5 to 7 minutes or until it's done. Divide into 4 portions and top with the remaining sauce.

PER SERVING:

Calories: 187	Fat: 5 g (24% of calories)	Cholesterol: 51 mg	Protein: 27 g
	Saturated Fat: <1 g	Sodium: 52 mg	Carbohydrate: 5 g

Judith Benn Hurley's
Chilled Haddock with
Snow Peas and Orange Vinaigrette   *4 servings*

☆☆☆☆☆☆☆☆☆☆☆☆☆☆☆☆ ☆☆☆☆☆☆☆☆☆☆☆☆☆☆☆☆☆☆

Judith Benn Hurley's cookbooks, Healthy Microwave Cooking *and* Garden-Fresh Cooking, *are International Association of Culinary Professionals R.T. French Tastemaker Award winners. She has a column in the* Washington Post *and has contributed to other publications, such as* The Surgeon General's Report on Nutrition and Health. *This fish recipe is very low in fat and, thanks to the orange and parsley, offers some vitamin C. The haddock must be refrigerated overnight, so plan ahead. Turn to page 188 for a chilly Hurley-created dessert.*

1 **pound haddock fillets**
1 **cup freshly squeezed orange juice (4 oranges)**
1 **teaspoon orange juice concentrate**
1 **teaspoon Dijon-style mustard**
2 **tablespoons cider vinegar**
1 **tablespoon minced fresh parsley**
2 **teaspoons olive oil**
¼ **cup chicken stock (see page 21) or low-sodium canned broth**
¼ **teaspoon grated orange peel**
¼ **pound snow peas, strings removed if necessary**

1. Set the haddock flat out in a 9-inch glass pie dish and pour the orange juice over it. Cover with vented plastic wrap and microwave on full power for about 4½ minutes (or put fish in nonstick frying pan, add orange juice, bring to a boil and let simmer for about 5 minutes). Let the haddock stand while you prepare the vinaigrette.
2. In a processor or blender, combine the concentrate, mustard, vinegar, parsley, oil, stock and orange peel and blend until smooth. Pour the vinaigrette over the haddock (undrained), cover and refrigerate overnight.
3. When you're ready to serve, rinse the peas and tip them into a medium bowl while still wet. Cover and microwave on full power for 45 to 60 seconds, depending on their size (or steam in covered pot for 5 minutes). Arrange the chilled haddock and vinaigrette on a serving plate with the peas alongside.

PER SERVING:
Calories: 167   Fat: 3 g (19% of calories)   Cholesterol: 65 mg   Protein: 23 g
                 Saturated Fat: <1 g   Sodium: 95 mg   Carbohydrate: 10 g

Barbara Kafka's
Fish Tangine
6 servings

☆☆☆☆☆☆☆☆☆☆☆☆☆☆ ☆☆☆☆☆☆☆ ☆☆☆☆☆☆☆☆☆☆☆☆ ☆☆☆☆☆☆☆☆☆☆

One taste of Barbara Kafka's Fish Tangine and you'll consider using your microwave for more than popcorn and frozen dinners. This is just one of many delectable recipes from her Microwave Gourmet Healthstyle Cookbook. *She also wrote* Party Food, The Opinionated Palate *and* Food for Friends. *Kafka is a multiple winner of the prestigious International Association of Culinary Professionals/Seagram award and writes regularly for newspapers and magazines. The cilantro and cayenne pepper make this recipe one of our favorites. Barbara says:*

There will be lots of delicious sauce—more than a quarter cup per person—that you can soak up with bread in traditional fashion or serve with a half cup of cooked rice. To keep the sauce under control, serve the fish in a rimmed soup dish with a big soup spoon. I would add a salad and consider mint tea as a drink. Leftovers are good cold.

FOR THE CHARMOULA:
- ¼ cup fresh cilantro leaves
- 2 cloves of garlic, mashed and peeled
- 1 tablespoon white wine vinegar
- 2 tablespoons fresh lemon juice
- ½ teaspoon paprika
- ½ teaspoon ground cumin
- 2 tablespoons water

- 6 flounder fillets (each 4 ounces), no more than ½ inch at the thickest point

FOR THE TANGINE:
- 1 tablespoon olive oil
- 2 teaspoons paprika
- 1 teaspoon ground cumin
- 3 cloves of garlic, mashed, peeled and minced
  large pinch of cayenne
- 4 stalks celery, trimmed, peeled and cut into 1½ x ¼ x ¼-inch matchstick strips
- 1 28-ounce can Italian plum tomatoes with liquid, coarsely chopped (no salt added)
- ½ teaspoon kosher salt
- 1 tablespoon fresh lemon juice

1. Combine the charmoula ingredients (except the fillets) in a food processor and chop coarsely. Transfer to a nonmetal dish. Rub the fillets on all sides with the charmoula and let stand while preparing the rest of the recipe.
2. Stir together oil, paprika, cumin, garlic and cayenne in a small bowl to make a paste. Place in the center of an 11 x 9 x 2-inch oval dish. Cook uncovered at 100% for 1 minute in a 650 to 700-watt oven.
3. Add celery and stir to coat with the spice mixture. Cook uncovered for 5

minutes. Stir in tomatoes and salt and cook, uncovered, for 8 minutes.

4. Roll up the fillets lengthwise and place them spoke fashion on top of the vegetables. Cover tightly with microwave plastic wrap. Cook for 7 minutes, or until fish is cooked through and opaque. Pierce plastic to release steam.

5. Remove from oven and uncover. With a slotted spoon, transfer fillets to a shallow serving bowl or individual plates. Stir lemon juice into sauce and spoon over fish.

For 400 to 500-watt ovens: In step 2, cook spice mixture uncovered for 2 minutes. Continue with step 3 and cook celery for 7 minutes. Add tomatoes and salt and cook for 12 minutes. In step 4, cook fillets for 9 minutes. Finish as in step 5.

PER SERVING:

Calories: 165	Fat: 4 g (24% of calories)	Cholesterol: 69 mg	Protein: 22 g
	Saturated Fat: 1 g	Sodium: 342 mg	Carbohydrate: 10 g

Kristine Kidd's
Grilled Fish Soft Tacos

6 servings

☆☆☆☆☆☆☆☆☆☆☆☆☆☆ ☆☆☆☆☆☆ ☆☆☆☆☆☆☆☆☆☆☆☆☆ ☆☆☆☆☆☆☆☆☆☆☆

Kristine Kidd says her love affair with food started as a teenager when her father opened up a country inn in Vermont. Ever since, Kristine has been creating delicious recipes—as a chef, caterer, cooking teacher and now as the food editor of Bon Appétit *magazine. Kristine served this recipe at the maiden dinner in her new home in Topanga Canyon, California, and says that it's a perfect warm-weather entree for outdoor dining. It's one of the most interesting ways we've seen of serving fish. The tomatoes and beans make up for the fish's lack of vitamin C and fiber.*

TOMATO AND AVOCADO SALSA:

 2 pounds tomatoes, seeded and chopped
 1 avocado, peeled, pitted and chopped
 ½ cup minced red onion
 ½ cup minced fresh cilantro
 2 jalapeño chilies, minced (wear gloves when mincing)
 2 tablespoons fresh lime juice
 2 teaspoons olive oil

SPICED WHITE BEANS:

 3 cups cooked dry white beans or two 15-ounce cans cannellini beans, rinsed and drained
 ½ cup minced fresh mint
 ½ cup minced red onion
 2 jalapeño chilies, minced
 3 tablespoons fresh lime juice

2 teaspoons olive oil
1 teaspoon ground cumin

FISH:

1½ pounds salmon, tuna or red snapper fillets
 ½ tablespoon olive oil
    fresh lime juice
    freshly ground black pepper

12 whole-wheat or corn tortillas
 1 head romaine or iceberg lettuce, shredded
   lime wedges
   yogurt, optional

1. For salsa: Combine all ingredients in a large bowl.
2. For beans: Combine all ingredients in another large bowl.   Season to taste with pepper.
3. For fish: Brush fish lightly with oil and lime juice.   Sprinkle with pepper. Let stand for 20 minutes.
4. Preheat oven to 350° and preheat barbecue or broiler.   Wrap tortillas in foil. Place in oven and heat while cooking fish.   Grill fish until cooked through, about 4 minutes per side.   Cut into ½-inch strips.   Place on heated platter. Sprinkle with additional lime juice.   Arrange salsa, beans, fish, tortillas, lettuce, lime wedges and yogurt on table.   Allow diners to assemble own tacos.

PER SERVING:

| Calories: 509 | Fat: 13 g (23% of calories) | Cholesterol: 35 mg | Protein: 36 g |
| | Saturated Fat: 2 g | Sodium: 76 mg | Carbohydrate: 65 g |

ℒౚ

Claude Lenfant's
Mediterranean Fish

4 servings

☆☆☆☆☆☆☆☆☆☆☆☆☆☆ ☆☆☆☆☆☆ ☆☆☆☆☆☆☆☆☆☆☆☆☆ ☆☆☆☆☆☆☆☆☆☆☆

Dr. Claude Lenfant is the director of the National Heart, Lung, and Blood Institute at the National Institutes of Health.   A prolific writer, Lenfant has published over 200 scientific articles.   He has received innumerable awards during his long and distinguished career.   Needless to say, Dr. Lenfant's scrumptious fish dish is low in fat and good for your heart!   He says, "Orange peel added to the classic Mediterranean-style tomato, onion and garlic sauce distinguishes this recipe."   Turn to page 157 for another low-fat main dish from Dr. Lenfant—this one with chicken.

2 teaspoons olive oil
1 large onion, sliced

1 16-ounce can whole tomatoes, drained (reserve juice) and coarsely chopped (no salt added)
1 bay leaf
1 clove of garlic
1 cup dry white wine
½ cup reserved tomato juice
¼ cup lemon juice
¼ cup orange juice
1 tablespoon fresh grated orange peel
1 teaspoon fennel seeds, crushed
½ teaspoon dried oregano, crushed
½ teaspoon dried thyme
½ teaspoon dried basil
¼ teaspoon freshly ground black pepper
1 pound ready-to-cook fish fillets (sole, flounder or perch)
   nonstick cooking spray

1. Heat oil in large nonstick skillet. Add onion and sautI over moderate heat 5 minutes or until soft. Add all ingredients except fish. Stir well; simmer for 30 minutes uncovered.
2. Arrange fish in a lightly sprayed 10 x 6-inch baking dish; cover with sauce. Bake uncovered at 375° about 15 minutes or until fish flakes easily.

PER SERVING:

Calories: 208	Fat: 4 g (17% of calories)	Cholesterol: 62 mg	Protein: 20 g
	Saturated Fat: <1 g	Sodium: 125 mg	Carbohydrate: 15 g

☙

Ralph and Rose Nader's
Baked Fish with Spices and Tarator Sauce

6 servings

☆☆☆☆☆☆☆☆☆☆☆☆☆☆ ☆☆☆☆☆☆ ☆☆☆☆☆☆☆☆☆☆☆☆ ☆☆☆☆☆☆☆☆☆☆☆☆

When you meet Rose Nader, a feisty woman if there ever was one, you have no doubt where some of her son's (consumer advocate Ralph Nader) inspiration and low threshold for outrage came from. The Nader passion applies to food as well as more political issues; Rose once told the New York Times, *"When you eat junk food, you feel irritated and you don't know why. It is all in the food; it all goes together."*

Baked fish with tarator, which was published originally in Rose's cookbook It Happened in the Kitchen, *is a rich and elegant way to prepare fish for a special evening. Colorful vegetables add to the presentation. The Naders' eggplant appetizer is on page 55.*

>   2 lemons
>   2 pounds white fish (for example, flounder, scrod, fillet of sole)
>   salt (optional) and pepper
>   ⅛ teaspoon tarragon or curry powder
> 2 to 3 cloves of garlic
>   ¼ teaspoon salt
>   ¼ cup tahini
>   juice of 2 lemons
>   2 tablespoons cold water
>   parsley for garnish

1. Slice lemons and arrange slices on bottom of baking dish. Place fish on top and season with salt, pepper and either tarragon or curry powder. Bake in 350° oven for no more than 10 minutes until flaky.
2. Pound garlic with ¼ teaspoon salt if desired. Add tahini and lemon juice and mix. Add cold water as needed and mix until smooth. Taste should be a little bit tart. Remove fish from oven, place on platter and serve immediately with tarator sauce and parsley garnish. Squeeze juice out of lemon slices onto fish.

Note: Alternatively, use a blender to blend garlic, salt, lemon juice and water. When that is smooth, blend in tahini.

PER SERVING:

Calories: 188	Fat: 7 g (32% of calories)	Cholesterol: 83 mg	Protein: 27 g
	Saturated Fat: 1 g	Sodium: 239 mg	Carbohydrate: 6 g

ༀ

Sushma Palmer's
Tandoori Fish   *4 servings*

☆☆☆☆☆☆☆☆☆☆☆☆☆ ☆☆☆☆☆☆ ☆☆☆☆☆☆☆☆☆☆☆☆ ☆☆☆☆☆☆☆☆☆☆☆☆

Sushma Palmer, a delightful, talented woman, was the director of the National Academy of Sciences's Food and Nutrition Board and in charge of the board's landmark 1989 report, Diet and Health. *She now commutes between the United States and Europe, where she works at the Central European Center for Health and the Environment. Sushma says this dish, one of her favorites, is a modified version of a traditional Indian recipe that includes more salt and spices in the marinade and more cream in the sauce. It is traditionally cooked in a tandoori—an Indian clay oven heated with charcoal. This version can be barbecued or broiled. Her Versatile Raita is on page 183.*

1 pound fish fillet (any sturdy white fish—preferably turbot or monkfish)

MARINADE:

2 tablespoons fat-free yogurt
1 tablespoon lemon juice
1 teaspoon vinegar
1 teaspoon oil
¼ teaspoon salt
½ teaspoon cayenne
¼ teaspoon mango powder (or substitute 1 tablespoon tamarind water)
1 teaspoon cumin seeds, freshly ground
1 teaspoon coriander seeds, freshly ground
1 teaspoon garlic, pressed
2 teaspoons grated fresh ginger
1 tablespoon cilantro, finely chopped

SAUCE:

½ teaspoon cumin seeds
½ teaspoon grated fresh ginger
1 tablespoon cilantro
4 ounces tomatoes, canned purée or freshly puréed (no salt added)
1 tablespoon lemon juice
1 teaspoon sugar
1 teaspoon mixed Indian spices (freshly ground mixture of equal parts cumin, cloves, nutmeg and cinnamon)

GARNISH:

lemon wedges
tomato slices

1. Wash and wipe the fish fillet dry and cut into serving-size pieces if desired. Place in a nonaluminum baking pan.
2. Make the marinade: Mix the yogurt with all the ingredients. The marinade should taste spicy and sour. Cover and marinate the fish for up to 2 hours at room temperature (refrigerate in hot weather), or overnight in the refrigerator.
3. Prepare sauce: In a saucepan pop the cumin seeds over a hot flame, add the ginger, 1 teaspoon of fresh cilantro and the tomato purée. Simmer covered for 10 to 15 minutes. Add the lemon juice and sugar; cook another 5 minutes.
4. Broil/barbecue the fish rapidly so as not to dry it. Do not cook for more than 10 minutes. Remove to a hot platter.
5. Add remaining marinade juices to the sauce, cook another 5 minutes, check seasoning, add the remaining fresh cilantro and mixed Indian spices and pour a few tablespoons on the fish.
6. Decorate the fish with the lemon wedges and tomato slices and serve with the sauce on the side.

Variation: Use the same marinade and sauce with chicken pieces from which skin has been removed. Marinate the chicken at least 6 hours or overnight.

PER SERVING:
Calories: 128   Fat: 2 g (17% of calories)   Cholesterol: 62 mg   Protein: 19 g
                Saturated Fat: <1 g   Sodium: 256 mg   Carbohydrate: 7 g

Joseph Piscatella's
Southwest Jambalaya
5 servings

☆☆☆☆☆☆☆☆☆☆☆☆☆☆ ☆☆☆☆☆☆ ☆☆☆☆☆☆☆☆☆☆☆☆ ☆☆☆☆☆☆☆☆☆☆

Author-lecturer Joseph Piscatella became an inspired healthy-food advocate after undergoing open-heart surgery at the tender age of 32. His three cookbooks, Don't Eat Your Heart Out, Choices for a Healthy Heart *and* Controlling Your Fat Tooth, *have sold over two million copies and reflect his commitment to recipes that are tasty, attractive and nutritious. Joe also does wellness consulting through his Institute for Fitness and Health.*

This cookbook's senior editor (M.F.J.) will forever be grateful to Joe for helping him out on a tour publicizing the editor's Fast-Food Guide. *During Detroit's biggest snowstorm in a decade, a taxi driver was supposed to be delivering the editor to a TV studio. Unfortunately, the driver went in the wrong direction. The editor was late to the show, but Joe had kindly explained to viewers the thrust of the fast-food book.*

This spicy Southwest Jambalaya is a delicious cross-hybrid of Tex-Mex and Italian cuisine.

    1 head garlic
    3 fresh Anaheim chilies or 1 large green pepper
    2 sweet yellow wax peppers
    2 large red peppers
    1 quart chicken stock (see page 21) or low-sodium canned broth
    6 cloves of garlic, minced
    ½ fresh jalapeño pepper, seeded, steamed and chopped (use gloves
       when handling raw)
    ½ teaspoon black pepper
    ½ teaspoon chili powder
    ¼ teaspoon ground mace
    ⅛ teaspoon cayenne pepper
    ½ pound medium prawns, shelled and deveined
    ½ pound halibut, cut into 2-inch cubes
    2 tablespoons quick-cooking tapioca
    2 cups cooked short-grain white rice
    2 cups cooked rotelle, wagon-wheel or tube-type pasta

1. Wrap garlic head in foil and arrange chilies and yellow and red peppers in a roasting pan. Broil 2 inches from heat for 15 to 30 minutes or until skins bubble and char on all sides. Transfer chilies and peppers to a paper bag; close bag and let cool 15 to 20 minutes. If garlic head is still firm after broiling, bake in a 400° oven until it feels soft when pressed; set aside.
2. When cool, pull off and discard stems, skin and seeds of broiled chilies and peppers. Cut into strips ¼ inch wide.
3. In a medium stockpot, combine chicken stock, garlic cloves and jalape:o pepper. Heat just to boiling (do not boil); reduce heat. Add black pepper, chili powder, mace and cayenne pepper; simmer 10 minutes. Return just to boiling; add skinned chilies and peppers, prawns, halibut and tapioca. Reduce heat and cook 3 to 4 minutes or until prawns are pink and halibut is just opaque.
4. Spoon ½ cup rice and ½ cup pasta into each soup bowl. Ladle jambalaya over top. Pull apart head of roasted garlic. Squeeze garlic from skin into the jambalaya.

Note: Anaheim chilies, also called Texas, California, New Mexico, Colorado, guijillo, long red or long green chilies, are usually available in Spanish and Mexican markets and in most supermarkets. Although the flavor will be slightly different, any other fresh hot chilies can be substituted. Variation: Substitute green peppers for yellow peppers and any medium-hot chilies for Anaheim chilies.

PER SERVING:

| Calories: 227 | Fat: 2 g (7% of calories) | Cholesterol: 70 mg | Protein: 22 g |
| | Saturated Fat: <1 g | Sodium: 111 mg | Carbohydrate: 41 g |

Ann Richards's
Tuna Steaks with Mango Salsa   *4 servings*

☆☆☆☆☆☆☆☆☆☆☆☆☆ ☆☆☆☆☆☆☆ ☆☆☆☆☆☆☆☆☆☆☆ ☆☆☆☆☆☆☆☆☆☆

   As she did in 1988, Texas Governor Ann Richards inspired the nation (or at least Democrats) again in 1992 with a sarcastic, no-nonsense speech at the Democratic National Convention. This former teacher, county commissioner and state treasurer has been a leader in health, civil rights, education and poverty issues. Besides being a great governor, mother of four and grandmother of four, Governor Richards obviously commands an excellent appreciation for healthy gourmet cuisine. This Texas Governor's Mansion recipe will delight your taste buds with a profusion of exotic flavors.

1½ pounds yellowfin tuna, cut into 4 portions
1 lime
1 lemon
1 orange
2 tablespoons ginger, grated
4 cloves of garlic, minced
2 tablespoons reduced-sodium soy sauce
1 tablespoon sesame oil

MANGO SALSA:
2 cups ripe mangos, peeled and diced into ¼-inch cubes
1 cup tomatoes, peeled, seeded and diced
¼ cup mixture of spearmint and cilantro leaves, finely chopped
juice of 1 lime
3 tablespoons pickled ginger, chopped
4 tablespoons minced red onion
1 teaspoon ground coriander
1 teaspoon cumin powder
3 serrano peppers, minced with seeds
pinch of salt, or to taste
cilantro or mint (for garnish)

1. Remove half the rind from the lime, lemon and orange with a peeler and cut into strips or grate the colored rind from the fruits. Squeeze the juice from the fruit into a stainless steel bowl. Add remaining ingredients to bowl and stir well. Pour into a shallow casserole dish and add tuna steaks, turning to coat. Cover with plastic wrap and refrigerate. Marinate 1 hour, turning once.

2. To make salsa, combine diced mangos and tomatoes. Fold in all the other ingredients. Flavors will develop best if the mixture can set for 2-3 hours.

3. To grill the tuna, first spray the grill or broiler with vegetable spray before heating. Discard marinade and place fish on the hot grill. Grill tuna for 3 minutes per side (or more depending on thickness) until just cooked through. Heat the salsa until warm or serve at room temperature.

4. To serve, prepare a rice mixture (I like to use half Lundberg Wild Blend and half Texmati or other white rice) with toasted chopped pecans. Place the tuna steak in the center of the plate with rice on the right and left of the steak and salsa at top and bottom. Cilantro or mint leaves make nice garnishes.

PER SERVING:

| Calories: 316 | Fat: 5 g (16% of calories) | Cholesterol: 63 mg | Protein: 36 g |
| | Saturated Fat: 1 g | Sodium: 511 mg | Carbohydrate: 31 g |

Bernd Schmitt's
Salmon with Poached Leeks, Capers and Chive Vinaigrette

4 servings

☆☆☆☆☆☆☆☆☆☆☆☆☆☆☆ ☆☆☆☆☆☆☆ ☆☆☆☆☆☆☆☆☆☆☆☆☆☆ ☆☆☆☆☆☆☆☆☆☆☆☆

Guests at the Canyon Ranch in Tucson, Arizona, are favored with the cooking of executive chef Bernd Schmitt. Prior to going to the ranch, the European-trained chef was at the Four Seasons Hotels in Dallas and Toronto. Bernd says he is "a strong advocate of better health and nutrition. My goal is to bring Canyon Ranch to the leading edge of spa food, where we intend to be number one in flair and flavor."

Americans certainly don't eat enough leeks—many folks wouldn't know a leek if it knocked on their door. This recipe is elegant, relatively simple to prepare and a great way to get to know a leek. Bernd contributed two other recipes to this book— Vegetable Strudel with Red Pepper Coulis (page 87) and Bread Pudding (page 197).

1 pound Atlantic salmon, cut into eight 2-ounce pieces
½ cup water
  juice of 1 lemon
½ teaspoon salt
2 leeks, cleaned and cut in half lengthwise

VINAIGRETTE:
½ cup chopped red onion
2 tablespoons chopped chives
½ teaspoon cracked black peppercorns
½ cup chicken stock (see page 21) or use low-sodium canned broth
½ cup balsamic vinegar
2 tablespoons lemon juice
2 teaspoons drained capers

GARNISH:
½ cup cooked beets (matchstick strips)
4 sprigs chervil

1. Spray large sauté pan with nonstick vegetable spray and sauté salmon until it begins to flake or to the degree of doneness you prefer. Set aside and keep warm.
2. In sauté pan, bring water, juice of 1 lemon and salt (at least 80% of the salt is discarded in the poaching liquid) to a boil. Add leeks, cover pan and cook until tender, approximately 5 minutes. Remove leeks, set aside and discard poaching liquid.
3. To prepare vinaigrette: In a medium saucepan, combine remaining ingredients and mix well. Bring to a boil and remove from heat.
4. Assemble plates by placing half of a leek on each plate. Arrange 2 pieces of salmon on top of leek and finish dish with 2 tablespoons of vinaigrette sauce. Garnish with beets and chervil.

PER SERVING:

| Calories: 172 | Fat: 5 g (28% of calories) | Cholesterol: 71 mg | Protein: 23 g |
| | Saturated Fat: 1 g | Sodium: 78 mg | Carbohydrate: 8 g |

Ringo Starr's
Chunky Fish
4 servings

☆☆☆☆☆☆☆☆☆☆☆☆☆☆ ☆☆☆☆☆☆☆☆ ☆☆☆☆☆☆☆☆☆☆☆ ☆☆☆☆☆☆☆☆☆☆☆☆

Ringo Starr joined the legendary rock music group The Beatles in 1960, replacing original Beatles drummer Pete Best. Ringo has his own band now—Ringo Starr and his All-Starr Band. He's more versatile than you might think—Ringo has acted with Richard Burton and Peter Sellers and starred in the public-television children's series "Shining Time Station." He is married to actress Barbara Bach, whose Green Salad recipe appears on page 40.

1½ **pounds ahi, swordfish, cod or firm white fish**
   nonstick cooking spray
  2 **teaspoons reduced-sodium soy sauce or tamari**
  1 **cup seedless grapes, red or green**

1. Remove any skin from fish and cut into 1-inch chunks. Spray an ovenproof dish with cooking oil. Arrange fish in 1 layer in the dish. Sprinkle the fish with the soy sauce. Slice the grapes in half and scatter over the fish.
2. Place under a preheated broiler for about 7 to 10 minutes. Serve with baked potato and vegetable of your choice (Ringo likes corn on the cob).

PER SERVING:

| Calories: 148 | Fat: 1 g (8% of calories) | Cholesterol: 59 mg | Protein: 25 g |
| | Saturated Fat: <1 g | Sodium: 194 mg | Carbohydrate: 8 g |

POULTRY AND OTHER MEAT

Gerald Berenson's
Chicken Breasts with Fennel Sauce   *4 servings*

☆☆☆ ☆☆☆☆☆ ☆☆☆☆☆☆ ☆☆☆☆☆☆☆☆☆☆☆☆☆☆☆☆☆☆☆☆☆☆☆☆

Gerald Berenson, M.D., is the director of the National Center for Cardiovascular Health at the Tulane School of Public Health. Formerly, he worked on the Bogalusa Heart Study at the Louisiana State University School of Medicine in New Orleans. That landmark study proved that America's high-fat diet caused arteries to begin clogging up in the teenage years. In both of Dr. Berenson's recipes, removing the chicken skin before cooking minimizes the fat level.

1 head crisp fennel (about ¾ pound)
¼ teaspoon salt
4 boneless, skinless chicken breast halves, trimmed of all fat, separated and flattened
  nonstick cooking spray
¼ cup green onions or shallots
¼ cup dry white wine (dry vermouth)
½ cup chicken stock (see page 21) or low-sodium canned broth
1 bay leaf
2 sprigs fresh thyme (or ¼ teaspoon dried)
3 dashes Tabasco sauce (about ⅛ teaspoon)
1 tablespoon margarine
  pepper to taste
4 fennel leaves, chopped finely

1. Trim the fennel, saving 4 leaves for chopping, leaving only the white bulb at the bottom. Cut the bulb into ¼-inch cubes (about 1½ cups). Stir in salt.
2. Spray a nonstick skillet with cooking spray and heat on medium. Add the chicken breasts and cook until lightly browned. Then add green onions or shallots.
3. Turn chicken breasts and scatter fennel around them. Continue cooking, shaking the pan, redistributing the fennel until it is evenly cooked (about 3 to 4 minutes). Add the wine, broth, bay leaf, thyme and Tabasco. Cover tightly and cook over medium heat for about 10 minutes. Turn pieces occasionally.
4. Transfer chicken to warm platter. Cover with foil to keep warm.
5. With slotted spoon, remove about ½ cup of the fennel cubes. Discard bay leaf and thyme. Pour remaining fennel mixture into blender or food processor. Add margarine and blend to a fine purée.
6. Pour mixture into saucepan and add pepper as needed. Add any liquid that has accumulated around the chicken. Add reserved fennel cubes and chopped fennel leaves. Bring to a simmer. Spoon sauce over chicken. Serve immediately.

PER SERVING:

Calories: 202   Fat: 6 g (28% of calories)   Cholesterol: 73 mg   Protein: 28 g
                 Saturated Fat: 1 g   Sodium: 261 mg   Carbohydrate: 5 g

ℱ⊃

Gerald Berenson's
Chicken New Orleans

4 servings

☆☆☆ ☆☆☆☆☆☆ ☆☆☆☆☆☆☆ ☆☆☆☆☆☆☆☆☆☆☆☆☆☆☆☆☆☆☆☆☆☆☆☆☆☆☆

Dr. Berenson served on a Center for Science in the Public Interest committee that set nutrition and food-safety guidelines for children's processed foods. This chicken recipe from Dr. Berenson gets an infusion of taste from fresh herbs and balsamic vinegar and some vitamin C from the red bell peppers.

1½ **tablespoons olive oil**
  4 **boneless, skinless chicken breast halves, flattened**
  ¼ **teaspoon salt, or more to taste**
      freshly ground black pepper to taste
  2 **small red bell peppers, thinly sliced**
  1 **onion, thinly sliced**
  2 **cloves of garlic, minced**
  1 **tablespoon minced fresh basil, or ¾ teaspoon dried**
  2 **teaspoons minced fresh oregano, or ½ teaspoon dried**
  2 **tablespoons balsamic vinegar**

1. Heat ½ tablespoon of the oil in a large skillet. Salt and pepper both sides of the chicken. Sauté both sides until golden brown. Remove chicken from the skillet.
2. Add remaining tablespoon of oil to skillet. Sauté peppers and onion for about 3 minutes. Add garlic, basil and oregano and sauté for 30 seconds. Do not brown. Taste and add salt and pepper.
3. Return chicken to the skillet and pour vinegar over it. Bring to just boiling, lower heat and simmer covered for 5 minutes until chicken is cooked through and vegetables are crisp-tender.
4. Serve the chicken with the vegetables and juices spooned on top, and some brown rice on the side.

PER SERVING:

Calories: 217   Fat: 9 g (36% of calories)   Cholesterol: 73 mg   Protein: 28 g
                 Saturated Fat: 2 g   Sodium: 199 mg   Carbohydrate: 6 g

ℱ⊃

Richard Carleton's
Baked Chicken
4 servings

☆☆☆ ☆☆☆☆☆☆ ☆☆☆☆☆☆☆ ☆☆☆☆☆☆☆☆☆☆☆☆☆☆☆☆☆☆☆☆☆☆☆☆☆☆☆☆☆

Richard Carleton, M.D., physician-in-chief at Memorial Hospital of Rhode Island, directed the acclaimed Pawtucket Heart Health Program, which promoted heart-healthy eating habits in the city of Pawtucket. Dr. Carleton has held many appointments at the National Institutes of Health, including the National Cholesterol Education Program. This recipe is basically a one-step meal, well-adapted to rapid preparation and easy cleanup for people on the go. Moderate in calories and low in fat, the taste is satisfying.

    4 boneless, skinless chicken breast halves
    ¼ teaspoon rosemary
      freshly ground black pepper to taste
    1 slice of large red onion
    1 large tomato, sliced
    4 medium potatoes, quartered

1. Place each chicken breast half on a 12 x 15-inch piece of aluminum foil. Sprinkle on the rosemary and black pepper.
2. Layer the circlets of onion and slices of tomato on the chicken. Surround the chicken with quarters of a medium-sized potato. Fold and seal the aluminum tightly. Repeat for each of 4 chicken breasts. Place the foil packets in an oven and cook for 45 minutes at 350°.
3. Serving the foiled dinner with a packet of microwave-prepared frozen sugar snap peas adds color and additional protein. The dinner may be removed from the foil to a plate or the foil may be placed directly on the plate to facilitate cleanup.

PER SERVING:

Calories: 370	Fat: 3 g (8% of calories)	Cholesterol: 73 mg	Protein: 32 g
	Saturated Fat: 1 g	Sodium: 82 mg	Carbohydrate: 53 g

ℬ

Katherine Eakin's
Malaysian Chicken Pizza
6 servings

☆☆☆☆ ☆☆☆☆☆☆☆ ☆☆☆☆☆☆☆☆ ☆☆☆☆☆☆☆☆☆☆☆☆☆☆☆☆☆☆☆☆☆☆☆☆☆☆☆☆

Katherine Eakin has been the editor of Cooking Light *magazine since its launch in 1987. She has edited many cookbooks, including the nineteen-volume* Southern Heritage Cookbook Library. *These two pizza recipes show that pizza can be heart healthy, as long as you don't use too much cheese and meat.*

¼ cup firmly packed brown sugar
¾ cup rice wine vinegar
¼ cup reduced-sodium soy sauce
3 tablespoons water
2 tablespoons chunky peanut butter
1 tablespoon peeled, minced ginger root
½ to ¾ teaspoon crushed red pepper flakes
4 cloves of garlic
nonstick cooking spray
½ pound boneless, skinless chicken breasts, cut into bite-sized pieces
½ cup Swiss cheese, shredded
¼ cup part-skim mozzarella cheese, shredded
1 whole-wheat pizza crust (see following recipe)
¼ cup chopped green onions

1. Combine first 8 ingredients in a bowl; stir well with a wire whisk. Set aside.
2. Coat a large nonstick skillet with cooking spray; place over medium heat until hot. Add chicken and sauté 2 minutes. Remove from pan; set aside.
3. Pour vinegar mixture into skillet; bring to a boil over medium-high heat. Cook 6 minutes or until slightly thickened (should be consistency of thick syrup; cook longer if it is too thin). Return chicken to skillet; cook 1 minute or until chicken is done.
4. Sprinkle cheeses over prepared crust, leaving ½-inch border; top with mixture. Bake at 500° for 12 minutes on bottom rack of oven. Sprinkle with green onions. Remove pizza to a cutting board; let stand 5 minutes.

PER SERVING:

| Calories: 290 | Fat: 8 g (23% of calories) | Cholesterol: 33 mg | Protein: 18 g |
| | Saturated Fat: 3 g | Sodium: 557 mg | Carbohydrate: 38 g |

Katherine Eakin's
Sausage, Garlic and Mushroom Pizza 6 servings
☆☆☆ ☆☆☆☆☆☆ ☆☆☆☆☆☆☆ ☆☆☆☆☆☆☆☆☆☆☆☆☆☆☆☆☆☆☆☆☆☆☆☆☆☆☆

Because the sausage is made of turkey, the fat content of this pizza is reasonable. You can cut the fat even more simply by using less sausage.

6 ounces Italian-flavored turkey sausage
nonstick cooking spray
4 cups finely chopped fresh mushrooms
½ cup diced onion
6 cloves garlic, minced

¼ cup evaporated skim milk
3 tablespoons chopped fresh parsley
½ cup shredded provolone cheese
1 12-inch whole-wheat pizza crust (see following recipe)
¼ cup grated fresh Romano cheese

1. Cook sausage in a large nonstick skillet over medium heat until browned, stirring to crumble. Drain and pat dry with paper towels; set aside.
2. Coat a skillet with cooking spray; place over medium-high heat until hot. Add mushrooms, onion and garlic and cook 7 minutes or until liquid evaporates. Add milk and parsley; cook an additional 2 minutes.
3. Sprinkle provolone cheese over prepared crust, leaving ½-inch border. Spread mushroom mixture evenly over cheese; top with sausage. Sprinkle Romano cheese over pizza. Bake at 500° for 12 minutes on bottom rack of oven. Remove to a cutting board; let stand 5 minutes.

PER SERVING:

Calories: 226	Fat: 7 g (26% of calories)	Cholesterol: 17 mg	Protein: 12 g
	Saturated Fat: 3 g	Sodium: 303 mg	Carbohydrate: 30 g

WHOLE-WHEAT PIZZA CRUST: *6 servings*

1 tablespoon honey
1 package dry yeast
1 cup warm water (105° to 115°)
2 cups whole-wheat flour, divided
1 cup all-purpose flour
¼ teaspoon salt
1 teaspoon olive oil
  nonstick cooking spray
1 tablespoon cornmeal

1. Dissolve honey and yeast in 1 cup warm water in a large bowl; let stand 5 minutes. Stir in 1¾ cups whole-wheat flour and next 3 ingredients to form a soft dough.
2. Turn dough onto a lightly floured surface. Flour hands and knead dough until smooth and elastic (about 5 minutes); add enough of remaining flour, 1 tablespoon at a time, to prevent dough from sticking to hands.
3. Place dough in a bowl coated with cooking spray, turning to coat top. Cover and let rise in a warm place (85°), free from drafts, for 1 hour or until doubled in bulk.
4. Punch dough down and divide in half. Roll each half into a 12-inch circle on a lightly floured surface. Place dough on a 12-inch pizza pan or baking sheet coated with cooking spray and sprinkled with 1 tablespoon cornmeal. Crimp edges of dough with fingers to form a rim. Let rise uncovered in a warm place (85°), free from drafts, 30 minutes. Top and bake according to recipe directions. Yields two 12-inch pizza crusts.

Note: Half of dough can be stored in freezer for up to 1 month. Let dough rise; punch down and divide in half. Dust half with flour; wrap in plastic wrap and store in a heavy-duty plastic bag in freezer. To thaw, place dough in refrigerator 12 hours or overnight; bring to room temperature and shape as desired.

PER SERVING:

Calories: 120	Fat: 1 g (8% of calories)	Cholesterol: 0 mg	Protein: 4 g
	Saturated Fat: 0 g	Sodium: 51 mg	Carbohydrate: 25 g

Al and Tipper Gore's
Chinese Chicken with Walnuts
6 servings

☆☆☆ ☆☆☆☆☆☆ ☆☆☆☆☆☆☆ ☆☆☆☆☆☆☆☆☆☆☆☆☆☆☆☆☆☆☆☆☆☆☆☆☆☆

Vice President Albert Gore, Jr., and Tipper Gore contributed this recipe shortly before he was tapped by then-Arkansas Governor Clinton to run in the 1992 election. Gore, a Tennessee Democrat, was elected to the Senate in 1984 and has been a great supporter of several issues advocated by the Center for Science in the Public Interest. For instance, he played a crucial role in obtaining warning labels on alcoholic beverages. His book on the environment, Earth in the Balance, *was on the best-seller list in 1992.*

Tipper, who has served on CSPI's board of directors, co-founded the Parents Music Resource Center to alert parents to violent and sexually exploitive lyrics in rock music. She authored Raising PG Kids in an X-Rated Society *and is an advocate for children, the homeless and the mentally ill. Tipper says, "This recipe has been a family favorite for several years. I hope that you will enjoy it as much as we have." Besides the great flavors in this dish, you'll appreciate the vitamin C, which is provided by the green peppers.*

  6 **boneless, skinless chicken breast halves**
2½ **tablespoons reduced-sodium soy sauce**
1½ **tablespoons water**
  2 **teaspoons cornstarch**
  2 **tablespoons dry sherry**
  1 **teaspoon sugar**
  1 **teaspoon grated fresh ginger root**
 ½ **teaspoon crushed red pepper**
 ¼ **teaspoon salt**
  1 **tablespoon peanut oil**
  2 **medium green peppers, cut into ¾-inch pieces**
  4 **green onions, diagonally-sliced into 1-inch lengths**
 ⅓ **cup walnut halves**

1. Cut chicken into 1-inch pieces and set aside. Mix soy sauce and water, then blend into cornstarch; stir in sherry, sugar, ginger root, red pepper and salt. Preheat wok or large skillet over high heat; add 2 teaspoons of peanut oil. Stir-fry green peppers and onions in oil for 2 minutes and remove. Add walnuts to wok and stir-fry for 1 to 2 minutes until golden brown and remove. Add another teaspoon of oil and stir-fry half of the chicken. Remove and stir-fry the remaining chicken for 2 minutes.
2. Return all the chicken to the wok and stir in the soy mixture. Cook and stir until bubbly.
3. Stir in vegetables and walnuts, cover and cook for 1 minute.

PER SERVING:

Calories: 230   Fat: 10 g (38% of calories)   Cholesterol: 73 mg   Protein: 29 g
                 Saturated Fat: 2 g   Sodium: 411 mg   Carbohydrate: 5 g

Tom Harkin's
Stuffed Pork Medallions *4 servings*

☆☆☆ ☆☆☆☆☆☆ ☆☆☆☆☆☆ ☆☆☆☆☆☆☆☆☆☆☆☆☆☆☆☆☆☆☆☆☆☆☆☆☆☆☆

The first recipe that Senator Tom Harkin sent us was loaded with fat. So, to serve up a nutritionally correct dish, he huddled with a Senate dietitian and offered this low-fat pork recipe. That kindness is characteristic of this Iowa Democrat, who won over many Americans when he competed in the 1992 Democratic presidential primaries. Senator Harkin was responsible for creating the Office of Alternative Medicine at the National Insitutes of Health. More recently, he sponsored legislation that would require the Surgeon General to publish biennial reports on nutrition and health. If, like Senator Harkin, you can't live without pork, make it tenderloin—the leanest of all cuts.

10 ounces lean pork tenderloin, cut into 1¼-inch-thick slices

STUFFING:
- ½ **cup whole kernel corn**
- ½ **cup whole-wheat bread crumbs (see page 79)**
  pinch of pepper
- ¼ **teaspoon salt**
- ⅛ **tablespoon parsley**
  pinch of sage
- ½ **tablespoon onion, chopped**
- ½ **cup apple, diced**
- 1 **tablespoon whole milk**
  nonstick cooking spray

BASTING SAUCE:
¼ **cup mustard**
¼ **cup honey**
¼ **teaspoon rosemary leaves**
  pinch of pepper

1. Combine stuffing ingredients. Slice tenderloin into 1¼-inch-thick medallions. Cut a pocket into the side of each medallion. Fill medallions with stuffing.
2. Brown medallions in a sprayed pan. Transfer to baking dish and bake uncovered at 350° for about 1 hour. Baste often with basting sauce mixture.

PER SERVING:

Calories: 233	Fat: 4 g (15% of calories)	Cholesterol: 44 mg	Protein: 18 g
	Saturated Fat: 1 g	Sodium: 448 mg	Carbohydrate: 31 g

David Horowitz's
Fight Back! Chicken
4 servings

☆☆☆ ☆☆☆☆☆ ☆☆☆☆☆☆☆ ☆☆☆☆☆☆☆☆☆☆☆☆☆☆☆☆☆☆☆☆☆☆☆☆☆☆☆

David Horowitz is the creator and host of the award-winning "Fight Back! With David Horowitz" television program, which was syndicated weekly for eighteen years. David is the author of seven books, including Fight Back! And Don't Get Ripped Off. *Not content merely to fight rip-offs in business and government, David is battling bad nutrition with his Fight Back! Chicken and Fight Back! Salad (page 93).*

2 **tablespoons dry vermouth**
4 **boneless, skinless chicken breast halves**
4 **small white onions, peeled**
1 **cup canned tomatoes**
  freshly ground black pepper to taste
1 **large green pepper, sliced**
1 **clove of garlic**
1 **cup sliced mushrooms**

1. Bring the dry vermouth to a boil in a nonstick frying pan. Add chicken and cook, turning occasionally until vermouth has evaporated and chicken has browned.
2. Add all ingredients except mushrooms to pan. Cover and simmer for 20 to 25 minutes. Add mushrooms and simmer for 10 minutes more or until chicken and vegetables are tender.

PER SERVING:

Calories: 172   Fat: 2 g (11% of calories)   Cholesterol: 68 mg   Protein: 29 g
                 Saturated Fat: 1 g   Sodium: 179 mg   Carbohydrate: 9 g

ℒ♋

Stephanie Kramer's
Portuguese Chicken
4 servings

☆☆☆ ☆☆☆☆☆☆ ☆☆☆☆☆☆ ☆☆☆☆☆☆☆☆☆☆☆☆☆☆☆☆☆☆☆☆☆☆☆☆☆☆☆

Stephanie Kramer is best known as Sergeant Dee Dee McCall—the tough-minded detective on the hit NBC-TV series "Hunter." At George Bush's inauguration, one of this cookbook's editors (J.C.D.) stood by as many of Stephanie's young admirers tried to capture her attention. Her fans may not know that Stephanie is an accomplished singer. In fact, she left "Hunter" after six seasons to pursue a music career and is working on her first album.

Stephanie says, "I serve this dish over rice with steamed vegetables on the side and sprinkled with Parmesan cheese. The recipe was given to me by a friend, and it is always well received at our home!"

　2　teaspoons olive oil
　4　boneless, skinless chicken breast halves
　½　onion, peeled and minced
　3　medium cloves garlic, minced
　¼　cup dry white wine
　¾　cup chicken stock (see page 21) or low-sodium canned broth
　1　(4-ounce) can pimientos, drained, cut into thin strips
　½　teaspoon ground cumin
　¼　teaspoon turmeric
　¼　teaspoon salt
　　　freshly ground pepper
　½　teaspoon ground arrowroot dissolved in 2 teaspoons water
　2　tablespoons cilantro, minced

1. In a large, nonstick skillet, heat 1 teaspoon of olive oil over medium heat. Cook the chicken in the oil for 3 minutes on each side and remove from pan.
2. Heat the remaining teaspoon of oil over medium heat. Add the onion and garlic; sauté five minutes to soften. Add the wine, broth, pimientos, cumin, turmeric, salt and pepper. Simmer for 5 minutes.
3. Place the chicken back into the pan. Cover and cook gently 4 minutes or until chicken is cooked through. Remove the chicken from the pan and keep warm.
4. Add the arrowroot to the sauce and cook 1 minute. Stir in the cilantro and spoon over chicken.

PER SERVING:

Calories: 187   Fat: 5 g (28% of calories)   Cholesterol: 73 mg   Protein: 27 g
                 Saturated Fat: 1g   Sodium: 199 mg   Carbohydrate: 3 g

🍃

Claude Lenfant's
Chicken Marsala
4 servings

☆☆☆ ☆☆☆☆☆☆☆ ☆☆☆☆☆☆☆☆ ☆☆☆☆☆☆☆☆☆☆☆☆☆☆☆☆☆☆☆☆☆☆☆☆☆☆☆☆☆☆☆☆

As the director of the National Heart, Lung, and Blood Institute, Dr. Claude Lenfant had best cook in a healthful way himself. The doctor does not disappoint. He provided a baked fish recipe (see page 138), and now offers Chicken Marsala, whose "rich wine sauce with tomato base lifts this dish out of the ordinary."

- **1 tablespoon margarine**
- **4 chicken breast halves, skin and fat removed**
  freshly ground black pepper and salt to taste (optional)
- **2 tablespoons scallions or shallots, finely chopped**
- **½ cup Marsala wine**
- **½ cup chicken stock (see page 21) or low-sodium canned broth**
- **2 cups tomatoes, peeled, seeded and chopped**
- **¼ cup fresh parsley, finely chopped**

1. Melt margarine in skillet. Brown chicken parts, both sides. Sprinkle with salt and pepper; remove from skillet.
2. Add scallions, wine, stock and tomatoes. Simmer until liquid is partially reduced, about 10 minutes. Return chicken to skillet, spooning sauce over chicken. Cover and simmer until chicken is tender, about 30 minutes.
3. Serve sauce over chicken. Sprinkle with chopped parsley.

PER SERVING:

Calories: 207   Fat: 6 g (27% of calories)   Cholesterol: 73 mg   Protein: 28 g
                 Saturated Fat: 1 g   Sodium: 118 mg   Carbohydrate: 6 g

🍃

Nancy Lopez's
Chicken Enchilada Casserole
8 servings

☆☆☆ ☆☆☆☆☆☆☆ ☆☆☆☆☆☆☆☆ ☆☆☆☆☆☆☆☆☆☆☆☆☆☆☆☆☆☆☆☆☆☆☆☆☆☆☆☆☆☆☆☆

Nancy Lopez first showed promise of golfing greatness at age eight in her home state of New Mexico. In 1978, the twenty-one-year-old claimed nine victories, including the Ladies Professional Golf Association Championship (LPGA). Nancy made a comeback in 1985, taking five tournaments. Her thirty-fifth victory came two years later, qualifying her for the LPGA Hall of Fame. Reflecting Nancy's Mexican-American heritage, this casserole combines the tortillas and chilies of Mexico with some convenience foods of America.

4	boneless, skinless chicken breast halves
	nonstick cooking spray
2	10-ounce cans low-sodium cream of chicken soup
1½	soup cans skim milk (about 2 cups)
3	small cans green chilies, chopped
10 to 12	flour tortillas
½	cup Longhorn cheese, grated
4	tablespoons onion, minced

1. In a sprayed medium-size frying pan, brown chicken breasts. Shred or dice and set aside.
2. In a large saucepan combine the soup, milk and chilies; cook over medium heat until mixture is well blended and smooth. Remove from heat and set aside.
3. Wrap the tortillas in foil; place in 300° oven to warm through. Remove from oven. Lay each tortilla flat and place 2 tablespoons of diced chicken in center and sprinkle with grated cheese and onion. Roll up and place in a lightly sprayed 9 x 13-inch baking dish. Continue with the rest of the tortillas until dish is full.
4. Pour soup mixture over all and baked covered at 350° for 30 minutes.

PER SERVING:

Calories: 314	Fat: 9 g (25% of calories)	Cholesterol: 48 mg	Protein: 22 g
	Saturated Fat: 3 g	Sodium: 595 mg	Carbohydrate: 37 g

૪ઽ

Harry Lorayne's
Chicken Tomatillo
4-6 servings

☆☆☆ ☆☆☆☆☆ ☆☆☆☆☆☆ ☆☆☆☆☆☆☆☆☆☆☆☆☆☆☆☆☆☆☆☆☆☆☆☆☆☆☆☆☆

This tangy chicken recipe comes from the hat of Harry Lorayne, who first gained fame as a professional magician. More recently he has written best-selling books on memory, including How to Develop a Super-Power Memory *and* Memory Book, *co-authored with Jerry Lucas of pro-basketball fame. If you read his books, you'll be able to fix this low-fat, one-dish meal by heart!*

By the way, the tomatillo is a vitamin A-rich fruit that resembles a green cherry tomato, but with a lemony-herbal flavor. It's used frequently in Mexican and Tex-Mex dishes.

4 boneless, skinless chicken breast halves
2 tablespoons olive oil
2 pounds tomatillos (husks removed)
2 bunches scallions
8 cloves of garlic, peeled and minced
1 cup cilantro
1 green chili pepper (hot or mild)
  salt to taste (optional)
4 cups cooked brown rice

1. Sauté chicken in oil until golden brown.
2. Cook tomatillos by placing them in cold water, then poaching gently, without simmering, until tender, 2 to 15 minutes, depending on the fruit. Put tomatillos, scallions, garlic, cilantro and chili pepper in a blender or food processor. Blend.
3. In a large pot, bring tomatillo mixture to a boil. Lower heat and simmer for 10 minutes or until soft.
4. Add chicken and simmer for 15 minutes or until chicken is cooked through and flavors have blended. Serve in bowls over brown rice.

PER SERVING (4 SERVINGS):

Calories: 498	Fat: 10 g (18% of calories)	Cholesterol: 73 mg	Protein: 35 g
	Saturated Fat: 2 g	Sodium: 68 mg	Carbohydrate: 68 g

ℬ

Walter and William Mondale's
Chicken Dijon
4 servings

☆☆☆ ☆☆☆☆☆☆ ☆☆☆☆☆☆☆ ☆☆☆☆☆☆☆☆☆☆☆☆☆☆☆☆☆☆☆☆☆☆☆☆☆☆☆☆☆

As this cookbook went to press, Walter Mondale, former senator from Minnesota and vice president under President Jimmy Carter, had been nominated by President Clinton to become Ambassador to Japan. This recipe was actually stolen from the recipe files of William Mondale (Mondale's son) and is a popular dish at the Mondale home in North Oaks, Minnesota. See page 99 for Walter Mondale's delicious, vitamin A-packed Shrimp Salad in Papaya with Fresh Fruit.

4 boneless, skinless chicken breast halves
¼ cup Gulden's or another lower sodium Dijon mustard
2 tablespoons finely minced ginger
½ teaspoon tarragon vinegar
  a few drops of Tabasco
1 tablespoon vegetable oil
½ cup whole-wheat bread crumbs (recipe on page 79)
  nonstick cooking spray

1. Remove all fat from the chicken breasts. Combine the mustard, ginger, vinegar, Tabasco and oil in a small dish. Coat the chicken with this mixture. Roll in bread crumbs.
2. Arrange chicken in pan or terra-cotta baking dish that has been lightly sprayed with vegetable oil. Bake for 30 minutes at 375°.

PER SERVING:

Calories: 193	Fat: 7 g (33% of calories)	Cholesterol: 73 mg	Protein: 27 g
	Saturated Fat: 1 g	Sodium: 273 mg	Carbohydrate: 4 g

ക

Jacques Pepin's
Pork Tenderloin
with Apples and Onions   *4 servings*

☆☆☆ ☆☆☆☆☆ ☆☆☆☆☆☆ ☆☆☆☆☆☆☆☆☆ ☆☆☆☆☆☆☆☆☆☆☆☆☆☆☆☆☆☆

The internationally renowned chef Jacques Pepin proves, if anyone needed any more evidence, that healthy gourmet cooking is not an oxymoron. This recipe (and his refreshing Melon with Lime Sauce on page 194) is taken from his book A Fare for the Heart, a low-sodium, low-fat, low-cholesterol cookbook that he wrote in conjunction with The Cleveland Clinic. Jacques is also the dean of special programs at the French Culinary Institute in New York City.

Though most pork is fatty, tenderloin is the leanest (as lean as chicken) and most tender portion of pork. Jacques says, "The pork is sautéed only for a short time, but continues to cook in its own heat, which gives excellent results. The richness of the meat is also complemented by the tartness of the apples, vinegar and seasonings."

    4 **4-ounce pieces pork tenderloin**
 ³⁄₄ **teaspoon freshly ground black pepper**
 ¹⁄₄ **teaspoon crushed dried thyme**
    1 **tablespoon corn, safflower or sunflower oil**
    6 **ounces onion, thinly sliced (2 cups)**
 ¹⁄₄ **cup cider vinegar**
 ¹⁄₄ **cup water**
    1 **teaspoon sugar**
 ¹⁄₂ **teaspoon ground cumin or caraway seeds**
    1 **pound Rome Beauty apples, cored, halved and thinly sliced**
 ¹⁄₂ **teaspoon salt**

1. Completely trim the pork of fat. Butterfly it and pound to a thickness of ½ inch. Season the pieces of pork on both sides with ½ teaspoon of pepper and the thyme.

2. Heat the oil in a nonstick skillet over high heat until very hot. Add the pork to the pan and cook 2 to 3 minutes on each side. Remove the meat from the pan and keep it warm. Add the onion to the pan and sauté for about 3 minutes, until it is softened.

3. In a bowl, mix together the vinegar, water, sugar and cumin or caraway and add to the pan along with the apples, salt and remaining ¼ teaspoon pepper. Cover and boil gently 4 to 5 minutes, until the liquid has almost evaporated and the apples are moist and tender. Return the pork steaks and any accumulated juices to the pan and reheat for 1 to 2 minutes. Serve.

PER SERVING:

Calories: 274	Fat: 8 g (27% of calories)	Cholesterol: 70 mg	Protein: 26 g
	Saturated Fat: 2 g	Sodium: 325 mg	Carbohydrate: 25 g

Tracy Pikhart Ritter's
Oatmeal-Crusted Chicken Roulade with Spaghetti Squash and Sesame-Snow Peas   *4 servings*

☆☆☆ ☆☆☆☆☆ ☆☆☆☆☆☆ ☆☆☆☆☆☆☆☆☆☆☆☆☆☆☆☆☆☆☆☆☆☆☆☆☆☆☆☆

Visitors to the Golden Door health spa in Escondido, California, are dazzled by Tracy Ritter's wizardry in the kitchen. Because she studiously avoids saturated fat, she was a perfect choice to be involved in the Kaiser Family Foundation's Project Lean (Low-fat Eating for America Now).

If you think chicken should provide beta-carotene and a little dietary fiber, genetic engineering might be one way, but this roulade is a lot easier and tastier. For an appetizer, see Tracy's Sun-Dried Tomato Crostini on page 63.

    4 boneless, skinless chicken breast halves
    1 spaghetti squash, quartered
    1 large carrot, cut into matchstick strips
    2 tablespoons mixed herbs
    ½ teaspoon freshly ground black pepper
    8 large white mushrooms, cut into matchstick strips
    1 tablespoon white or black sesame seeds
    ½ cup uncooked oats
    ¼ cup whole-wheat flour
    2 tablespoons wheat germ
    1 tablespoon roasted cumin
    1 teaspoon chili powder
    4 egg whites, lightly beaten
    2 teaspoons dark sesame oil

¼ **pound snow peas**
1 **tablespoon grated orange rind**

1. Clean chicken breasts and carefully flatten between 2 sheets of plastic wrap.
2. Steam spaghetti squash. Add carrot toward the end of the cooking time to soften slightly. Run carrot sticks under cold water to stop cooking.
3. With a fork or spoon clean out center of spaghetti squash and reserve. Sprinkle chicken breasts with mixed herbs and pepper; add spaghetti squash, carrot and mushrooms. Reserve extra spaghetti squash. Roll chicken up and squeeze tightly shut. Refrigerate for ½ hour or overnight.
4. Combine next 6 ingredients to make breading. Dip chicken in egg whites and then roll in the oat breading. Place on a pan and refrigerate for ¼ hour before cooking.
5. Spray a nonstick pan lightly and brown the chicken roulade on all sides. Transfer to a baking pan and finish in the oven for 15 minutes. They should be slightly firm to the touch.
6. Sauté snow peas in sesame oil with minced orange rind. Reheat remaining squash. Slice the chicken rolls diagonally and serve with peas and squash. Sprinkle with additional sesame seeds if desired.

PER SERVING:

Calories: 318	Fat: 8 g (24% of calories)	Cholesterol: 73 mg	Protein: 36 g
	Saturated Fat: 2 g	Sodium: 139 mg	Carbohydrate: 24 g

Geraldo Rivera's
Puerto Rican Beans
6 servings

☆☆☆ ☆☆☆☆☆☆ ☆☆☆☆☆☆ ☆☆☆☆☆☆☆☆☆☆☆☆☆☆☆☆☆☆☆☆☆☆☆☆☆☆☆

Geraldo Rivera's controversial syndicated talk show "Geraldo" examines vital—and not-so-vital—issues of our times. Now one of America's best-known television journalists, Geraldo started learning the ropes in 1970 as an investigative reporter at WABC in New York City. Afterward, he reported for ABC-TV's "Good Morning America" and "20/20" and produced and hosted a series of live specials. His work has produced ten Emmys. We think you'll enjoy this spicy bean recipe, which was actually created by Millie Marquez, Geraldo's housekeeper.

1 **pound dry red kidney beans**
2 **tablespoons olive oil**
¼ **pound extra lean ham, diced**
3 **cloves of garlic, minced**
2 **tablespoons chili powder**
1 **8-ounce can tomato sauce, no salt added**

1 green pepper, diced
5 small little peppers (ajicitos), optional
2 tablespoons Mi Secreto sofrito, optional
½ teaspoon dried red pepper flakes
1 onion, diced
½ teaspoon salt
¼ teaspoon black pepper
2 small diced potatoes
  Tabasco, if desired

1. Wash beans and cover with water. Bring to a boil and boil for 2 minutes. Turn off the heat and let stand covered for one hour. Drain beans and add fresh water. Cook over medium heat until tender, about 1 hour. Add more water as necessary.
2. In a separate saucepan, fry ham in oil until brown. Add garlic and chili powder and cook for 2 minutes. Stir in tomato sauce, green pepper, ajicitos, Mi Secreto sofrito, red pepper flakes and onion. Cook slowly for 20 minutes.
3. When beans are tender, drain, add salt (leave out for lower sodium), pepper and ham/tomato mixture. Add potatoes and simmer until potatoes are tender and sauce is thick. Stir in a few drops of Tabasco if beans are not hot enough for you.

PER SERVING:

Calories: 347	Fat: 7 g (17% of calories)	Cholesterol: 10 mg	Protein: 19 g
	Saturated Fat: 1 g	Sodium: 432 mg	Carbohydrate: 53 g

ℛ

Mikie and Max Runager's and Sarah and Curtis Strange's
Grilled Chicken or Fish with Sesame Marinade

4 servings

☆☆☆ ☆☆☆☆☆☆ ☆☆☆☆☆☆☆ ☆☆☆☆☆☆☆☆☆☆☆☆☆☆☆☆☆☆☆☆☆☆☆☆☆☆

Outstanding professional athletes Max Runager and Curtis Strange are neighbors in Williamsburg, Virginia. Their wives, Mikie and Sarah, sent us this recipe that they say is great for chicken or fish. Max Runager played in the National Football League for eleven years as a punter and was a member of the 1984 Super Bowl-winning San Francisco 49ers. Golfer Curtis Strange won the U.S. Open in 1988 and 1989 and has a total of seventeen PGA Tour victories.

½ cup unsweetened white grape juice
1½ tablespoons reduced-sodium soy sauce
¼ cup dry white wine
1 tablespoon sesame seeds
1 tablespoon vegetable oil
¼ teaspoon garlic powder
1 teaspoon freshly grated ginger (or substitute ¼ teaspoon ground ginger)
freshly ground black pepper to taste
⅛ teaspoon lemon juice
4 boneless, skinless chicken breast halves

1. Combine first 8 ingredients in shallow dish and mix well. Add chicken, turning to coat; cover and marinate in refrigerator at least 2 hours.
2. Remove chicken, reserving marinade. Grill 4 to 5 inches from medium-hot coals about 15 minutes. Turn and baste frequently. This marinade is also perfect for fish.

PER SERVING:

Calories: 222	Fat: 8 g (32% of calories)	Cholesterol: 73 mg	Protein: 28 g
	Saturated Fat: 1 g	Sodium: 297 mg	Carbohydrate: 6 g

George Stephanopoulos's
Lime and Yogurt Marinated Chicken   *4 servings*

☆☆☆ ☆☆☆☆☆☆ ☆☆☆☆☆☆☆ ☆☆☆☆☆☆☆☆☆☆☆☆☆☆☆☆☆☆☆☆☆☆☆☆☆☆

During the 1992 presidential election campaign, most Americans were wowed by then-Arkansas Governor Bill Clinton's boyish-looking press secretary, George Stephanopoulos. After the election, George was the White House communications director for several months, then was named the president's senior advisor for policy and strategy. Judging from his tasty, very low-fat chicken dish, we think George could also give President Clinton some culinary advice.

1 green onion, minced
3 garlic cloves, minced
¾ teaspoon cumin
¼ teaspoon caraway seeds
1 teaspoon coriander seeds
1 teaspoon lime zest (skin of the lime)
1½ teaspoons lime juice
½ cup plain non-fat yogurt
salt and pepper, if desired
4 boneless, skinless chicken breast halves

1. Mix together all ingredients except chicken. Put mixture in a large glass baking dish.
2. Add chicken and turn to coat with marinade. Let stand for 20 minutes as broiling rack heats.
3. Broil on rack, turning once until done (10 to 20 minutes). Slice ¼ inch thick across the grain and serve immediately.

PER SERVING:

Calories: 163	Fat: 3 g (19% of calories)	Cholesterol: 74 mg	Protein: 28 g
	Saturated Fat: <1 g	Sodium: 85 mg	Carbohydrate: 3 g

VEGETABLE SIDE DISHES

Shana Alexander's
Corn Kathy
6 servings

☆☆

Shana Alexander, a liberal, will long be remembered for her television debates with James Kilpatrick, a dyed-in-the-wool conservative, on CBS-TV's "60 Minutes." She also was an editor of McCall's *magazine and reported for* Life *magazine, later writing a column called "The Feminine Eye." Her books include* Appearance of Evil: The Trial of Patty Hearst *and* Very Much a Lady: The Untold Story of Jean Harris and Dr. Herman Tarnower.*

Shana's vegetable side dishes offer simple ways to enjoy corn and potatoes without adding fat. Shana says, "We live on the edge of a cornfield, and when I'm writing, this corn, with salt only, is my working-at-desk lunch. I find it nourishes me beautifully and interrupts my writerly flow of thoughts scarcely at all."

   6 fresh ears of corn (unhusked)
      salt or margarine (if desired)

1. Buy any just-picked, same-day corn. Heat oven to 375° and toss in as many unhusked ears as you wish, just so long as you make certain that no ear touches another while cooking; the hot air must be able to circulate freely.
2. After 20 minutes, remove corn. Wearing a pair of potholder-gloves, strip down husks, cut at stalk and serve with salt or margarine or neither. You'll find that the corn has steamed to perfection in nature's own juices.

PER SERVING (1 EAR):

Calories: 77	Fat: 1 g (12% of calories)	Cholesterol: 0 mg	Protein: 3 g
	Saturated Fat: <1 g	Sodium: 14 mg	Carbohydrate: 17 g

Shana Alexander's
Potatoes Fred
6 servings

☆☆

Potatoes are naturally low-fat, but in this country we like to saturate them with fatty toppings like butter, sour cream and cheese. Shand's recipe shows a healthier way to dress up potatoes.

  12 very small red potatoes
       nonstick cooking spray
     6 cloves of garlic, peeled, minced
     1 tablespoon dried rosemary
       black pepper, freshly ground
   ¼ teaspoon salt (or to taste)

1. Parboil the potatoes for 15 minutes and drain.
2. Preheat oven to 375°.
3. Spray a glass baking dish with nonstick cooking spray. Cut the unpeeled potatoes into quarters and spread in one layer on the bottom of the baking dish. Use a large enough dish so that the pieces do not overlap.
4. Sprinkle minced garlic over potatoes. Sprinkle with rosemary, pepper and salt. Place in oven until brown (about 25 minutes).

PER SERVING:

| Calories: 105 | Fat: <1 g (1% of calories) | Cholesterol: 0 mg | Protein: 3 g |
| | Saturated Fat: 0 g | Sodium: 94 mg | Carbohydrate: 24 g |

Millie Bancroft's
Stuffed Peppers
8 servings

☆ ☆

Okay, so Millie Bancroft isn't a household name. But we wouldn't have had actress Anne Bancroft without her! Anne's mom uses reduced-fat cheddar cheese for this recipe—use less to reduce the fat (and sodium) even more.

  4 large green peppers, cut in half lengthwise, seeds removed
½ tablespoon vegetable oil
  1 clove of garlic, minced
  1 large onion, chopped
  2 large ripe tomatoes, peeled and chopped
1½ cups cooked brown rice
  2 tablespoons capers, rinsed and drained
¾ cup reduced-fat (75% less fat) cheddar cheese, shredded

1. Steam peppers until tender but still firm, about 5 to 10 minutes.
2. Heat vegetable oil and sauté garlic and onion. When almost tender, add tomatoes. Mix rice and capers, add to onion mixture and let simmer until warm.
3. Stuff mixture into peppers. Sprinkle with cheese and bake at 350° for 25 minutes in covered casserole.

PER SERVING:

| Calories: 110 | Fat: 5 g (25% of calories) | Cholesterol: 8 mg | Protein: 5 g |
| | Saturated Fat: 1 g | Sodium: 104 mg | Carbohydrate: 15 g |

Marian Burros's
Warm Potatoes Vinaigrette
4 servings

☆☆☆☆☆☆☆☆☆☆☆☆☆☆☆☆☆☆☆☆☆☆☆☆☆☆☆☆☆☆☆☆☆☆☆☆☆☆☆

Marian Burros is probably the premier food writer in the country. She reviews restaurants, cookbooks and recipes with the best of them, but in addition is a top-notch investigative reporter when she's digging into the deeds and misdeeds of manufacturers, Congress, the Food and Drug Administration and Department of Agriculture.

With its vitamin C and fiber, her Warm Potatoes Vinaigrette goes well with her other recipe in this cookbook, Tuna with Tomatoes and Capers (page 132).

    1 **pound tiny new potatoes**
    4 **teaspoons olive oil**
    3 **tablespoons tarragon vinegar**
    4 **scallions**
      freshly ground black pepper to taste

1. Scrub potatoes, leaving skins on. Boil until tender, about 20 minutes.
2. Beat oil with vinegar. Slice scallions into rings and stir into dressing; season with pepper.
3. When potatoes are cooked, drain and cut in halves or quarters; stir with dressing and serve.

PER SERVING:

Calories: 140	Fat: 5 g (30% of calories)	Cholesterol: 0 mg	Protein: 3 g
	Saturated Fat: 1 g	Sodium: 4 mg	Carbohydrate: 23 g

Dom De Luise's
Cabbage and Beans
4 servings

☆☆☆☆☆☆☆☆☆☆☆☆☆☆☆☆☆☆☆☆☆☆☆☆☆☆☆☆☆☆☆☆☆☆☆☆☆☆☆

If you saw the exciting road adventures of Smokey and the Bandit II, *the guy who kept you laughing was Dom De Luise, who has appeared on Broadway, screen and television for the past twenty years. His film credits include* The Best Little Whorehouse in Texas *and* Brighton Beach Memoirs, *and his culinary credits include this cabbage and bean dish. Cabbage is a great way to get vitamin C (and lots of other goodies), and beans provide a good slug of dietary fiber.*

    1 **head savoy cabbage, cleaned**
    1 **quart water**
    ½ **cup chopped onion**

½ teaspoon celery seed
¼ teaspoon black pepper
1 potato, peeled
2 cloves of garlic, chopped
1 19-ounce can great northern beans
½ tablespoon olive oil

1. Remove outer leaves of cabbage. Tear cabbage into pieces. Put into 5- to 6-quart pot. Add water, onion, celery seed and black pepper. Cut potato in half and add to cabbage. Add garlic. Cook at least 20 minutes.
2. Take potato out and mash. Return to pot and add beans (with liquid in can) and olive oil. Simmer for 10 minutes.

PER SERVING:

Calories: 225	Fat: 3 g (14% of calories)	Cholesterol: 0 mg	Protein: 11 g
	Saturated Fat: <1 g	Sodium: 303 mg	Carbohydrate: 42 g

M.F.K. Fisher's
Quick Belarussian Salad

4 servings

☆☆☆

In her loving tribute to M.F.K. Fisher, Washington Post *restaurant critic Phyllis Richman said the "grande dame" of food writers "wrote about food and sounded as if she were writing of life, death and love. Which of course she was." Fisher, who died in 1992 at age 83, produced 26 books and compilations of writings, among them* Serve It Forth *and* How to Cook a Wolf. *Her work, which appeared in* The New Yorker *and other magazines, blended her passion for gastronomy with reveries, observations and recipes. W.H. Auden called her "the best prose writer in America." Fisher contributed this recipe just months before she died, saying, "I loathe 'healthy' foods, but send you a favorite recipe of mine. I like to assume that it is fresh and good always. That's enough. This is a fast, easy recipe, equally good with cucumbers, chunks of green pepper, or green onions or young zucchini...or all mixed."*

3 small cucumbers
1 onion, sliced
   fresh dillweed
2 cups water
6 tablespoons wine vinegar
¼ cup sugar
½ teaspoon salt
1 clove of garlic, crushed or minced

1. Wash the cucumbers and slice lengthwise about ½ inch thick. Lay in a little casserole. Lay the sliced onion on top. Sprinkle with dillweed.
2. Mix a brine of water, wine vinegar, sugar, salt and garlic. Bring brine to a boil and let it cool for crisper pickles. Add brine hot for limper ones. Cover vegetables, and make more brine if needed, making strong or weak to taste. Let stand at least 6 hours. Store in refrigerator.
3. Drain well before eating as a salad or relish. Use fingers or fork. Will keep 10 days in brine in the refrigerator.

Note: This recipe depends solely on the brine, which one doesn't eat anyway. It has no oil, and the amount of sugar and salt depends on one's tastes and needs. Be sure to use a good vinegar, wine or not. Much of the sodium is left in the brine and not consumed.

PER SERVING:

Calories: 79	Fat: <1 g (1% of calories)	Cholesterol: 0 mg	Protein: <1 g
	Saturated Fat: 0 g	Sodium: 273 mg	Carbohydrate: 20 g

ℒᵌ

Michael Foley's
Sweet and Sour Cabbage

8 servings

☆☆

Having grown up in the restaurant business, Michael Foley's hard work (as butcher, bus boy, cashier—you name it) has paid off. Now Michael helps run Printer's Row restaurant in Chicago, has won several culinary awards and has served on the New England Culinary Institute Advisory Board. With this recipe, Michael proves that cabbage, a good source of vitamin C, can easily be made into a healthful, tasty side dish. His Pot-au-Feu of Root Vegetables with Tortellini is on page 71.

  1 tablespoon olive oil
  1 medium onion, minced
  1 28-ounce can of Italian tomatoes
  1 3-pound head of green cabbage
¼ cup wine vinegar
  2 tablespoons sugar
    salt and pepper (optional)

1. Heat oil in a saucepan. Sauté onion until golden. Add tomatoes, cabbage and vinegar.
2. Bring to a boil, reduce heat and cook covered for 20 minutes. Add sugar and mix well. Add salt and pepper to taste.

PER SERVING:

| Calories: 75 | Fat: 2 g (28% of calories) | Cholesterol: 0 mg | Protein: 2 g |
| | Saturated Fat: <1 g | Sodium: 163 mg | Carbohydrate: 14 g |

Senator John Glenn's
Harvest Festival Squash
5 servings

☆☆

When he's not spinning around the globe in a spaceship or globetrotting on a congressional mission, U.S. Senator (and former astronaut) John Glenn is busy eating this fabulous squash dish. The Ohio Democrat has served in the Senate since 1974 and is chairman of the Governmental Affairs Committee. This colorful dish, a squash-lover's delight, is rich in both fiber and beta-carotene.

> 2 cups cooked acorn or butternut squash (about 1 large)
> 1 cup fresh or thawed frozen cranberries
> ¼ cup sugar
> ¼ cup water
> 2 medium-sized fresh apples, coarsely grated
> grated rind and juice of 1 orange
> ½ cup whole uncooked cranberries, for garnish
> ¼ teaspoon ground allspice, for garnish

1. Slice squash in half and steam or bake for 40 minutes. Place 1 cup cranberries and sugar in small saucepan; add ¼ cup water and simmer for 15 minutes.
2. Mix squash, cooked cranberries, grated apples, orange rind and juice. Put in 1½-quart casserole, garnish with whole cranberries and sprinkle with allspice. Bake 20 minutes at 325°.

PER SERVING:

| Calories: 125 | Fat: <1 g (1% of calories) | Cholesterol: 0 mg | Protein: 1 g |
| | Saturated Fat: 0 g | Sodium: 0 mg | Carbohydrate: 21 g |

Jean Hewitt's
Marinated Vegetables

8 servings

☆☆☆

Stick with acclaimed cookbook writer Jean Hewitt's recipes and you'll be making headway on the National Cancer Institute's recommendation to eat five or more servings of vegetables or fruit each day (see the dessert section for recipes with fruit). In addition to this all-veggie dish, she gave us a delicious vegetable soup on page 24.

Jean says, "Buffets set out on my large butcher block center island are my favorite way to entertain in the country. Instead of a green salad or vegetables that have to be cooked at the last moment, I prefer this make-ahead recipe."

    2 single stalks broccoli, cut into small florets (save stalks for soup)
    2 cups small cauliflower florets
    2 carrots, cut into ¼-inch-thick rounds
    4 stalks celery, sliced
    ½ pound button mushrooms
    2 small zucchini or yellow squash, cut into ¼-inch slices
    1 bunch scallions, chopped
    2 tablespoons olive oil
    ¼ cup balsamic vinegar
    2 cloves garlic, crushed
      salt and pepper to taste
    ¼ cup chopped Italian parsley

1. Steam broccoli and cauliflower about 3 minutes, plunge into ice water, drain. Steam carrots over the same water for 4 minutes, plunge into ice water, drain.
2. Place steamed vegetables into a glass or ceramic bowl. Add celery, mushrooms, zucchini and scallions.
3. In a jar with a tight-fitting lid, combine the oil, vinegar, garlic, salt and pepper. Shake to mix. Pour over vegetables, toss to mix. Refrigerate several hours, tossing several times. Stir in parsley.

PER SERVING:
Calories: 80   Fat: 4 g (45% of calories)   Cholesterol: 0 mg   Protein: 4 g
                 Saturated Fat: <1 g   Sodium: 48 mg   Carbohydrate: 10 g

Jim Hightower's
The Anarchist's Great Potato Grate   *4 servings*

☆ ☆

When Jim Hightower directed the Agriculture Accountability Project in Washington in the early 1970s, he gained this cookbook's senior editor's (M.F.J.) eternal gratitude by introducing him to bluegrass and old-time country music. At AAP, he authored Hard Tomatoes, Hard Times *and* Eat Your Heart Out. *He then moved back to Texas to edit the* Texas Observer *and prove that he was one of the best (and funniest) political orators in the country. He served as Texas's elected Agriculture Commissioner from 1983-91, advocating the interests of small farmers and the environment. Dubbed the "nation's preeminent populist" by the* San Francisco Examiner, *Hightower recently started a syndicated radio show. This dish is loaded with fiber and vitamin C. Hightower says:*

> This is tasty, easy, healthy, cheap, fun food. There are no rules for it— enjoy for breakfast, brunch, a side dish, a main course or just for the hell of it. It's readily adaptable to your own taste choice of spuds; turnip or not; any veggie you like thrown in; whatever herbs, spices and oils suit your mood; more or less of any ingredient. It's cookbook anarchy.

1½ **cups grated, unpeeled potatoes (yellowfin, Yukon gold, sweet potato, russet, red, a mix of them—whatever seems right)**
½ **cup grated turnip**
¼ **cup finely chopped scallion or sweet onion**
¼ **cup finely chopped red bell or pimiento pepper**
¼ **cup coarsely chopped fresh Italian parsley (or a tablespoon or so of chopped fresh dill, coriander or other favorite herb)**
  salt (optional) and pepper to taste
2 **tablespoons top quality olive, canola or corn oil**

1. Mix together grated and chopped veggies and herbs in a bowl and add salt (if desired) and pepper. (If you prefer a tightly bound patty, you can add an egg white to the mix at this point; I find that the potatoes have enough stick-um to hold the ingredients without an egg, but I'm a pretty loose kind of guy.)
2. Heat the oil in a 10- to 12-inch nonstick pan over medium-high heat. Dump the whole load into the skillet and use a wooden spoon or spatula to form a 1-inch-or-so patty covering bottom of skillet. For prissier presentation, form the potato-grate into 4 separate patties.
3. Cook till golden brown on one side (5 minutes; a bit longer if you fancy darker, crispier patties). Turn and do the same for the other side.

PER SERVING:
| Calories: 240 | Fat: 7 g (27% of calories) | Cholesterol: 0 mg | Protein: 4 g |
| | Saturated Fat: 1 g | Sodium: 28 mg | Carbohydrate: 41 g |

Lady Bird Johnson's
Stuffed Squash
6 servings

☆☆☆

Lady Bird Johnson was First Lady from 1963 to 1969. She is also a longtime and ardent environmentalist, who has helped beautify the countryside by planting flowers and unplanting billboards. This stuffed squash recipe will beautify your table and satisfy your taste buds (vegetarians can substitute sauteed mushrooms for the bacon).

    2 pounds yellow squash
    2 onions, chopped
    1 clove garlic, minced
    ¾ cup toasted whole-wheat bread crumbs, rolled finely (recipe on page 79)
    6 slices bacon, fried, blotted dry and crumbled
    1 teaspoon sugar
    ¼ teaspoon salt
       freshly ground black pepper to taste
       dash cayenne pepper
    1 teaspoon Worcestershire sauce

1. Cook whole squash with onions and garlic until tender. Drain well.
2. Halve squash and scoop out pulp. Arrange halves in baking dish. Mash pulp and mix with bread crumbs, bacon (or sautéed mushrooms) and seasonings.
3. Fill squash halves and bake at 350° for 15 minutes.

PER SERVING:

Calories: 145	Fat: 5 g (29% of calories)	Cholesterol: 6 mg	Protein: 6 g
	Saturated Fat: 2 g	Sodium: 293 mg	Carbohydrate: 23 g

ॐ

Lady Bird Johnson's
Spiced Tea
16 servings

☆☆☆

Tea lovers will find this delightful recipe a refreshing alternative to regular tea.

    6 teaspoons tea (or 8 tea bags)
    2 cups boiling water
    1 small can frozen lemonade
    1 small can frozen orange juice
    8 cups water
    1 stick cinnamon

1. Pour boiling water over tea and let cool. Strain and add remaining ingredients.
2. Simmer mixture for 20 minutes. If too strong, add water. Add extra sugar to taste. This recipe makes 16 to 20 cups.

PER SERVING:

Calories: 50   Fat: 0 g (0% of calories)   Cholesterol: 0 mg   Protein: 0 g
               Saturated Fat: 0 g   Sodium: 4 mg   Carbohydrate: 12 g

Graham Kerr's
Golden Threads Squash

6 servings

☆☆☆

Graham Kerr, television's "Galloping Gourmet," says, "What a great natural invention: The so-called spaghetti squash has a unique internal thread-like structure—and bright color! The classic recipe uses a sausage filling, but we've kept the meat out so we'd have another wonderful vegetable dish. With one brimming cup per head, it will serve six. We like some freshly steamed broccoli on the side." See page 12 for Graham's heart-healthy update of usually cholesterol-rich quiche.

 1 4½-pound spaghetti squash
 1 tablespoon extra-light olive oil with a dash of sesame oil
 2 cloves of garlic, crushed
 2 medium peeled carrots, julienne-cut (matchstick strips)
 1 red bell pepper, seeded and julienne-cut
 1 green bell pepper, seeded and julienne-cut
¼ cup chicken stock (see page 21)
1½ tablespoons finely chopped fresh basil
 4 tablespoons freshly grated Parmesan cheese
    freshly ground black pepper to taste
 1 tablespoon arrowroot mixed with 2 tablespoons chicken stock

GARNISH:
½ ounce cracked filberts
 1 sprig of fresh basil

1. Pierce the squash on one side, allowing it to "breathe." Place it on a baking sheet and bake at 325° for 80 minutes. Remove and dip it in an icy water bath to prevent it from overcooking by retaining heat.
2. Put the squash on one side and cut a long lid. Remove the lid and scoop out and discard the seeds. Carefully scrape the spaghetti-like threads out of the shell. Put these golden threads on a plate and set aside.
3. Put the empty squash shell on a serving platter. If the shell won't stay in place, scoop some remaining pulp from the sides, and put it on the plate

as a base to hold the shell stable.

4. Heat the oil in a wok and fry the crushed garlic. Add the carrots, peppers and chicken stock. Gradually stir in the golden threads of reserved spaghetti squash. Sprinkle with the basil and half of the grated cheese and stir lightly to mix. Add some freshly ground black pepper.

5. Remove from the heat and add arrowroot paste. Return the wok to the heat and stir until thickened. Tip the mixture into the squash shell and garnish with the remaining cheese, the filberts and the basil sprig.

PER SERVING:

Calories: 92	Fat: 6 g (55% of calories)	Cholesterol: 3 mg	Protein: 2 g
	Saturated Fat: 1 g	Sodium: 80 mg	Carbohydrate: 9 g

Phil and Jill Lesh's
Broccoli-Stuffed Potatoes

2 servings

☆☆

Phil Lesh plays bass for The Grateful Dead and is a co-founder of the legendary musical group. When one of this cookbook's editors (J.C.D.) asked Phil if he were a vegetarian like his more famous fellow band member, Jerry Garcia, Phil said, "No, he's a vegetarian like me!" Phil and his wife Jill and their two children eat this as a side dish, lunch or a meal in itself. Their Risotto with Asparagus and Shiitake Mushrooms is on page 113.

- 1 cup broccoli florets, chopped
- 1 teaspoon margarine
- ½ cup mushrooms, chopped
- ½ cup scallions, chopped
- 2 potatoes, baked
- ½ cup non-fat plain yogurt
- 2 ounces reduced-fat cheddar cheese

1. Steam broccoli until tender. In a medium skillet melt butter, add mushrooms and scallions and cook until soft. Add broccoli and cook 2 more minutes.

2. Cut potatoes in half lengthwise. Scoop out pulp from potato halves and put in a large bowl and mash.

3. Add yogurt and cheese to potatoes and mix well. Stir in vegetable mixture and combine gently. Spoon into potato shells. Place filled shells on a nonstick baking sheet and broil until potatoes are heated and browned (about 5 minutes).

PER SERVING:

Calories: 383	Fat: 7 g (17% of calories)	Cholesterol: 21 mg	Protein: 19 g
	Saturated Fat: 4 g	Sodium: 296 mg	Carbohydrate: 62 g

Paul and Linda McCartney's
Zucchini with Apples
4 servings

☆☆

Linda McCartney was famous first for being married to Beatle Paul McCartney, but then acquired fame in her own right as author of Linda McCartney's Home Cooking. *Linda and Paul are vegetarians and active in the animal-rights group People for the Ethical Treatment of Animals (PETA). This recipe is perfect for anyone looking for an easy, new way to cook zucchini.*

1½ pounds small zucchinis, thinly sliced
1 tablespoon butter
1 medium onion, chopped
2 eating apples, peeled and chopped
2 fresh tomatoes, peeled and chopped
2 tablespoons chopped fresh parsley
½ teaspoon salt
   freshly ground black pepper to taste

1. Set a small pan of water to boil. Drop the zucchini slices into the boiling water for 30 seconds. Remove immediately and drain.
2. Melt the butter in a large pot and sauté the onion until it is transparent. Add the apples and stir well. Add the tomatoes and the blanched zucchini. Stir well, then add the parsley.
3. Season the mixture with salt (use less to cut the sodium) and pepper and leave it to cook, covered, over a gentle heat for 5 to 10 minutes, until the zucchini is soft. Serve hot.

PER SERVING:

Calories: 150	Fat: 4 g (22% of calories)	Cholesterol: 8 mg	Protein: 3 g
	Saturated Fat: 2 g	Sodium: 277 mg	Carbohydrate: 28

ℛ

Harold McGee's
Jerusalem Artichokes
4 servings

☆☆

What happens when you cross a scientist with a chef? Happily, if that scientist is Harold McGee, you get the fascinating, encyclopedia-like tome, On Food and Cooking: The Science and Lore of the Kitchen. *This recipe requires a good deal of delayed gratification, but is one of the simplest and most interesting. As the following quotation demonstrates, Harold has a knack for giving clear, detailed explanations of culinary facts, historical information and the scientific basis of cooking:*

Our digestive systems can't handle inulin [a starch-like substance], of course, which is why certain vegetables tend to cause gassy discomfort. While trying to figure out a way of reducing the inulin content of Jerusalem artichokes, a notorious offender, I came across the method by which peoples indigenous to the American West and Northwest used to prepare camas bulbs, whose carbohydrate content is also mainly inulin. Lewis and Clark described this slow pit-cooking method back in 1806. In the 1970s, researchers at the University of Michigan School of Public Health found that after forty-eight hours of pit-cooking, nearly all the inulin in camas bulbs has been converted to its constituent fructose units, which are digestible. What follows is a 24-hour adaptation for the Jerusalem artichoke. It transforms appearance and flavor as well as the inulin-fructose balance: the off-white tubers turn brown and almost translucent, like a cloudy aspic, and they develop a sweet, rich, caramel-like flavor. By the way, Jerusalem artichokes are unusually rich in iron—they are comparable to meats in this respect—though to my knowledge, no one has studied how absorbable it is.

Jerusalem artichokes
salt to taste

1. Put the whole artichokes in a casserole dish with a little water in the bottom and cover tightly with foil.
2. Cook in a 200° oven for 24 hours, checking periodically to replenish the water if necessary. Use as you would boiled yams or sweet potatoes.

Note: For a sweet, oil-free snack, slice cooked tubers lengthwise into thin strips, salt lightly, and dry on a rack in a 200° oven for 2 hours, or until just crisp.

PER SERVING (1 CUP):

Calories: 115	Fat: 0 g (0% of calories)	Cholesterol: 0 mg	Protein: 3 g
	Saturated Fat: 0 g	Sodium: 3 mg	Carbohydrate: 26 g

Mark Miller's
Jumpin' Jalapeño Beans   *6 servings*

☆☆

People in Sante Fe and Washington, D.C., are lucky to live close to Mark Miller-owned restaurants. The creative, scrumptious vegetarian offerings make his Red Sage restaurant one of this cookbook editor's (J.C.D.) favorite eating establishments. Even bean haters may become legume aficionados with this recipe, which gives you a good supply of fiber and burn-the-tongue, delight-the-taste buds deliciousness. Mark also provided Wild Mushroom and Sun-Dried Tomato Salsa on page 54.

  1 cup dried mixed beans, such as pintos, limas, flageolets and black beans
  4 cups water
  1 tablespoon virgin olive oil
  ½ small onion, peeled and cut into ¼-inch dice (about ¼ cup)
  ¼ small red bell pepper, seeded and cut into ¼-inch dice (about 2 tablespoons)
  ½ poblano chili, seeded and cut into ¼-inch dice (about 2 tablespoons)
  1 jalapeño chili, with seeds, cut into ⅛-inch dice (about 1 tablespoon)
  1 cup vegetable stock (see page 21) or use low-sodium canned broth or water
  ½ teaspoon salt
  1 tablespoon chopped chives

1. Carefully sort through the beans and remove any foreign objects. Rinse in a sieve and soak overnight.
2. Drain and rinse the beans, place in a large pot and add the 4 cups water (or enough water to cover the beans by at least 2 or 3 inches).
3. Slowly bring to a simmer and continue to cook at a low simmer until just tender, about 1½ to 2 hours. Add more water as necessary to keep the beans covered. When cooked, there should be about 2½ cups beans. Drain the beans.
4. Heat the olive oil in a large pan and sauté the onion, bell pepper, poblano and jalapeño over medium heat for 3 to 5 minutes until softened.
5. Stir in the cooked beans, add the stock or water and cook for 10 minutes; the liquid will have reduced. Season with salt and add the chives.

PER SERVING:

Calories: 136	Fat: 3 g (19% of calories)	Cholesterol: 0 mg	Protein: 7 g
	Saturated Fat: <1 g	Sodium: 204 mg	Carbohydrate: 21 g

ℰ𝔞

Mark O'Meara's
Cabbage Ramen Salad   *12 servings*

☆☆

Golf devotees know well the stellar career of Mark O'Meara. In 1992, Mark won the AT&T Pebble Beach National Pro-Am tournament for the fourth time. He has been a member of three Ryder Cup teams, as well as the U.S. vs. Japan and Nissan Cup squads. Mark keeps fit by eating healthful foods, and cabbage, which this recipe features, is one food that most of us eat much too rarely. Chicken is used more as a condiment than as the main feature of this recipe, just as nutritionists have been recommending. Don't be fooled by the high percentage of calories that fat represents; a serving has only five grams. The vitamin C and complex carbohydrate from the cabbage complement the protein from the chicken, making this a well-rounded dish.

2 packages instant ramen, crumbled
1½ cups water
½ small head of green cabbage, finely sliced
¾ small head of red cabbage, finely sliced
½ pound skinless, boneless chicken breast, cooked and shredded
6 green onions, thinly sliced

FOR DRESSING:
5 tablespoons apple juice
2 tablespoons salad oil
5 tablespoons vinegar
¾ teaspoon salt
¼ teaspoon black pepper
1½ tablespoons sesame oil
2 tablespoons toasted sesame seeds

1. Soak noodles (ramen) in water overnight.
2. Combine the salad ingredients. Combine the dressing ingredients and mix thoroughly. Toss noodles, salad and dressing lightly, cover and chill several hours.

PER SERVING:
Calories: 157   Fat: 6 g (32% of calories)   Cholesterol: 12 mg   Protein: 8 g
                 Saturated Fat: <1 g   Sodium: 237 mg   Carbohydrate: 20 g

Carolyn O'Neil's
New South Green Beans
4 servings

☆☆

Carolyn O'Neil has interviewed staffers of the Center for Science in the Public Interest many a time on issues ranging from Food and Drug Administration regulation of food labeling to risks related to caffeine. She anchors "On the Menu," Cable News Network's weekly show on food, nutrition and cuisine, and is managing editor and correspondent for food and health news. Her broadcasts have won awards from the American Heart Association and the American Dietetic Association. O'Neil, a registered dietitian, says her recipe is "a great way to capture the old-fashioned taste of bacon-flavored green beans, while serving modern palates a fresh and healthy vegetable side dish." Green beans are a well-rounded, low-calorie source of fiber and contain moderate amounts of vitamin C, beta-carotene, B vitamins and several minerals.

1 pound fresh green beans, washed and trimmed
2 tablespoons bacon bits
2 teaspoons margarine
  salt and pepper to taste

1. Fill vegetable steamer or large saucepan with thin layer of water. Sprinkle the bacon bits in the water. Place steamer basket in pan. Bring to a boil and add the green beans. Cook 7 to 10 minutes or until tender.
2. Remove steamer with beans. Pour off water and bacon bits; discard. Melt margarine in the pan and then toss in the green beans. If desired, add salt and pepper to taste.

PER SERVING:
Calories: 60   Fat: 2 g (29% of calories)   Cholesterol: 0 mg   Protein: 2 g
                Saturated Fat: <1 g   Sodium: 26 mg   Carbohydrate: 4 g

꽈

Sushma Palmer's
Versatile Raita
8 servings

☆☆

Sushma Palmer, former director of the National Academy of Sciences's Food and Nutrition Board, contributed a fantastic Tandoori Fish recipe (page 140) and now shares another healthful version of a traditional Indian recipe.

  2 **cups fat-free yogurt**
  1 **tablespoon lemon juice**
  1 **tablespoon finely chopped fresh cilantro or 2 teaspoons mint**
  1 **teaspoon cumin seed, dry roasted on griddle and crushed with wooden spoon**
2 to 3 **cups combination of boiled potatoes, cucumbers, frozen thawed peas and fresh tomatoes, all chopped into approximately ½-inch pieces**
  fresh cilantro or mint leaves for decoration

1. Beat the yogurt in a glass or plastic bowl. Add lemon juice, cilantro or mint and half of the crushed cumin. Add the vegetables and mix well.
2. Decorate with a few cilantro or mint leaves, sprinkle with the remaining cumin seeds and serve.

Variations:
A. Dilute with water or add a few ice cubes, adjust seasoning and use as a summer soup.
B. Serve the yogurt sauce alone without the vegetables as an accompaniment to meat, fish or poultry.
C. Use the yogurt sauce as a salad dressing or substitute it for the mayonnaise and sour cream (uncooked) in recipes, e.g., pasta salads, rice salads, etc.
D. Substitute 2 to 3 cups of a combination of other chopped raw or cooked vegetables (e.g., cauliflower, carrots, celery, broccoli, green beans, eggplant, etc.)

PER SERVING:
Calories: 70   Fat: <1 g (3% of calories)   Cholesterol: 1 mg   Protein: 5 g
                  Saturated Fat: 0 g   Sodium: 72 mg   Carbohydrate: 11 g

ℰ⁊

Abigail Van Buren's
Divine Stewed Okra
6 servings

☆☆☆

Abigail Van Buren was born Pauline Esther Friedman, but is better known as Dear Abby. Her column appears in over eight hundred newspapers worldwide. As one of America's most popular syndicated advice givers (or "agony aunts," as the British say), Dear Abby's fiercest competition comes from her sister, Eppie Friedman (AKA Ann Landers). Dear Abby's advice for today is to give okra a try!

    3 10-ounce packages frozen whole baby okra
    1 6-ounce package French-cut string beans or fresh string beans
    6 cups canned tomatoes (no salt added)
    1 tablespoon fresh basil (or 1 teaspoon dried basil)
    1 large onion, diced
    3 teaspoons Wyler salt-free chicken broth mix
    1 6-ounce can V-8 juice
    2 cups very hot water
    2 heaping teaspoons prepared minced garlic
    1 teaspoon dried basil
    1 teaspoon ground cinnamon
1 to 2 teaspoons fennel seed
    ½ teaspoon ground ginger

1. Combine all ingredients in a large soup kettle and bring to a boil, stirring occasionally.
2. Reduce heat to medium-low and continue cooking and stirring until okra turns from bright to dull green. Delicious plain, as a side dish, or over pasta. Or can be served with cooked shrimp over brown rice as a main course. Also freezes well.

PER SERVING:
Calories: 132   Fat: 1 g (8% of calories)   Cholesterol: 0 mg   Protein: 7 g
                   Saturated Fat: <1 g   Sodium: 144 mg   Carbohydrate: 29 g

DESSERTS

Ellen Brown's
Apricot Soufflé
6 servings

☆☆

Award-winning cookbook writer Ellen Brown says, "The dried apricots combined with the fresh apricots give this almost guiltless dessert a mellow, intense fruity flavor heightened by the orange liqueur." The "A" in apricots is for vitamin A (or, at least, the copious amounts of beta-carotene that the body converts to vitamin A). This recipe is taken from Ellen's Gourmet Gazelle Cookbook. *She has another wonderful dessert on the next page and her Baked Grouper in Herb Crust with Mustard Sauce is on page 131.*

6 ounces dried apricots
1 pound ripe fresh apricots
2 tablespoons Triple Sec or Cointreau
   nonstick cooking spray
6 egg whites, room temperature
   pinch of cream of tartar

1. Place the dried apricots in a mixing bowl and cover with boiling water. Let them hydrate for 15 to 20 minutes, or until soft. Drain in a colander, squeezing with the back of a spoon to extract as much liquid as possible.
2. While the apricots are soaking, bring a large pot of water to a boil. Place the fresh apricots in a colander, and place in the boiling water for 1 minute. Remove, and run under cold water until cool enough to handle. Peel and dice the apricots.
3. Combine the dried apricots, fresh apricots and liqueur in a blender or food processor fitted with a steel blade. Purée until smooth, scraping down the sides a few times. Refrigerate until well chilled, at least 1 hour.
4. Preheat the oven to 400°. Spray a 2-quart soufflé dish with nonstick cooking spray and dust with granulated sugar, shaking over the sink to eliminate the excess.
5. Place the egg whites in a copper bowl (or in a stainless or glass bowl) with a pinch of cream of tartar and beat until stiff peaks form. Beat ¼ of the meringue into the apricot mixture to lighten it, and then gently fold in the remaining meringue.
6. Transfer to the soufflé dish, place it in the center of the oven and immediately turn the heat down to 375°. Bake for 25 to 35 minutes, depending on if you like soufflés moist or dry. The soufflé will have puffed, and the top will be brown. Serve immediately.

Note: The apricot mixture can be made up to 3 days in advance and kept refrigerated, covered with plastic wrap.

PER SERVING:
Calories: 130   Fat: <1 g (3% of calories)   Cholesterol: 0 mg   Protein: 5 g
                 Saturated Fat: 0 g   Sodium: 54 mg   Carbohydrate: 26 g

Ellen Brown's
Dried Fruit Bars
20 servings

☆ ☆

Ellen says she serves these dried fruit bars as an alternative to muffins at breakfast. They also make a nice dessert, and the dried fruit and wheat bran provide plenty of fiber.

　3 **tablespoons unsalted butter, softened**
½ **cup firmly packed brown sugar**
　1 **egg**
　2 **egg whites**
1¾ **cups wheat bran**
　1 **cup buttermilk**
　1 **cup all-purpose flour**
　2 **teaspoons baking soda**
¼ **teaspoon salt**
½ **cup dried currants**
¾ **cup dried figs, cut into ½-inch chunks**
¼ **cup chopped pecans, toasted**
½ **cup golden raisins**
　　nonstick cooking spray

1. Preheat oven to 375°. Spray a 9 x 13-inch pan with nonstick cooking spray. Cream butter and brown sugar in large bowl until light and fluffy. Beat in egg and egg whites, then add wheat bran, buttermilk, flour, baking soda and salt. Beat well.
3. Stir in currants, figs, pecans and raisins.
4. Spread into pan and bake for 20 minutes, or until edges are lightly browned. Cool in pan on cooling rack, then cut into rectangles.

PER SERVING:

Calories: 145	Fat: 3 g (20% of calories)	Cholesterol: 19 mg	Protein: 3 g
	Saturated Fat: 1 g	Sodium: 53 mg	Carbohydrate: 27 g

Annemarie Colbin's
Spiced Glazed Pears
with Tofu Cream
6 servings

☆ ☆

Once she finally found rice syrup (look in a health food store), one of this cookbook's editors (J.C.D.) tested cookbook writer Annemarie Colbin's recipe and found it superb. Annemarie says, *"The reduction of the pear cooking juices creates a most delicious syrupy glaze for this sophisticated dessert."* Another of Annemarie's gourmet creations, Curried Apple-Squash Bisque, is on page 18.

   8 firm pears, preferably Bosc
1½ cups unfiltered apple juice or cider
   2 teaspoons ground cardamom
 ¼ teaspoon ground cloves
 ¼ teaspoon ground ginger

TOFU CREAM:
   8 ounces soft tofu
 ¼ cup rice syrup
¼ to ½ cup water
     ground cinnamon for garnish

1. Preheat oven to 350°. Quarter the pears, slicing off the core. Slice each quarter in half lengthwise to make 8 slices. Place in a 9 x 14-inch shallow baking dish.
2. In a small saucepan, heat the apple juice or cider. Stir in the spices. Pour the mixture over the pears and bake, covered with aluminum foil, for 35 to 40 minutes or until the pears are tender when pierced. With a slotted spoon, remove pears to a bowl and allow to cool to room temperature.
3. To make a glaze, pour the pan juices into a 3- to 4-quart saucepan, leaving the spice residue behind to discard. Bring to a boil over high heat and keep boiling, uncovered, for about 40 minutes, or until the juice is reduced to about ½ cup. Spoon 1 tablespoon glaze over each serving.
4. Place the tofu and rice syrup in a blender and blend until smooth, adding water as needed to reach a consistency similar to whipped cream. Serve over the spiced glazed pears, with a dusting of ground cinnamon for garnish.

PER SERVING:

Calories: 210	Fat: 3 g (12% of calories)	Cholesterol: 0 mg	Protein: 4 g
	Saturated Fat: <1 g	Sodium: 11 mg	Carbohydrate: 47 g

Judith Benn Hurley's
Cucumber and Cantaloupe Ice   *4 servings*

☆ ☆

    The recipes in Judith Hurley's cookbooks and other writings tantalize your taste buds while effortlessly improving your diet. This light, vitamin-rich dessert, from her Garden-Fresh Cooking *cookbook, is a perfect ending to a healthful summertime meal. Her Chilled Haddock with Snow Peas and Orange Vinaigrette is on page 135.*

1 cup water
⅓ cup honey
3 sprigs mint
1 pound cucumbers, peeled, halved and seeded
½ medium-size cantaloupe
1½ tablespoons lime juice

1. In a small saucepan, combine water, honey and mint and bring to a boil. Boil gently for 5 minutes. Remove from heat and let cool. Cover and refrigerate until chilled.
2. In a food processor or blender, purée cucumbers until smooth (you should have about 1¼ cups purée). Pour into a medium-size bowl and set aside while you prepare marinade.
3. Remove rind and seeds from cantaloupe and cut it into cubes. In a food processor or blender, purée until smooth (you should have about 1 cup purée). Stir in lime juice. Add cucumbers, stir and chill.
4. Stir honey syrup into cucumber mixture. Pour into chilled container of an ice cream maker and freeze according to manufacturer's directions. You can also still-freeze the ice. Simply pour the mixture into a 9-inch square pan and cover with foil. Then freeze it until firm, 3 to 4 hours. Break into small pieces and spoon half of the mixture into a chilled food processor bowl. Beat with a metal blade until light and fluffy but not thawed. Repeat with remaining frozen mixture. Serve immediately or return to pan and freeze until firm.)

PER SERVING:
Calories: 130   Fat: <1 g (2% of calories)   Cholesterol: 0 mg   Protein: 1 g
                 Saturated Fat: 0 g   Sodium: 11 mg   Carbohydrate: 33 g

Joan Lunden's
Cranberry-Strawberry-Pineapple Dessert   4 servings

☆☆ ☆☆ ☆☆☆☆☆ ☆☆☆☆☆☆☆☆☆☆☆☆☆☆☆☆☆☆☆☆☆☆☆☆☆☆☆☆☆☆☆☆☆☆☆☆

Joan Lunden has been an early-morning visitor in people's homes since 1980, when she first co-hosted ABC-TV's "Good Morning America." One of the most visible women in the country, Joan is also one of the best-known working mothers. She has three children and has hosted two programs on parenting and won TV Guide's Best Parenting Video of the Year award. We're delighted to include her simple and tasty side dish. You can also make this recipe with fresh fruit.

1 cup whole cranberries (or rehydrated dried cranberries)
1 16-ounce bag frozen strawberries, defrosted, drained
1 20-ounce can crushed pineapple, drained
2 tablespoons chopped walnuts

Mix all ingredients in a bowl and chill.

PER SERVING:

Calories: 253	Fat: 2 g (8% of calories)	Cholesterol: 0 mg	Protein: 2 g
	Saturated Fat: <1 g	Sodium: 6 mg	Carbohydrate: 60 g

₰

Abby Mandel's
Strawberry Sherbet
4 servings

☆ ☆

Cookbook author Abby Mandel offers this tasty way to end a meal. The recipe is from her cookbook More Taste Than Time *and it's fat free (OK, it does have a little sugar). Abby, who also provided a great soup recipe (page 30), says:*

This is one of my favorite uses for the food processor. Fresh fruit, at the peak of perfection, is frozen, then whipped into a fluffy sherbet bursting with flavor. It's low calorie, high impact, loaded with fresh fruit and endlessly variable, depending on what fruit is in season. Three cups of almost any fruit can be used solo or in combination. Bananas are sensational, especially with fresh pineapple or peaches; oranges and mangos tropical and delicious; apples and raspberries a rare treat. Liqueur is optional and helps define the flavor. Pick one that enhances the fruit you're using.

    3 cups strawberries
¼ to ½ cup sugar
    ⅓ cup plain low-fat yogurt (or 1 large egg white)
    1 tablespoon kirsch or framboise (optional)

1. Hull the berries and cut them in quarters or halves depending on their size. Arrange them on a baking sheet lined with wax paper and freeze until solid. Once they are frozen, they can be used right away or double-wrapped in plastic bags and frozen for several months.
2. Put the frozen berries in a food processor with the sugar, adding according to taste as well as the sweetness of the fruit. Pulse the machine on and off several times to chop the fruit, then process continuously until the berries are minced into tiny frozen chips. You may have to stop several times to scrape down the sides of the bowl with a rubber spatula.

3. With the machine on, pour the yogurt (or egg white) through the feed tube and process until the mixture is completely smooth and fluffy, up to 2 minutes. Add the liqueur, if using, and mix well. The sherbet can be served immediately or frozen. If it is frozen for more than 12 hours, let it soften just to the point where it can be spooned back into the work bowl. Process again until smooth, to eliminate ice crystals.

Note: Any fruit you use should be cut into 1-inch pieces, then frozen, like the strawberries. Peaches, nectarines and apricots do not need to be peeled.

PER SERVING:

Calories: 115	Fat: 1 g (8% of calories)	Cholesterol: 1 mg	Protein: 2 g
	Saturated Fat: <1 g	Sodium: 14 mg	Carbohydrate: 27 g

Meredith McCarty's
Dried Fruit Compote

7 servings

☆ ☆

Master macrobiotic chef Meredith McCarty gave us two delightful fruit compotes. One or the other would be a great ending to a dinner based around her Pasta with Red Lentil Sauce (page 114). Meredith says:

Compotes are fruits cooked in syrup. This winter version is actually dried fruit stewed in water. Dried fruits are so much sweeter than fresh ones that any extra sweetener makes the outcome seem overdone. Still served in New England inns, compotes have been enjoyed historically by many cultures from Germans to the Chinese.

    4 cups dried fruit, single or mixed fruit (1 pound mixed dried fruit)
    1 quart water
    cinnamon (2- to 3-inch stick)
1 to 2 teaspoons lemon rind, freshly grated

1. Place all ingredients in a saucepan and bring to a boil.
2. Turn heat down, cover and simmer until fruit is plump and juicy and liquid has become syrupy, 15 to 30 minutes.

Variation: Serve compote garnished with ½ cup toasted, chopped hazelnuts (adds 5 grams of fat per serving).

PER SERVING:

Calories: 175	Fat: <1 g (2% of calories)	Cholesterol: 0 mg	Protein: 2 g
	Saturated Fat: 0 g	Sodium: 5 mg	Carbohydrate: 46 g

Meredith McCarty's
Fresh Strawberry Compote

3 servings

☆☆

Forget the whipped cream—here's an easy, healthful way to dress up fresh strawberries.

- 1   pint strawberries (2 to 3 cups), rinsed, stems pinched off and berries halved or quartered depending on size
- ¼   cup brown rice syrup
- ¼   cup strawberry-apple juice or strawberry cider
- 1   teaspoon orange rind, freshly grated
- 1   teaspoon ginger root, peeled and freshly grated
    fresh mint or lemon balm sprigs for garnish

Whisk all ingredients (except strawberries) together. Pour over strawberries and marinate at least 1 hour. Fruit releases its juices and becomes submerged in syrup. Stir occasionally.

PER SERVING:

Calories: 140	Fat: 1 g (6% of calories)	Cholesterol: 0 mg	Protein: 1 g
	Saturated Fat: 0 g	Sodium: 3 mg	Carbohydrate: 36 g

Maureen McGovern's
Fresh Fruit Cobbler

10 servings

☆☆

Singer Maureen McGovern has been called "the quintessential interpreter of Gershwin," but for our purposes, she is the quintessential interpreter of fresh-fruit cobbler. She says "it satisfies my insatiable sweet tooth—a great dessert without the grief." All that fruit sugar must give Maureen inexhaustible energy. She seems to be on the move constantly—in motion-picture cameos, appearing with symphonies, recording albums, appearing in musicals and starring in television specials. Maureen is probably most well known for her interpretation of "The Morning After," the Academy award-winning song from The Poseidon Adventure.

- 1   pint blueberries
- 6 to 8   fresh peaches, pitted and chopped
- ½   cup raisins
- ¼   cup apple, apricot or peach juice
- 1   teaspoon cinnamon
- 1   cup rolled oats

½ **cup chopped almonds**
2 **tablespoons sesame seeds**
¼ **cup sunflower seeds**
1 **tablespoon safflower oil**
   pinch or 2 of nutmeg

1. Preheat oven to 350°. Combine all fruits and fruit juice. Spoon into greased 9 x 13-inch baking pan. Sprinkle with cinnamon.
2. In separate bowl, mix oats, almonds and seeds. Add oil and blend with fork. Sprinkle over fruit, then sprinkle with nutmeg. Bake for 1 hour.

PER SERVING:
Calories: 155   Fat: 6 g (32% of calories)   Cholesterol: 0 mg   Protein: 4 g
                Saturated Fat: <1 g   Sodium: 4 mg   Carbohydrate: 25 g

Jeremy Miller's
Fresh Fruit Pops   *6 servings*

☆☆ ☆☆ ☆☆☆☆☆☆☆ ☆☆☆☆☆☆☆☆☆☆☆☆☆☆☆☆☆☆☆☆☆☆☆☆☆☆☆☆☆☆☆☆

Starting at age eight, Jeremy Miller starred as Ben Seaver in the ABC-TV sit-com "Growing Pains" and has played the voice of Linus in several "Peanuts" television specials. Even though his big break came in a McDonald's commercial, Jeremy, now a teenager, writes for Healthy Kids *magazine and advocates healthful eating. Jeremy describes his fresh fruit pops as "a cool and fruity treat that's good anytime!"*

½ **cup orange juice**
1 **medium red apple, quartered and cored**
1 **medium orange, peeled and sectioned**
1 **small banana, peeled and cut up**
6 **3-ounce paper cups**
6 **wooden popsicle sticks**

1. Combine fruits and juice in blender or food processor. Cover and blend until smooth.
2. Pour equal amounts into paper cups. Cover with aluminum foil and insert sticks. Place in freezer for 4 to 6 hours.

Note for the messy or environmentally conscious: Omit the wooden sticks and use an ice cube tray instead of paper cups.

PER SERVING:
Calories: 60   Fat: <1 g (5% of calories)   Cholesterol: 0 mg   Protein: <1 g
               Saturated Fat: <1 g   Sodium: 0 mg   Carbohydrate: 15 g

Marion Nestle's
Baked Pears
6 servings

☆☆☆

If you want to impress your friends with an elegant dessert—but not overwork your-self—try Marion Nestle's delicious baked pears. This dish is not for people with alcohol problems, but its absence of fat is an unusual bonus for a fancy dessert and reflects one of Marion's chief nutritional concerns. Marion says, "Here is a favorite dessert, elegant but effortless, good for all seasons and always successful. I've written it for six but it can be expanded readily to meet the needs of a dinner party of any size."

Marion, one of most outspoken and respected experts in the nutrition and food policy field, also has a Root Vegetable Medley recipe on page 80.

> 3 **pears (Bosc work well)**
> 1 **cup full-bodied red wine**
> 1 **cup water**
> **cinnamon, a 2-inch stick or ½ teaspoon ground**
> 1 **tablespoon dark brown sugar**
> **non-fat vanilla frozen yogurt (optional)**

1. Wash pears, slice them in half lengthwise and scoop out the cores.
2. Place the wine, water, cinnamon and sugar in a pan large enough for pears to be laid out in a single layer, cut side up. Spoon sauce over pears. Cover pan. Either cook on stove over low heat or place in 350° oven. Cook until pears are tender, about 30 to 40 minutes, basting occasionally.
3. Remove pears to individual serving dishes or platter. Continue cooking sauce until it is concentrated to a thin syrup, about 10 to 20 minutes uncovered on top of stove. Pour syrup over pears and serve while they are still warm. For a summer dessert, refrigerate the pears until ready to serve; then place a scoop of non-fat vanilla frozen yogurt on each pair half, spoon the syrup over the yogurt and garnish with a sprig of fresh mint.

PER SERVING:

Calories: 80	Fat: 1 g (5% of calories)	Cholesterol: 0 mg	Protein: 1 g
	Saturated Fat: 0 g	Sodium: 3 mg	Carbohydrate: 14 g

క్ల

Jacques Pepin's
Melon with Lime Sauce
6 servings

☆☆☆

Chef Jacques Pepin, who earlier provided a low-fat pork tenderloin recipe (page 160), now gives us a little lesson on converting an ordinary melon recipe into an ele-

gant dessert. Cantaloupe contains far more vitamins A and C than honeydew melon. We won't argue that the rum and sugar add anything in the way of nutrition, although the lime juice adds a little vitamin C.

- 4 cups cantaloupe and/or honeydew balls
- 1 large lime
- 1 tablespoon rum
- 1 tablespoon sugar
  mint or lime wedges for garnish

1. Cut the melon in half and remove the seeds. Use a melon baller to make the balls and place them in a large bowl.
2. With a vegetable peeler, remove the green part of the lime skin. Stack the strips of lime together and cut into fine matchstick strips. Add strips to the melon balls.
3. Squeeze the lime and mix the juice (approximately ¼ cup) with the rum and sugar. Stir into melon. Allow the mixture to set for 1 hour or as long as 24 hours in the refrigerator.
4. At serving time, spoon the melon into bowls and garnish with mint or lime wedges.

PER SERVING:

Calories: 70	Fat: <1 g (7% of calories)	Cholesterol: 0 mg	Protein: 1 g
	Saturated Fat: <1 g	Sodium: 13 mg	Carbohydrate: 15 g

Fred Rogers's
Corn Pudding
10 servings

☆☆

Fred Rogers has delighted children nationwide since 1970, when PBS picked up his show, "Mister Rogers' Neighborhood." Fred, a Presbyterian minister, was immortalized by The Smithsonian Institution in 1984 when his sweater was placed in the National Museum of American History. He says that his Grandmother Rogers used to make this recipe every Christmas.

- 1 16-ounce can of cream-style corn, no salt added
  Egg Beaters equivalent of 2 eggs (or another egg substitute)
- 2 tablespoons flour
- 2 tablespoons sugar
- ½ teaspoon salt
- ½ cup skim milk
- 1 tablespoon melted butter or margarine
  nonstick cooking spray

1. Preheat oven to 350°. Beat the Egg Beaters. Then add all the other ingredients and mix well.
2. Place into a sprayed casserole dish. Bake for 1 hour or until well set.

PER SERVING:

| Calories: 70 | Fat: 1 g (16% of calories) | Cholesterol: 3 mg | Protein: 2 g |
| | Saturated Fat: <1 g | Sodium: 142 mg | Carbohydrate: 14 g |

Lorna J. Sass's
Lemon Poppyseed Cake
10 servings

☆☆☆☆☆☆☆☆☆☆☆☆☆☆☆☆☆☆☆☆☆☆☆☆☆☆☆☆☆☆☆☆☆☆☆☆☆☆

Lorna Sass's other recipe, Red Bean Salad Ole (page 45), would fit easily into her no-animal-product, no-sugar cookbook, Recipes from an Ecological Kitchen. *Lorna accomplished a more difficult culinary feat with the creation of this luscious cake. She says:*

Sugar-, dairy- and egg-free baking is quite a challenge—particularly when your standards are high and you are not willing to settle for a dessert that tastes "healthy" rather than delicious. I hope that you'll agree that this recipe would win the approval of any ardent cake lover. The secret ingredient is flaxseed, which acts as a binder and gives the cake a moist, rich texture. You'll no doubt be hearing more about flaxseed soon, as it is a fine source of high-quality protein, fiber and the two essential fatty acids. Since its oil content is high, store flaxseed in the freezer and grind as needed. It is readily available in health-food stores.

   oil and flour for preparing cake pan
5 tablespoons flaxseed, ground
1 cup apple juice
2 cups whole-wheat pastry flour
1 cup unbleached white flour
½ cup poppy seeds
4 teaspoons double-acting, nonaluminum baking powder, such as Rumford's
2 tablespoons grated lemon rind
½ teaspoon salt
¼ cup canola or safflower oil
¾ cup maple syrup
½ cup lemon juice
4 tablespoons unsweetened applesauce

1. Brush oil onto the bottom, sides and center of a 9-inch tube pan. Dust lightly with flour, tip out the extra and set aside. Set the flaxseed in the bowl of a blender (preferably) or food processor and add the apple juice. Process for 30 seconds. Set aside.

2. In a large bowl, combine the whole-wheat and white flours, poppy seeds, baking powder, lemon rind and salt. Blend the oil, maple syrup, lemon juice and applesauce into the flaxseed mixture and process for about 10 seconds. Blend the liquid ingredients into the dry ingredients, mixing just until all the flour is absorbed. Preheat oven to 375°.

3. Transfer the batter to the prepared tube pan and gently smooth the top with a spatula. Bake on the center shelf of oven until top of cake springs back when gently touched and a skewer inserted into the center comes out clean, about 35 to 40 minutes.

4. Set on a rack to cool for 30 minutes. Then run a knife along the outside and center edges and unmold. Set the cake on the rack to cool completely before serving.

Note: It's best to use organic lemons, free of any pesticide residues. To obtain the grated rind, use a sharp old-fashioned potato peeler with a gentle, sawing motion to remove strips of the peel. Avoid the white pith underneath which is somewhat bitter. Either finely chop the peel by hand or use a mini-chopper. A less efficient but workable approach is to grate the peel on the finest side of a box grater.

PER SERVING:

Calories: 305	Fat: 9 g (27% of calories)	Cholesterol: 0 mg	Protein: 6 g
	Saturated Fat: 1 g	Sodium: 249 mg	Carbohydrate: 52 g

Bernd Schmitt's
Bread Pudding

6 servings

☆ ☆

This yummy pudding is courtesy of Bernd Schmitt, the executive chef at Canyon Ranch, one of the nation's leading health spas. You can mix the ingredients in five minutes and have your pudding in another thirty. The small amount of fat in this pudding will, perhaps, excuse the moderate amount of sugar. If you need a main dish to precede this pudding, try Bernd's Salmon with Poached Leeks on page 145 or Vegetable Strudel with Red Pepper Coulis on page 87.

- 6 slices whole-wheat bread diced into ¼-inch cubes
- 2 cups non-fat milk
- 2 tablespoons melted margarine
- 6 egg whites
- ⅓ cup fructose

1 tablespoon vanilla
1 tablespoon cinnamon
¼ cup seedless raisins
nonstick cooking spray

1. Combine bread cubes and milk in a bowl and set aside to soak.
2. Preheat oven to 350°. In another bowl, combine margarine, egg whites, fructose, vanilla and cinnamon together and mix well. Add raisins and mix again.
3. Combine egg mixture and bread mixture. Pour into sprayed 8 x 8 x 2-inch pan. Bake for 30 minutes or until solid.

PER SERVING:
Calories: 210 | Fat: 5 g (20% of calories) | Cholesterol: 1 mg | Protein: 9 g
| Saturated Fat: 1 g | Sodium: 317 mg | Carbohydrate: 34 g

Richard Simmons's
Pineapple Bavarian Cream

6 servings

☆ ☆

Your guests might think you're on a feeding frenzy of fat when you serve this colorful dish from diet and exercise guru Richard Simmons. But what looks like a no-no is actually a fruit-filled, virtually no-fat dessert—so, go ahead and indulge. For another fruity recipe from Richard, turn to page 47, where you'll see his Classic Citrus Salad.

1 envelope unflavored gelatin
2 tablespoons cold water
¼ cup boiling water
1¼ cups low-fat cottage cheese
½ cup evaporated skim milk
¼ cup apple juice concentrate or honey
1½ teaspoons vanilla
2½ cups canned crushed pineapple, unsweetened
1½ cups frozen or fresh blueberries

1. In small bowl, soften gelatin in cold water. Add boiling water and stir until gelatin is completely dissolved.
2. In blender container, blend gelatin mixture with remaining ingredients except fruit. Stir in pineapple including juice. Mix well.
3. Arrange most of blueberries in base of glass dessert dish, or divide into 6 parfait glasses. Pour pineapple mixture over blueberries. Top with remaining blueberries and refrigerate until firm, at least 2 hours.

PER SERVING:
Calories: 160   Fat: 1 g (7% of calories)   Cholesterol: 5 mg   Protein: 10 g
    Saturated Fat: 1 g   Sodium: 223 mg   Carbohydrate: 28 g

The Vegetarian Resource Group's
Bulgur and Fruit Salad
5 servings

☆ ☆

Charles Stahler, the co-founder of the Vegetarian Resouce Group, first got the senior editor (M.F.J.) of this cookbook thinking about vegetarianism when he managed the Center for Science in the Public Interest's mail room in the 1970s. He then moved to Baltimore where he helped create one of the liveliest vegetarian groups around. Debra Wasserman is the other co-founder of VRG and editor of the group's Vegetarian Journal. *Debra is the author of several books, including* Simply Vegan: Quick Vegetarian Meals.

Charles and Debra say, "The wonderful thing about this recipe is that it is easy to prepare and can be served for breakfast, as a salad or snack and even as a dessert. Feel free to substitute different fruits and to add raisins or chopped dates."

1 **cup uncooked bulgur**
2 **cups fruit juice (apple, grape, etc.)**
¼ **pound seedless grapes, cut in half**
1 **peach, chopped**
1 **apple, chopped**
1 **pear, chopped**
¾ **teaspoon cinnamon**
⅛ **teaspoon nutmeg**

Soak bulgur in fruit juice until soft (best to do overnight). Add remaining ingredients and stir well. Serve chilled.

PER SERVING:
Calories: 240   Fat: 1 g (4% of calories)   Cholesterol: 0 mg   Protein: 4 g
    Saturated Fat: <1 g   Sodium: 5 mg   Carbohydrate: 57 g

Ernst Wynder's
Apricot Tart

12 servings

☆☆ ☆☆ ☆☆☆☆☆☆ ☆☆☆☆☆☆☆☆☆☆☆☆☆☆☆☆☆☆☆☆☆☆☆☆☆☆☆☆☆☆☆☆

If you're looking for new ways to use dried apricots (other than munching on them directly from the bag), try this easy, vitamin A-rich recipe from Ernst Wynder, founder of the American Health Foundation. Ernst's low-fat Creamy Oriental Cheese Dressing can be found on page 48.

1 pound dried apricots
½ cup golden raisins
1 cup frozen apple juice concentrate, thawed
2 cups dry, crunchy, whole-grain cereal
   juice of 1 lemon
2 tablespoons cinnamon

GLAZE:
  1 cup apple juice concentrate
  1 cup water
  2 tablespoons arrowroot

1. Preheat oven to 400°. In large saucepan, cover apricots and raisins with water. Bring to boil, then reduce heat and simmer for 20 minutes.
2. Meanwhile, pour half of the apple juice into sheet pan; cover with cereal and let absorb until moist. After apricots and raisins have finished simmering, combine with lemon juice, remaining apple juice and cinnamon. Pour onto cereal crust and cover with foil. Bake for 30 minutes or until apricots take on rich color.
3. To make glaze, combine juice, water and arrowroot in a small saucepan. Stir over low heat until thick. Remove sheet pan from oven and brush with glaze.

PER SERVING:
Calories: 210   Fat: <1 g (2% of calories)   Cholesterol: 0 mg   Protein: 2 g
                Saturated Fat: 0 g   Sodium: 77 mg   Carbohydrate: 53 g

INDEX

Center for Science in the Public Interest

The Center for Science in the Public Interest is one of the nation's leading health-advocacy organizations.

CSPI was founded in 1971 by three public-interest scientists, Albert Fritsch, James Sullivan and Michael Jacobson. They began with a borrowed desk in a friend's office, what little savings they had accumulated and dreams of contributing to a better nation. Today, CSPI has a full-time staff of 30 dedicated people. CSPI's *Nutrition Action Healthletter*, which began as a free, bi-monthly newsletter for a handful of progressive nutritionists, today brings reliable nutrition advice to over 600,000 subscribers and key journalists.

CSPI has worked on issues ranging from toxic chemicals in the environment to America's wasteful lifestyle, and from examining the effects of chemicals on behavior to promoting solar energy. Now CSPI focuses on improving the safety and nutritional quality of our food supply and on reducing the carnage caused by alcoholic beverages.

CSPI exemplifies how a small organization can leverage its modest resources to change the attitudes and policies of a huge nation and change the practices of multi-billion-dollar corporations. That's exactly what CSPI has done in the areas of nutrition and alcohol.

CSPI encouraged whole-grain, low-fat eating when Jell-O was in and tofu unknown. At first CSPI was labeled by the "Establishment" as a bunch of nutrition nuts, but CSPI's work helped put nutrition on the map. Due to the efforts of CSPI and innumerable others, the message caught on. Now, it's impossible to avoid discussions of nutrition on TV talk shows, in magazines and in conversations with friends.

CSPI's efforts have resulted in real changes that mean better health for everyone. Because of CSPI's work:

- ☑ fast-food chains stopped frying foods in beef fat (even fruit pies were fried in beef fat!), offer grilled chicken sandwiches and fat-free yogurt and disclose ingredient and nutrition information;
- ☑ major food manufacturers stopped using heart-disease-promoting coconut and palm oils;
- ☑ dozens of dishonest food labels and ads were eliminated;
- ☑ Congress passed laws mandating more informative food labels;
- ☑ warnings were required on alcoholic-beverage containers;
- ☑ the FDA banned sulfites—an additive that killed more than a dozen individuals in the 1980s—from most fresh foods.

CSPI has been a major educator. Millions of copies of CSPI's consumer-oriented books, videotapes, software and reports have been used by parents, health professionals and teachers. CSPI sponsored National Food Day, which was celebrated in hundreds of communities in 1975, 1976 and 1977.

The 1977 Food Day was capped by a buffet dinner in the White House.

In addition to executive director Michael Jacobson, two staff members have played particularly important roles in CSPI's accomplishments. Bonnie Liebman has been CSPI's director of nutrition since 1977. She started her work by petitioning the Food and Drug Administration to list sodium on food labels. Since then she has written articles for *Nutrition Action Healthletter* on topics ranging from heart disease to vitamin supplements to cookies. She is relied upon by journalists nationwide for thoughtful analyses of nutrition controversies.

Bruce Silverglade has been CSPI's director of legal affairs since 1980 and has spearheaded CSPI's successful efforts to halt deceptive food labeling and advertising. He also led the coalition that won a 1990 law mandating improved food labeling.

Though CSPI's books, congressional testimonies, and other writings are scientifically based and serious, a sense of humor pervades much of CSPI's work. For instance, in the mid-1970s CSPI conferred the annual Bon Vivant Vichyssoise Memorial Award (named after a botulism-tainted soup) on food manufacturers that "did the most to promote bad nutrition." In 1977, CSPI attached a plastic bag filled with 170 extracted, decayed teeth to a formal, legal petition asking the Federal Trade Commission to ban junk-food ads on children's television shows. Michael Jacobson's TV appearances are often enlivened by the large tubes of fat he uses to illustrate the fat content of fast-food meals. And the "Food Porn" column—a humorous look at the best and worst food of the month—has long been one of the most popular features in *Nutrition Action Healthletter*.

In the 1990s CSPI will continue to promote safer, healthier diets, whether people buy natural foods processed foods or eat at restaurants. In addition, CSPI will support organic farming, oppose food irradiation, provide sensible advice about vitamin and mineral supplements and improve the quality of foods marketed to children. And perhaps even more importantly, CSPI hopes to continue fostering a better-informed citizenry, improved corporate practices and more enlightened governmental policies...all through the use of science in the public interest.

CSPI Publications

Cooking with the Stars: You'll be a star in the eyes of the lucky person to whom you give a gift copy of this book. The more than 175 recipes will allow them to brag about having the dinner of (if not with) President Carter, Anne Bancroft, Ringo Starr, or Chris Evert. $12.95.

Nutrition Action Healthletter: CSPI's flagship publication brings the latest nutrition news and insights to 600,000 subscribers ten times a year. *Nutrition Action* rates the nutritional value of fresh and processed foods, provides the lowdown on vitamin supplements and tells readers how they can influence government officials and food manufacturers. $24 per year. (Subscribers receive a ten percent discount on all other publications.)

Wall charts 18 x 24 inches. Paper version: $5; plastic laminated: $10.
Nutrition Scoreboard: CSPI has distributed over one million copies of this stylish neon-and-black poster. It provides nutrition scores for about 300 foods. A baked sweet potato tops the scoreboard with a score of +184. Bulgur and wheat germ top the grain category. Skinless turkey breast rates 10 points, while pot roast's score is -114. Ben & Jerry's ice cream scores -183.
Fast-Food Guide: This colorful poster is really a book on one giant page. It is based on CSPI's fast-food book (see below).

CSPI's Healthy Eating Pyramid: This colorful three-dimensional pyramid divides foods into "Anytime," "Sometimes," and "Seldom." It is one of the best guides to better nutrition ever developed. Sturdy paper version: 7 inches high, $4. Plastic version: 7-1/2 inches high, $15.

The Completely Updated and Revised Fast-Food Guide: by Michael F. Jacobson and Sarah Fritschner (Workman Publishing): This book tells you everything you wanted (and didn't want) to know about the foods offered by all the major chains. Complete lists of ingredients and nutritional values, comparisons of burgers, chicken, fries and much more. The book uses a unique "Gloom" score to rate the overall nutritional quality of every food (a plain baked potato scores 0; a large double-cheeseburger has a very gloomy score of 83). 333 pages, $7.95

Kitchen Fun for Kids: by Michael F. Jacobson and Laura Hill (Henry Holt Co.): This is the perfect cookbook for 7- to 12-year-olds (or beginning cooks of any age). Fifty-five fun recipes for tasty, nutritious foods. Kids can start out with Muffin Pizzas, then move on to a Mouse-in-the-House Salad and maybe a little Hummus is Among Us. Hardcover, 136 pages, $14.95.

CSPI Order Form

☐ CSPI's latest catalog of publications (no charge)

☐ Cooking with the Stars _____ @ $ 12.95 = _____

☐ 1-year subscription to *Nutrition Action*
Healthletter *(includes membership in CSPI)* MI _____ @ $ 24.00 = _____

☐ Nutrition Scoreboard poster (paper) 82 _____ @ $ 5.00 = _____

☐ Nurition Scoreboard poster (laminated) 82L _____ @ $ 10.00 = _____

☐ Fast-Food Guide poster (paper) 94 _____ @ $ 5.00 = _____

☐ Fast-Food Guide poster (laminated) 94L _____ @ $ 10.00 = _____

☐ CSPI's Healthy Eating Pyramid (paper) HEP1 _____ @ $ 4.00 = _____

☐ CSPI's Healthy Eating Pyramid (plastic) HEP2 _____ @ $ 15.00 = _____

☐ The Completely Updated and Revised
Fast-Food Guide (FF) _____ @ $ 7.95 = _____

☐ Kitchen Fun for Kids (KFFK) _____ @ $ 14.95 = _____

Shipping & handling $ 2.00 = $2.00

SUBTOTAL = _____

Are you a *Nutrition Action* subscriber (CSPI member)?
If so, deduct 10 percent. (10% of subtotal) = _____

☐ Donation = _____

TOTAL ENCLOSED = _____

_____
Name

_____
Street   Apt.

_____
City   State   Zip

Mail this form and a check made payable to CSPI for the total amount to:
CSPI Publications
1875 Connecticut Avenue, N.W., #300
Washington, DC 20009-5728
(202) 332-9110 (ext. 393)

Allow four to six weeks for delivery.

CC93